Praise for *Attack Surface Management*

In today's cybersecurity landscape, professionals are inundated with guidance and recommendations but receive very little in the way of practical advice that can be executed to minimize risk and defend against threats. *Attack Surface Management* provides a pragmatic and practical approach to identifying, classifying, and protecting an organization's most critical assets in a way that aligns with and augments published best practices and risk management frameworks. This is an ideal methodology for transitioning from "checking the boxes" to implementing security practices that actually provide value.

—*Jeremy Faircloth, Sr., CyberSecurity Consultant/Architect*

Everyone who deals with security learns that it's a Sisyphean task: every day we work to make our systems stronger and safer, but every day there are new challenges that undermine our efforts. *Attack Surface Management* provides a framework for reevaluating the landscape so that anyone with a job that involves information security, which seems to be all of us these days, can approach the work in a sustainable and effective way. I've already put ideas from this book into practice with my own work, and I look forward to seeing this approach to cybersecurity spread more widely in the future.

—*Chris Devers,*
Technical Lead of Sustaining Engineering, EditShare

Attack surface management is a term often heard but rarely comprehensively explained to people new to the subject. Ron and MJ have done an incredible job of building foundational knowledge of ASM, and they progress readers to a level of understanding that allows them to leverage the knowledge in the field. I wish I had this book ten years ago; it would have saved me an incredible amount of time and effort.

—*Dane Grace, Sr., Cybersecurity Product Manager*

You can't protect what you don't know about. This book delivers a practical framework to help you identify and understand your attack surface. A must-read for those serious about understanding how to minimize and protect their exposed edge.

—*Steve Winterfeld, Advisory CISO, Cyber Vigilance Advice*

Attack Surface Management

*Strategies and Techniques for
Safeguarding Your Digital Assets*

Ron Eddings and MJ Kaufmann

O'REILLY®

Attack Surface Management

by Ron Eddings and MJ Kaufmann

Copyright © 2025 Ronald Eddings, Melody Ann Jones "MJ" Kaufmann. All rights reserved.

Printed in the United States of America.

Published by O'Reilly Media, Inc., 1005 Gravenstein Highway North, Sebastopol, CA 95472.

O'Reilly books may be purchased for educational, business, or sales promotional use. Online editions are also available for most titles (*http://oreilly.com*). For more information, contact our corporate/institutional sales department: 800-998-9938 or *corporate@oreilly.com*.

Acquisitions Editor: Simina Calin	**Indexer:** BIM Creatives, LLC
Development Editor: Jill Leonard	**Interior Designer:** David Futato
Production Editor: Beth Kelly	**Cover Designer:** Karen Montgomery
Copyeditor: J.M. Olejarz	**Illustrator:** Kate Dullea
Proofreader: Dwight Ramsey	

May 2025:   First Edition

Revision History for the First Edition

2025-05-19:   First Release

See *http://oreilly.com/catalog/errata.csp?isbn=9781098165086* for release details.

978-1-098-16508-6

[LSI]

Table of Contents

Part II.   Identification and Classification

Part IV. Adapting and Monitoring

Preface

Cybersecurity is a never-ending race—one where the finish line keeps moving. Every time we think we've secured our systems, attackers find new ways in. Every innovation, convenience, cloud service, or connected device we adopt opens up new opportunities—not just for businesses but also for adversaries. This is where attack surface management (ASM) comes in.

ASM isn't just another security buzzword; it's a fundamental shift in how organizations approach cybersecurity. In a world where digital transformation is happening at breakneck speed, the old ways of securing networks and endpoints are no longer enough. Our attack surfaces have evolved from a handful of well-defined servers and firewalls to a sprawling, interconnected ecosystem of cloud environments, third-party SaaS applications, APIs, IoT devices, remote workforces, and supply chain dependencies. The modern attack surface is vast, fragmented, and constantly changing. Everything that it encompasses is a prime target for cybercriminals looking for gaps in our defenses.

But the challenge isn't just about scale—it's about visibility. Security teams are drowning in alerts and vulnerabilities, trying to protect assets that in some cases they don't even know exist. ASM provides the strategic framework to cut through the noise, helping organizations discover, analyze, and manage their exposure before attackers can exploit it.

By understanding and actively managing your attack surface, you're not just reacting to threats but anticipating them. You're reducing risk before it becomes an incident, securing what you know and what you didn't realize was exposed. This book is about taking control—helping security professionals, IT teams, and business leaders confidently navigate the ever-expanding digital frontier.

The game has changed. ASM is how we stay ahead.

Who Should Read This Book

Cybersecurity is no longer confined to a single department or a specialized team locked away in a security operations center. The responsibility of securing an organization's assets is now shared across IT, security, DevOps, compliance, and even business leadership. If you're reading this, chances are you play a role in protecting your organization's digital footprint—whether you realize it or not.

This book is for security professionals—CISOs, security engineers, SOC analysts, and AppSec teams who are constantly fighting to reduce risk, respond to threats, and improve security posture across an increasingly complex digital environment. If your job involves monitoring security alerts, managing vulnerabilities, investigating breaches, or designing security policies, this book will give you the tools to approach ASM in a structured, proactive way.

It's also for IT administrators who manage infrastructure, endpoints, and cloud environments. You're responsible for keeping systems running smoothly, ensuring they are secure, and managing configurations. However, with shadow IT, third-party SaaS applications, and evolving cloud services, staying ahead of security gaps can feel impossible. ASM provides a framework for visibility, automation, and control—helping IT teams eliminate blind spots before they turn into security incidents.

DevOps teams will also find this book invaluable. Modern application development moves too fast for traditional security models to keep up. Continuous integration and continuous deployment (CI/CD) pipelines, containerized applications, and API-driven architectures have expanded attack surfaces in ways most security teams struggle to manage. This book will help DevOps teams embed security into their workflows, ensuring that security is not an afterthought but an integrated part of software development.

For compliance officers and risk managers, ASM provides a way to map security efforts to regulatory frameworks such as GDPR, HIPAA, PCI DSS, and NIST. Understanding where sensitive data lives, who has access to it, and what external dependencies exist is crucial for maintaining compliance. This book will help compliance professionals work alongside security and IT teams to operationalize security controls and maintain regulatory alignment.

Finally, this book is for anyone involved in cybersecurity strategy—business leaders, product managers, and technology decision-makers who need a clear understanding of attack surfaces, digital risk, and security investments. ASM is not just a technical challenge; it's a business imperative. Leaders who understand the importance of ASM can drive smarter security investments, improve incident response, and align security efforts with business objectives.

What You Need to Know

This book assumes a basic understanding of security principles, network architecture, and risk management concepts. You'll find it easy to follow along if you're familiar with common security frameworks, basic networking, and how applications interact in cloud environments. However, we've structured this book to be practical, accessible, and actionable, ensuring that even those new to ASM can grasp and apply the key concepts effectively.

Regardless of your role, one thing is certain: the attack surface is growing, and managing it is no longer optional. Whether you're securing infrastructure, developing software, monitoring threats, or ensuring compliance, this book will help you turn ASM from a reactive burden into a proactive advantage.

Why We Wrote This Book

Every cybersecurity professional knows that securing an organization is a constant battle. Attackers innovate as fast—if not faster—than defenders, and keeping up feels like running on a treadmill set to full speed. As digital transformation accelerates, organizations are expanding their IT environments across cloud platforms, SaaS applications, APIs, and mobile devices—yet many struggle to answer a fundamental question: What, exactly, are we trying to protect?

This is the challenge of ASM. Organizations know they need it, and security teams understand the risks of unmanaged, unknown, or misconfigured assets. Yet, when faced with the question of "Where do we even begin?" most don't have an answer.

That's why we wrote this book.

What You'll Learn

Despite the increasing importance of ASM, there isn't a go-to resource that security teams can turn to for practical guidance. Some organizations think they're doing ASM, but they're just running vulnerability scans or cataloging assets without a true strategy. Others know they need ASM but get overwhelmed by the complexity and don't know how to start. This book is meant to fill that gap—to provide both the high-level strategy and the day-to-day tactics that make ASM actionable.

The book offers:

Real-world use cases and industry best practices
   ASM is more than just theory. Throughout this book, you'll find examples of how organizations manage their attack surfaces, what works, and what doesn't.

A balance of strategic and tactical guidance

This book provides a clear, structured road map for implementing ASM, whether you're starting from scratch or looking to improve an existing program.

A framework for integrating ASM into security operations

ASM isn't just a security tool or a one-time project—it's a process that must be embedded into incident response, vulnerability management, DevOps, and compliance efforts. This book shows you how.

The goal of the book is to help security teams make the shift from reacting to threats to getting ahead of them. By the time you finish reading, you'll have a clear understanding of ASM, a practical framework for implementation, and the confidence to take control of your attack surface—before attackers do.

Navigating This Book

ASM is a journey, not a single destination. It requires a strategic foundation, practical execution, and continuous adaptation to keep pace with evolving threats. This book is structured to take you through that journey step by step, from understanding what an attack surface is to implementing a scalable, proactive ASM program.

We've divided the book into four key parts, each focusing on a critical phase of ASM. Whether you're new to the concept or refining an existing approach, you can follow along in sequence or jump to the sections that align with your immediate needs.

Part I: Foundations of ASM

Before you can manage your attack surface, you need to understand what it is and why it matters. This section establishes the core concepts of ASM, setting the stage for everything that follows.

Chapter 1 lays the groundwork, defining attack surface management and explaining how the digital landscape has changed, why traditional security approaches no longer suffice, and why ASM has become essential for modern cybersecurity.

Chapter 2 explores the different types of attack surfaces, from traditional IT assets to cloud environments, SaaS applications, APIs, IoT, and third-party dependencies. Understanding the scope of exposure is the first step in securing it.

Chapter 3 connects ASM to risk management, outlining how organizations should prioritize threats based on real-world impact rather than blindly chasing every vulnerability.

By the end of Part I, you'll have a strong strategic understanding of ASM and why it must be an integral part of security operations.

Part II: Identification and Classification

Once you understand the scope of your attack surface, the next step is to find and classify everything that needs protection. This part focuses on visibility—because you can't protect what you don't know exists.

Chapter 4 covers asset discovery—how organizations identify all their digital assets, whether in on-premises infrastructure, the cloud, or shadow IT.

Chapter 5 dives into automation and classification, showing how organizations can move beyond manual asset inventories to scalable, real-time attack surface monitoring.

By the end of Part II, you'll know how to map your attack surface comprehensively and categorize assets based on risk, business impact, and exposure.

Part III: Prioritization and Remediation

Discovery is just the beginning—not every asset carries the same level of risk. Part III focuses on prioritizing vulnerabilities and exposures so that organizations can focus resources where they matter most.

Chapter 6 introduces prioritization frameworks, including crown jewel analysis and business context mapping. Instead of treating every vulnerability equally, organizations must focus on what attackers are most likely to target.

Chapter 7 provides methods for measuring attack surface exposure, showing how security teams can quantify and track changes over time.

Chapter 8 covers remediation strategies, from proactive risk reduction to reactive incident response. It also explains how to validate remediation efforts to ensure security fixes are effective.

By the end of Part III, you'll have a systematic approach to reducing risk efficiently—without getting lost in alert fatigue or low-priority issues.

Part IV: Adapting and Monitoring

Attack surfaces aren't static. They expand, contract, and evolve as organizations grow, adopt new technologies, and integrate third-party services. Part IV focuses on long-term attack surface management—how to continuously monitor, adapt, and improve security posture.

Chapter 9 examines strategies for minimizing the attack surface—how organizations can design their environments to reduce unnecessary exposure and limit attacker opportunities.

Chapter 10 explores continuous monitoring, automation, and AI-driven security strategies. It explains how organizations can set alert thresholds, integrate ASM with incident response, and automate security operations to keep up with ever-changing threats.

By the end of Part IV, you'll understand how to sustain an ASM program over time, making it an ongoing part of security operations rather than a one-time effort.

Looking Ahead

Cybersecurity never stands still, and neither does ASM. Chapter 11 looks toward the future of attack surface management—how emerging technologies like AI, automation, and predictive analytics will shape the next evolution of ASM. It also explores how security teams can stay ahead of evolving attacker tactics.

How to Use This Book

This book is designed to be a structured guide and a practical reference. If you're new to ASM, we recommend reading Parts I and II first to build a strong foundation before diving into the technical details. If you're already familiar with ASM and need help operationalizing it, you might find Parts III and IV most useful.

No matter where you start, one thing is certain: the attack surface is always growing, shifting, and under threat. By implementing the principles in this book, you can take control of your organization's exposure, reduce risk, and stay ahead of attackers—today and in the future.

Conventions Used in This Book

The following typographical conventions are used in this book:

Italic
    Indicates new terms, URLs, email addresses, filenames, and file extensions.

> This element signifies a general note.

O'Reilly Online Learning

O'REILLY® For more than 40 years, *O'Reilly Media* has provided technology and business training, knowledge, and insight to help companies succeed.

Our unique network of experts and innovators share their knowledge and expertise through books, articles, and our online learning platform. O'Reilly's online learning platform gives you on-demand access to live training courses, in-depth learning paths, interactive coding environments, and a vast collection of text and video from O'Reilly and 200+ other publishers. For more information, visit *https://oreilly.com*.

How to Contact Us

Please address comments and questions concerning this book to the publisher:

O'Reilly Media, Inc.
1005 Gravenstein Highway North
Sebastopol, CA 95472
800-889-8969 (in the United States or Canada)
707-827-7019 (international or local)
707-829-0104 (fax)
support@oreilly.com
https://oreilly.com/about/contact.html

We have a web page for this book, where we list errata, examples, and any additional information. You can access this page at *https://oreil.ly/attack-surface-management*.

For news and information about our books and courses, visit *https://oreilly.com*.

Find us on LinkedIn: *https://linkedin.com/company/oreilly-media*.

Watch us on YouTube: *https://youtube.com/oreillymedia*.

Acknowledgments

Both authors would like to thank all of the technical reviewers whose suggestions, advice, and criticisms have helped refine this book and make the content shine:

- Chris Devers
- Jeremy Faircloth
- Dane Grace
- Robin Smorenburg
- Josh Summitt
- Sean Sun
- Diana Volere
- Steve Winterfeld

Ron Eddings

To my wife and my rock, Monika Eddings, for putting up with my endless stream of cybersecurity ideas and for being the best mother to our daughter, Ava Rose. Your patience, support, and encouragement made my contributions to this book possible. I would not be where I am without you by my side.

MJ Kaufmann

Deepest thanks to my husband, Kurt Kaufmann, for his unwavering support, advice, and constructive criticism during the writing of this book; to my closest friends, Andrew Matchett, Blanca Betances, Jaime Lumsden, and Dionne Lister, for keeping me grounded, believing in me, and inspiring me; and to my mother-in-law, who is my biggest cheerleader. Big shout-out to my tribe of ladies who've had my back, encouraged me from page one, and stayed by me to the final chapter: Anne Gotay, Michelle Fleming, Sonia Awan, Jen VanAntwerp, Lea Rabinowitz, Gianna Whitver, Karen Walsh, and Joanna Ochoa. To Sean Sun, Todd Kamp, and Evan Davis, a special thanks for keeping my spirits up, never letting me give up, and making me laugh even when things were tough. Thanks to Dane Grace, Diana Volere, and Josh Summitt for helping me look at things from a different perspective and technical advice that really brought out the best in this book. Special thanks to Nabeel Nizar for mentoring me and pushing me to be my absolute best. Thanks to our wonderful editor, Jill Leonard, without whom this book would not exist, and to Simina Calin for believing in our vision.

PART I

Foundations of ASM

In these early chapters, we're setting the stage for understanding attack surface management (ASM), a concept that has become essential in the industry. Whether you're just starting out in the field or have been in it for years, the first three chapters cover ASM basics everyone needs to know. They ensure we are all on the same page before diving deeper. We start by answering the key question: *What exactly is an attack surface?*

You'll discover the answer is not just about networks and servers anymore—attack surfaces include everything from software and hardware to people and processes. Essentially, attack surfaces are all the entry points that someone could use to access your systems, and managing them is about knowing where those points are, what risks they pose, and how to protect them.

We'll dive into the details of how IT environments have evolved, including cloud services, IoT devices, and even employee smartphones. So many advances have expanded attack surfaces in ways we couldn't have imagined a decade ago. This shift introduces new security challenges, and we'll break down how organizations can address them. We'll also introduce you to risk management strategies, which help you prioritize the vulnerabilities you tackle first based on their potential impact. By the time you finish Part I, you'll have a strong understanding of ASM fundamentals and be well equipped to move forward, no matter your experience level.

CHAPTER 1

Laying the Groundwork: An Overview of Attack Surface Management

Attack surface management (ASM) is more than just a cybersecurity buzzword that can help you sound savvy in meetings. Respected industry analysts like Gartner have recognized ASM as a valuable framework for managing emerging threats and organizational attack surfaces since 2022. The US government (*https://oreil.ly/hpRhG*), National Institute of Standards and Technology (NIST) (*https://www.nist.gov*), and other regulatory bodies (*https://oreil.ly/UG6Xl*) have increasingly emphasized the importance of reducing risk and minimizing your attack surface. ASM is designed to provide actionable insights that deepen visibility into the vulnerabilities and risks of your organization's digital footprint. The purpose of ASM is to proactively identify threats and mitigate vulnerabilities before they become entry points for attackers. Doing this across multiple environments is complex, critical, and challenging. For this reason, it has emerged as a strategic imperative for security teams in organizations of all sizes.

Attack Surface Management: What It Is and Why It Matters

ASM plays an essential role in efficiently managing cybersecurity programs, reducing risk, improving compliance, and proactively improving your organizational security posture to ensure business continuity and build cyber resilience. This framework encompasses several aspects designed to help determine where attacks may occur and what kind of impact they may have. It does this through a process of identifying, classifying, prioritizing, and securing all points of potential vulnerability within your organizational ecosystem—collectively known as the *organizational attack surface*.

While many organizations already have standard risk assessment methodologies, they can augment them with ASM. ASM complements and enhances standard risk assessment methodologies by providing a focused, continuous approach to identifying and mitigating potential vulnerabilities within an organization's digital and physical realms. Unlike traditional risk assessments that occur periodically, ASM offers a dynamic, real-time evaluation of threats as they evolve, aligning closely with the NIST Risk Management Framework's (RMF) phases.

For instance, during the Categorize phase, ASM aids in categorizing assets based on their exposure levels, feeding into more accurate risk determinations. In the Implement and Assess phases, ASM's ongoing monitoring capabilities ensure that the selected security controls are implemented and effective against current threats.

By integrating ASM into a risk framework such as NIST's, organizations can break free from the more rigid assessments and more agilely adapt their security posture to proactively address known and emerging threats.

We'll walk through each piece of the framework and use cases later, but first, let's break down what exactly we mean when we say attack surface.

What Do We Mean by Attack Surface?

Attack surface is a comprehensive term that describes any and every point within an organization where an unauthorized user or attacker could gain access or extract data from an environment or hijack resources for malicious purposes. We intentionally say *user* and *attacker* because there is an important distinction between the two. Attacks are often assumed to be from external third parties, generally malicious individuals or bad actors, but unintentional attacks can come from users within your organization. An attack surface includes physical hardware and software-based systems, such as servers, networks, applications, and machine-automated processes. It also encompasses the human elements—the people who interact with these systems and the business processes through which the systems are operated, as well as the environment and physical security elements. When referring to all the potential entry points to your technology within your organizational ecosystem, the phrase *organizational attack surface* is normally used.

It's easy to focus on just the core IT components, such as servers and endpoints, when discussing attack surfaces. However, it is important to understand that the overall attack surface of an IT ecosystem is far broader. Public and private network interfaces serve as gateways for data exchange and can be potential entry points for unauthorized access. Unpatched software vulnerabilities offer cybercriminals opportunities to exploit outdated systems. Exposed databases that contain sensitive information can be targeted for data breaches. Cloud services and web applications expand the organizational attack surface further, and are all too often not properly managed and secured. The complexity of the attack surface increases when you consider things like remote work, bring-your-own-device (BYOD) policies, the Internet of Things (IoT), and the supply chain. Today, our IT paradigm has shifted to ephemeral virtual infrastructure and resources where employees can access organizational resources from anywhere, rather than in a server room or on physical computers within an office space managed directly by an IT team. This means nearly any device used by your employees, whether personal or professional, can be connected to your company's network from any place around the world. Each of these variables increases the number of potential entry points into your organizational ecosystem (as mentioned earlier, this is holistically viewed as the organizational attack surface). The larger or more complex the total organizational attack surface, the more opportunities there are for bad actors to exploit vulnerabilities and breach an organization.

Managing the intricacies of an organizational attack surface is challenging even if an organization remains entirely static. However, the goal of most companies, even small and medium businesses, is growth, and modern ones are continuously changing. There are a lot of internal factors that cause changes to the IT ecosystem. Factors that you might not think of as relating to the attack surface, such as adopting new software, technical debt, or onboarding a new employee, do, in fact, have an impact. Other less common internal factors might include adding new hardware, changing security policies, or adjusting employee access permissions.

External factors, such as the broader technology landscape—from the way COVID accelerated cloud migration to evolving cyberthreats, like the emergence of ransomware-as-a-service (RaaS)—alter an organizational attack surface. Unlike internal factors, these variables are outside of a company's control. The most well-known external factor is cybercriminals constantly discovering vulnerabilities in existing applications or developing new techniques and tools for bypassing security controls.

This brings us to the concept of *attack vectors*. Attack vectors enable hackers to exploit system vulnerabilities, and much like with attack surfaces, this also includes the human element.

Attack Vectors Versus Attack Surfaces

When planning and carrying out an attack on a system, the attacker needs to identify weaknesses that they can exploit and methods for doing so. We refer to these weaknesses as attack surfaces and the methods as attack vectors. Attack vectors refers to all the tools, tactics, and techniques used to exploit your attack surfaces. Attack surfaces are the targets or locations where malicious actors apply attack vectors. You might hear people use them interchangeably, but they are not synonymous. They are related but different.

Think of an attack vector as a bow and arrow while the attack surface is the bull's-eye. This concept is illustrated in Figure 1-1. In this illustration, we have a selection of various attack vectors and related attack surfaces, but it is important to note that these are not all-encompassing; organizations may break them down differently, such as dividing malware into smaller vectors like ransomware, spyware, etc. Very rarely does one attack vector target every attack surface, but those surfaces that are more exposed may be more targeted.

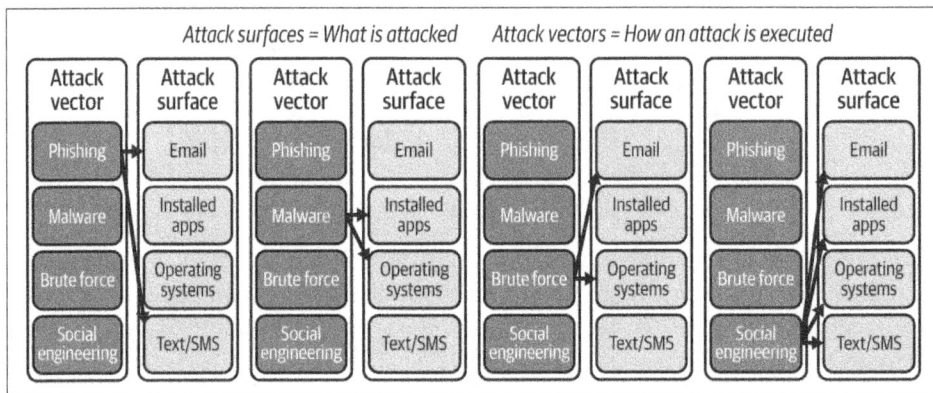

Figure 1-1. Examples of both attack surfaces and attack vectors.

Attack vectors encompass a broad spectrum of attack types, ranging from cunning social engineering attacks to sophisticated technical exploits. The popularity and usage of each vary based on the attack surface and the attacker's preference. Attack vectors may change as new vulnerabilities are discovered, allowing cybercriminals to take advantage of security gaps and leaving security teams racing to mitigate them. As the organizational attack surface expands, potential attack vectors increase exponentially. Conversely, reducing the attack surface by minimizing vulnerable points reduces the number of potential attack vectors.

This may seem very abstract, but the consequences are very real. To give you a better idea of the relationship between attack surfaces and attack vectors, we've listed several examples of vectors below. In each example, we noted the real-world breaches that resulted from the successful use of each type of vector as well as the attack surface:

Social engineering attack

These attacks manipulate individuals into revealing confidential information or gaining unauthorized access to systems. They often involve deceptive communication methods like phishing or impersonation:

- Example: In Q3 2023, a surge in social engineering attacks was noted, with the K2A243 (Scattered Spider) group using sophisticated email phishing scams, including attacks via Microsoft Teams using DarkGate malware.

Employees with access to the systems and email as the secondary attack surface were the primary exploited attack surface. The employees were tricked through social engineering into exposing their credentials via SMS.

The email component was used to help deliver messages convincing them to install the tools and malware. Without an effective defense, nothing prevented the attackers from getting through. Each of these elements was necessary to the success of this complex attack.

Attacks like this contributed to a rise in social engineering and an increase in business email compromise (BEC), where cybercriminals deceive employees into transferring money or providing sensitive information.

- Attack vector: Emails and text messages
- Primary attack surface: Employees
- Secondary attack surface: Email systems, Teams, phones via SMS

Software exploits

These are attacks that exploit weaknesses or vulnerabilities in software or hardware to gain unauthorized access or cause disruptions. They often involve sophisticated hacking techniques:

- Example: In December 2021, the Kaseya ransomware attack exploited a vulnerability in the company's software, impacting over 1,000 companies globally. Orchestrated by the REvil group, the cybercriminals demanded $70 million to decrypt the data.

  In this case, the primary attack surface are the vulnerabilities in the Kaseya software that was exploited by REvil. This provided the entry point to inject ransomware into the system. Without this opening, many of the systems that fell victim would have been otherwise untouchable.

  The servers that automatically ran software updates from Kaseya, configured to automatically trust the provider, were an additional component of the attack surface. They could not have installed the tainted software without this inherent trust, which allowed the attack to take place.

- Attack vector: Modified software
- Primary attack surface: Kaseya software
- Secondary attack surface: Servers running Kaseya

Malware attacks

Malware attacks involve malicious software such as viruses, worms, trojans, and ransomware being installed on a victim's system without their knowledge. These can lead to data theft, system damage, or unauthorized network access:

- Example: The University of California, San Francisco, faced a malware attack in November 2021. The Conti ransomware group used a phishing email to install malware, resulting in data theft and file encryption, with a ransom demand of $1.14 million.

The Conti group used the email system as their primary attack surface, sending infected emails to it. This allowed malware to spread to employees who opened the emails because no filtering software was implemented that could detect the malicious emails. This meant the Conti group was able to launch the payload and infect devices. As these organizational devices had no sufficient means to stop the malware, their vulnerability was exploited, making them an additional part of the attack surface.

- Attack vector: Emails
- Primary attack surface: Employees
- Secondary attack surface: Email systems, end user devices

Man-in-the-middle (MitM) attacks
In these attacks, the threat actor secretly intercepts and possibly alters the communication between two parties who believe they are directly communicating with each other. This can lead to data theft or manipulation:

- Example: In April 2018, Dutch authorities caught four Russian intelligence officers from the GRU cyberhacking team attempting to conduct a MitM hacking operation targeting the WiFi network of the Organisation for the Prohibition of Chemical Weapons.

  The attack surface was the OPCW network infrastructure that allowed individuals to hijack the network and intercept traffic. The infrastructure lacked appropriate controls to detect a rogue access point that could intercept user traffic.

- Attack vector: WiFi
- Primary attack surface: Network infrastructure

Insider threats
These occur when someone within the organization, such as an employee or contractor, abuses their access to compromise the organization's security, intentionally or unintentionally:

- Example: In April 2023, the FBI arrested a member of the Massachusetts Air National Guard for leaking top secret and classified documents online.

  This individual used overly permissive access rights to steal data. Failure to adhere to the principle of least privilege, coupled with the inability to adequately detect suspicious usage patterns, allowed this exposure of sensitive data to take place.

- Attack vector: Misuse of access rights
- Primary attack surface: Access privileges
- Secondary attack surface: Data storage systems

While this is not a complete list of attack vectors, these high-profile breach examples highlight the wide range of unique threats to organizational security and demonstrate the need for distinct prevention and mitigation strategies. One key aspect to note here is that a single attack vector can target multiple attack surfaces. Attack surfaces and attack vectors rarely have a one-to-one relationship—it's often many-to-many.

The fluid nature of attack vectors is notable. These are in a constant state of evolution as criminals find new paths around organizational defenses. This reality underscores the need for continuous vigilance; there is no silver bullet, no defense that is one hundred percent foolproof. No matter how innovative our security measures become, cybercriminals will find ways to circumvent them. This is why we must be prepared for emerging threats and zero-day attacks.

That's not to say threat actors won't use tried-and-true exploits of long-existing vulnerabilities. In fact, that is usually where they start. However, they don't stop there. Once well-known exploits and low-effort attacks fail, cybercriminals double down on their efforts, seeking out novel and inventive methods to breach defenses. This is part of what makes attack surface management challenging and crucial for any growing organization.

What Is Attack Surface Management?

Now that we better understand attack surfaces and attack vectors, let's take a look at exactly what attack surface management is and why it matters. ASM is the fundamental understanding, analysis, and management of attack surfaces. It covers identifying, assessing, and mitigating vulnerabilities across an organization's digital footprint.

So why does this matter to your organization? ASM helps you understand your entire organizational attack surface and correctly prioritize the protections that allow you to get the best possible results from your cybersecurity investment. It's a well-known fact that we can't stop every attack. Additionally, cybersecurity teams operate with finite resources, which means that we can either play Whack-a-Mole with cyberattacks or adopt a strategic, organized approach to handling threats and vulnerabilities and reducing risk. This is where ASM comes in.

The strategic nature of ASM accommodates the constantly evolving threat landscape and the less dynamic organizational attack surface that, while generally static for periods, does shift to keep pace with new technologies and changing business processes. By encompassing these aspects of an organization's digital presence, ASM provides a holistic approach to defending organizations against a wide array of cyberthreats. The ongoing nature of ASM, through monitoring and adapting, ensures that as vulnerabilities are identified, they are assessed in terms of their potential impact. Once assessed, either the vulnerabilities can be eliminated or their impact can be effectively mitigated to holistically improve the quality of cybersecurity defenses.

The attack surface of modern organizations has undergone significant change in recent years. A multitude of global factors initiated a shift from strictly traditional office roles to a mix of traditional, remote, and hybrid workforce models as well as driving the acceleration of cloud adoption. These, in turn, eliminated the reliance on the once-trusted corporate perimeter, where much of the security was provided by internal networks. Employees now access corporate resources both on-premises and in the cloud, from a range of geographical locations and leveraging public and personal networks, sometimes even using personal devices. All of which renders traditional defenses like firewalls and access control lists less effective.

With remote operations, organizations can maintain some devices' security by enforcing patching and security policies. Still, they cannot extend that level of control to the vast array of the networks employees now use, such as those at home, in coffee shops and libraries, or in hotels. This expansion of the possible attack surface has necessitated a combination of old and new security strategies focusing on reducing external connection risk. Virtual private networks (VPNs) have long been a standard for ensuring safe connections between the client and the office. Companies had to expand on this to incorporate access monitoring, threat detection, and more robust access controls to account for threats where the device or user's credentials were compromised.

There has also been a significant increase in collaboration and communication platforms like Slack, Microsoft Teams, and Zoom to facilitate the global workforce. These platforms have become indispensable tools for facilitating effective communication and collaboration across geographies and time zones.

However, with this reliance comes inherent risks and an expanded attack surface, particularly concerning the sharing and storage of information. While enhancing productivity and connectivity, these platforms can also be potential targets for data breaches, unauthorized access, and information leaks, especially if sensitive or proprietary information is shared. The ability to rapidly collaborate and share data also allows for the rapid sharing of dangerous content, including files infected with hidden threats such as ransomware, rootkits, or malware.

Along with challenges in remote access and collaboration, organizations have transitioned from traditional on-premises IT environments to cloud-based services and tools, which is a significant shift in how they manage their data and operations. This shift has been driven by the need for better access to a global workforce, the desire for faster development cycles, and the advantages of scalable, cost-effective operations.

Cloud-based services offer unparalleled flexibility and efficiency, allowing organizations to rapidly scale up or down based on their needs. However, adopting cloud technologies brings unique challenges, particularly in terms of security.

One of the primary security implications of widespread cloud adoption is the shift to shared responsibility models. In these models, the cloud service provider and the client organization are responsible for different security aspects. Many organizations, however, were not fully prepared for this shift and found that their existing tools and technologies were not always compatible with cloud environments or as effective in securing them. Compounding this was a move toward newer technologies, such as containerization, where traditional IT security teams struggle due to lack of training or preparation, causing the attack surface to grow and creating massive exposures. This lack of preparedness can lead to vulnerabilities in safeguarding sensitive data.

Compounding this is multitenant cloud environments, where resources are shared among multiple users, such as in many software-as-a-service (SaaS) environments. The risk here is twofold: firstly, sensitive data could potentially be exposed to other tenants or the cloud provider itself, and secondly, if the cloud provider suffers a breach, it could lead to the exposure of an organization's data. Understanding what data is stored in these places is a core part of managing the cloud attack surface.

Special attention must be given to the array of heterogeneous devices populating the modern network environment. IoT sensors, operational technology (OT) systems, and smartphones represent diverse, often less-secured nodes that significantly expand an organization's attack surface. These devices vary widely in their operating systems, security protocols, and susceptibility to threats, making securing them uniquely challenging.

It is important to remember that even though most of the technology discussed so far pertains to internal operations, the attack surface extends well into customer-facing infrastructure. This shift is particularly pronounced with APIs and online services that interact directly with customers. These interfaces often serve as critical gateways to organizational data and services, making them attractive targets for cyberattacks.

Part of the drive for ASM is the evolution of cyberthreats over time. These threats have increased in sophistication and diversity, fundamentally altering the cybersecurity landscape. Initially, cyberthreats were relatively straightforward and limited in scope, often targeting specific, well-defined system vulnerabilities. However, with technological advancements and the increasing complexity of IT environments, these threats have become more intricate and varied, encompassing everything from advanced malware and ransomware to complex social engineering and state-sponsored cyberattacks. Observing these developments, you may recognize a similar evolution in your own organization's challenges. This shifting paradigm underscores the importance of rethinking our cybersecurity strategies. Traditional security approaches are often inadequate against these sophisticated threats. For this reason, many organizations adopt a strategic and dynamic methodology like ASM.

One change that has driven this need for proactive defense is the significant evolution of cybercrime through the emergence of advanced persistent threats (APTs) and targeted attacks. APTs represent a new level of threat, typically but not exclusively state-sponsored or originating from highly organized criminal entities, focusing on prolonged and stealthy operations against specific targets. These attacks often aim at espionage, data theft, or causing long-term damage to critical infrastructure, distinguishing themselves from more opportunistic cybercrime through their persistence, level of sophistication, and the significant resources behind them. APTs tend to leverage a combination of tactics simultaneously to create numerous points of ingress, allowing them recurring access to targets, even if a few ways get shut down.

A similar trend is evident in the realm of malware. In RaaS attacks, the RaaS groups are not focused purely on malware delivery, but often thoroughly breach an environment before they ever start deploying ransomware payloads. They establish future points of entrance, and plant hidden inactive malware allowing them to restart future attacks with ease, even after defenders believe their organization has survived an attack.

This evolution of malware reflects a parallel escalation in the methods used by cybercriminals, moving beyond traditional attack vectors to more insidious and hard-to-detect techniques. These attacks are no longer just simple email attachments. They now frequently leverage complex phishing schemes, exploiting human vulnerabilities to gain access to networks or uploading infected files via trusted pathways, such as web portals used by contractors or third parties, making detecting and preventing these attacks more challenging.

The XZ (*https://oreil.ly/diU7p*) attack did just this, compromising open source software libraries that were assumed to be trustworthy, subverting them to embed a malicious payload into software using the compression libraries. The libraries' repository was assumed safe and was managed through the crowd-sourced process that open source code relies upon. But malicious actors manipulated the process by being "helpful," allowing the toxic code payload to be inserted and approved into the codebase.

To complicate this further, bad actors have developed new malware strains and attack vectors, including advanced ransomware and rootkits, as well as hidden threats embedded in seemingly safe file types like documents. This evolution has rendered traditional solutions less effective, as the rapid change in methods means that signature-based detection often can't keep up. Even behavioral identification techniques, which look for patterns of malicious activity, are being circumvented by newer, more sophisticated threats.

Phishing attacks, mirroring the evolution of malware, have undergone a significant transformation to become highly sophisticated and targeted. Gone are the days of generic, easily spotted phishing emails; today, cybercriminals craft deceptive messages meticulously tailored to individual recipients or specific organizations. This customization increases the difficulty of distinguishing between legitimate communications and malicious ones.

Criminals often conduct thorough research to personalize their approach, leveraging social media and publicly available information to create convincing scenarios. They expertly mimic communications' tone, language, and visual design from trusted entities, such as financial institutions, government agencies, or familiar corporate entities. By exploiting social engineering tactics, these advanced phishing attacks effectively manipulate recipients into revealing confidential information, such as login credentials or financial details, or unwittingly execute actions that compromise the organization's security, like transferring funds or granting access to restricted systems.

As we see with the advanced techniques used in APTs, malware, and phishing, the cyberthreat landscape continually evolves, becoming more complex and challenging to navigate. This trend paves the way for emerging threats, which harness the latest technological advancements such as artificial intelligence (AI) and machine learning (ML). These emerging threats represent the next frontier in cybercrime.

While AI and ML technologies have significantly advanced threat detection and response, they have also opened doors to new vulnerabilities. For instance, cybercriminals can harness these technologies to develop adaptive malware. Such malware could use machine learning algorithms to analyze and understand the defense mechanisms it encounters, allowing it to modify its code on the fly to evade detection by antivirus software. An example of this is polymorphic malware, which can change its underlying code and signature, making it incredibly challenging for traditional, signature-based antivirus solutions to identify and neutralize it.

Furthermore, AI and ML can be exploited for large-scale, automated cyberattacks. Threat actors could deploy AI-driven bots to conduct widespread phishing campaigns, where each message is uniquely crafted to target specific individuals, increasing the likelihood of success. These bots can learn and improve, adapting their messages based on user interactions to become more convincing. AI can also be used in more complex cyberattacks like distributed denial of service (DDoS), where it optimizes strategies in real time, making them more disruptive and harder to counter. The use of AI in such scenarios represents a significant escalation in the cyber arms race, as it equips criminals with tools that can analyze vast amounts of data, identify vulnerabilities faster, and execute attacks with unprecedented efficiency and scale.

This evolution across multiple vectors has dramatically expanded the potential attack surfaces for organizations. As these modern threats no longer just target traditional internal IT infrastructure, companies must account for vulnerabilities in cloud services, mobile devices, IoT devices, and human elements, making attack surface management necessary. This might lead you to think that ASM is just another form of vulnerability management, but it would be more correct to say that vulnerability management is actually a small part of the ASM framework.

Vulnerability management, while essential, operates with a limited scope focused primarily on identifying and mitigating specific system vulnerabilities. When utilized independently, this approach can overwhelm organizations with extensive lists of vulnerabilities, making it difficult to prioritize effectively without a broader strategic context. In contrast, ASM enriches information from vulnerability management solutions by integrating it within a wider organizational framework, enabling security teams to focus efforts where they can most significantly improve security posture without negatively impacting business objectives.

Vulnerability Management

Vulnerability management is a fundamental component of ASM, but it has a narrow focus on discovering and mitigating vulnerabilities within a specific system, application, or network. This process involves scanning for weaknesses, identifying them, and then taking steps to address these issues. However, when vulnerability management is used by itself, organizations are often overwhelmed by an extensive list of findings. Without a broader context, this can result in a challenging situation where prioritizing which vulnerabilities to address first becomes a daunting task.

Without integrating additional layers of analysis and insight, vulnerability management alone may lead to a reactive approach, where organizations constantly try to patch issues without a strategic plan or understanding of their broader impact. This never-ending hamster wheel causes them to spend most of their time addressing urgent and important problems without having time to address the important ones proactively before these become critical. Vulnerability management zooms in on specific issues leading to awareness and possibly actionable advice on mitigation, but attack surface management assesses the overall risk landscape and all potential weak points.

ASM leverages the findings from vulnerability management solutions and contextualizes them within the broader framework of the organization's operations and business objectives. This means identifying problems, understanding how they fit into the attack surface, and assessing their potential impact on the business. By doing so, ASM enables organizations to prioritize vulnerabilities based on their relevance and potential damage, ensuring that resources and efforts are focused on areas that yield the most significant impact on the investment. This approach transforms vulnerability management from a simple checklist of security gaps into a strategic tool, aligning cybersecurity efforts with business goals and facilitating a more proactive and effective defense against cyberthreats.

The Components of ASM

ASM comprises six core steps that help establish a baseline of what assets exist and their overall value to the organization. These steps build on each other, creating a foundation of data that feeds into subsequent steps, as shown in Figure 1-2. The steps cover everything from the initial discovery of the attack surface to monitoring and management. Using ongoing monitoring, we can identify and adapt security controls, policies, or procedures as needed to continuously improve our risk posture. Like many processes in cybersecurity, ASM is not a one-time project but a cyclical one, requiring repetition, particularly when the IT ecosystem changes or the threat landscape evolves. We'll break down ASM into its components and discuss each in more detail.

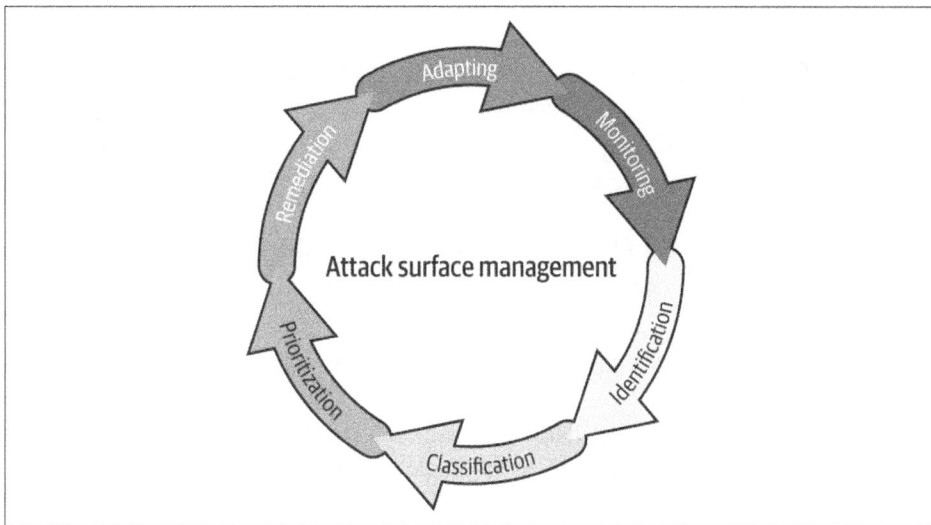

Figure 1-2. As with many security processes, ASM contains multiple components; effectively managing your attack surface is a continuous process of identifying, classifying, prioritizing, and remediating all of the various points where an attacker can try to enter or extract data from an organizational environment.

Identification

The first step in ASM primarily focuses on understanding what exists within the organizational ecosystem. This process entails a thorough exploration in which each technology is systematically identified and cataloged. This includes recognized systems as well as those that are unknown or possibly overlooked, often termed *shadow IT*. Identifying these assets forms a solid foundation for developing a baseline security strategy.

While similar to traditional asset management in IT, there are core differences in how ASM handles this process of inventory assessment. Let's detail those differences:

The scope and nature of assets

Traditional asset management focuses primarily on tangible IT assets within the organization, such as hardware, software applications, and network devices. This approach involves maintaining a detailed inventory of these assets, tracking their usage, and managing their life cycle. Conversely, ASM expands the scope to include intangible assets like data, user accounts, and cloud services, as well as external elements like third-party services and supply chain components. ASM aims to identify all potential attack points, including assets often overlooked in traditional asset management, thereby providing a more comprehensive view of the organizational attack surface.

Identifying unknown and dynamic assets

A traditional asset management inventory is simple and relies on a static mapping of known and regularly tracked assets. However, ASM goes beyond the standard IT stack, looking for known and unknown assets, including brief and dynamic ones, such as temporary cloud instances or containers. ASM leverages dynamic discovery and constant monitoring to keep pace with the rapidly changing nature of modern IT environments, especially the cloud, ensuring that no potential vulnerabilities are overlooked.

Achieving visibility and coverage

The visibility in standard asset management is often limited to assets within the controlled IT environment. ASM, however, seeks broader visibility, extending its reach to include BYOD or shadow IT and emphasizing the understanding of an asset's external exposure. ASM tools employ advanced techniques like external scanning and threat intelligence to identify assets exposed to potential attackers, thus providing a more holistic view of an organization's vulnerabilities.

Understanding asset context

Context for traditional asset management is concerned with operational aspects of assets, such as performance, maintenance, and compliance. ASM takes a deeper dive into the security context of assets, focusing on how they could be exploited and assessing their security posture and significance in the overall attack surface. The information gathered by this approach is vital for understanding the security implications of each asset and how it contributes to the organization's susceptibility to cyberthreats.

Taking a proactive security-centric approach

Goals of standard asset management processes highlight information about asset utilization, cost, and life cycle management. With ASM's security-centric approach, prioritization is placed on identifying vulnerabilities, misconfigurations, and potential attack vectors so remediation can be prioritized and managed proactively.

Classification

While asset identification establishes what exists in the environment, it does not provide context on the importance of each asset. This step addresses this issue by grouping assets into categories. This involves classifying assets based on various criteria, such as data type, compliance requirements, functions, and relevance to security.

To effectively manage an organization's attack surface, we need to differentiate between asset classification and data classification. While both processes involve categorizing elements based on sensitivity and risk, asset classification focuses on the devices, software, and systems as a whole, considering factors such as their role in business operations, vulnerability to threats, and potential impact of compromise. In contrast, data classification explicitly addresses the type of data an asset handles—such as confidential, private, or public information—and the security measures necessary to protect it.

The classification of an asset can indeed be influenced by the type of data it processes or stores; however, the criteria and implications of classifying assets versus data are distinct. Understanding this distinction is vital for teams to implement appropriate security controls and compliance measures, ensuring that their assets and data are adequately protected.

Let's consider what this means:

Tailoring security controls
> Different assets have different security needs, and asset classification allows organizations to tailor security controls appropriately. For example, consider two organizational databases, one containing sensitive data and the other managing publicly accessible data. While both may require strict access controls and regular backups, the one with sensitive data requires encryption of sensitive fields. The asset classification highlights the different needs, allowing organizations to implement adequate security controls where they matter most. This helps organizations avoid broadly scoped security rules that overprotect assets that don't need it or underprotect those that do.

Determining compliance needs
> Security needs don't just focus on the challenges from outside adversaries; these often have to include compliance with governance, legal, and regulatory requirements. Asset classification plays a pivotal role in ensuring these meet current needs. Categorizing assets must have a data focus highlighting when a given data type falls into a regulated category. For instance, an asset containing personal

health information would be classified for HIPAA compliance and require specific security and privacy controls. Without factoring in these needs, it would be easy to overlook required controls, leading to penalties, fines, and damage to the organization's reputation.

Planning for incident response and recovery

Asset classification also highlights what is most important to business operations, helping improve business continuity by developing incident response plans that prioritize these assets to ensure faster recoveries with less downtime. An example would be restoring web services and their supporting infrastructure that is indispensable to customer operations. This prioritization in planning helps organizations maintain operational continuity even in the face of security incidents, minimizing the impact on business functions and reputation.

Prioritization

ASM recognizes that not all vulnerabilities or exposures carry the same level of risk, especially when considering the associated assets. It is necessary to prioritize vulnerabilities based on their potential impact versus the asset's value to the organization. This approach ensures the effective allocation of limited resources to manage the attack surface. There are many ways to establish this prioritization, and we will explore these more thoroughly in Chapter 5, including discussing quantitative and qualitative risk assessment methods and their role in the prioritization process.

Servers containing sensitive data or systems that are externally accessible and other high-risk systems are given priority in applying security controls. These systems are prioritized using measures such as frequent patching, robust monitoring, and stringent access controls. This does not mean that other systems are ignored; it just shifts the focus to those that need it most. By ensuring the most vitally important assets are prioritized for protection, organizations gain the most significant reduction in risk for their resource investment.

Remediation

Once priorities are established, the next step is remediation by securing high-priority attack surfaces. This involves remedying vulnerabilities and misconfigurations that expose the asset, which includes implementing targeted controls to address exposures within the attack surface. Given the resource constraints most organizations face, ASM underscores the importance of strategic security measures—securing everything perfectly is not feasible, hence the need for a focused approach.

One of the core drivers of ASM is the need for organizations to balance their limited resources with the need to secure their attack surface. The information from the identification and classification phases helps to drive the prioritization by determining vulnerabilities and misconfigurations that pose the greatest threat. The difference between this and standard vulnerability management is that ASM leverages a deep understanding of the organization's security posture and the potential impact of different threats. In contrast, traditional vulnerability management simply focuses on prescribed scores.

Organizations face a flood of data from vulnerability management tools, leading to more vulnerabilities than can be efficiently tackled. Even if an organization focuses purely on high-priority weaknesses, eliminating them may not effectively reduce risk. For example, eliminating 20 critical vulnerabilities on a legacy server that is about to be retired and that only resides on the internal network is likely less effective than removing one on the publicly exposed API for the organization's e-commerce site. ASM uses business context information so organizations can target security controls in areas where they will yield the highest reduction in actual risk, rather than just checking off boxes for security.

Adapting

In tandem with monitoring, ASM involves regular adaptation to the changing landscape. As organizations grow and their digital footprints evolve, so does their attack surface. Periodic reassessment and adjustment of security strategies is necessary to keep pace with these changes, ensuring the organization's security posture remains robust and responsive.

As we've mentioned previously, traditionally organizations often have a fairly static attack surface for extended periods, but over time, especially in a growing organization, events or situations occur that necessitate changes to the IT ecosystem. However, modern organizations are built on fast-growing and evolving IT infrastructures, with CI/CD pipelines pushing constantly changing code, teams adding new supply chain vendors, and even marketing people pushing random scripts onto the main site without security review, causing the attack surface to be constantly in flux.

Even for more static organizations, standing up new physical or virtual systems, adding new software, adopting a new service provider, and even building out a new satellite office are all examples of common changes that might expand the attack surface. It's important to note that change does not always grow the attack surface; sometimes it shrinks it, such as by deprecating old systems, removing unused software, or eliminating unused ports.

When there is advance knowledge of these impending changes, they can be planned for. Planning makes it easier to work through the ASM framework and adapt current security controls, policies, or procedures to meet the needs of the modified attack surface to maintain a robust security posture.

Monitoring

The use of continuous monitoring is crucial to an ASM practice. It leverages ongoing surveillance of all network assets, detecting changes in the attack surface, and identifying new vulnerabilities as they emerge. Organizations can promptly respond to new threats, patch vulnerabilities, and adjust their security strategies by implementing tools and protocols that provide real-time or near-real-time monitoring. This proactive approach not only helps in immediate threat detection but also contributes significantly to the adaptability of ASM.

The need for continuous monitoring is also driven by the perpetual evolution of cybercriminals. An organization never has a permanently "secure" state, as the threat landscape is ever-changing. Continuous monitoring feeds into this adaptability, offering insights into emerging trends and potential future threats, enabling organizations to stay ahead of malicious actors, and continuously refining and updating their defense mechanisms to remain in line with the latest security developments.

The Strategic Role of ASM in Cybersecurity

It's important to consider the role of an attack surface as a strategic road map for cybersecurity teams. This becomes increasingly valuable in the context of limited resources and the overwhelming volume of data generated by existing security tools because it allows teams to focus their security efforts. ASM acts as a road map, showing the vulnerable spots that need protection. In today's cybersecurity landscape, organizations face a deluge of vulnerabilities and potential issues, far exceeding their capacity to mitigate them all.

This reality is further compounded by the prevalent shortage of skilled cybersecurity professionals, leading to teams that are often understaffed and overburdened. In such an environment, understanding and mapping the attack surface is not just beneficial; it's imperative. By prioritizing key vulnerabilities, cybersecurity teams can strategically allocate their limited resources, directing their efforts toward implementing targeted security measures where they are most needed.

Lastly, managing the attack surface is essential for compliance with regulations and standards such as PCI DSS, HIPAA, GDPR, and SOX. These standards require strict adherence to security procedures that prevent the dissemination of customer data. Data breaches or other security incidents caused by inadequate controls will have significant legal consequences that can directly affect an organization's bottom line through fines, lawsuits, or costly mandatory remediation plans.

Regulatory failures also come with less direct costs such as SEC materiality guidance, class action lawsuits, impacts to the stock price, and loss of customer trust. Customers are savvier and factor how well their data is protected into whether they wish to do business with a company. Organizations that are victims of a data breach, especially if due to their own mismanagement, suffer a loss of customers, and regaining them takes more than waiting it out. It requires showing a fundamental change in how the organization prioritizes security, such as what is provided by ASM.

Adopting the Attacker's Perspective

Attack surface management represents a significant shift in cybersecurity, moving from a purely defensive posture to one that incorporates elements of offensive strategy. By adopting an attacker's perspective, ASM offers a more comprehensive and proactive approach to securing IT environments by incorporating offensive strategy elements into traditional defense postures. Beyond this, it also helps validate that security controls are working and delivering the necessary protection.

Changing Your Point of View

ASM represents a transformative concept. Most organizations focus their security with a defense-centric mindset, sometimes called a blue team. The blue team is aimed at protecting information systems against cyberattacks by identifying vulnerabilities, implementing security measures, and doing continuous monitoring. Some organizations also leverage an offense-centric approach, or a red team, in which members aim to circumvent and penetrate defenses, highlighting where controls are insufficient or altogether lacking.

ASM requires a significant shift to include thinking like an attacker. However, making this transition can be challenging. As security professionals, we are traditionally conditioned to focus on defense. We're taught to prioritize safeguarding assets, monitoring activities, and responding to threats.

Cybercriminals, typically driven by goals like financial gain, hacktivist mentalities, or political motivations, often aim for minimal effort and maximum anonymity. This spurs creativity and strategic thinking. They search for the weak point that offers the most leverage in an attack. Embracing the attacker's point of view requires a fundamental change in approach and innovative thinking. Moving to this more offensive perspective involves several key steps. First is the identification of vulnerabilities within the system. Then, a thorough analysis of why these vulnerabilities might be attractive.

Next is the pivotal step of adopting the adversaries' mindset and considering questions such as, "If I were the attacker, which targets would appear most attractive? What tactics would I employ to exploit these vulnerabilities?" Engaging in this kind of strategic thinking is mandatory for shifting from a reactive to a proactive stance in cybersecurity, allowing for the anticipation of potential attacks rather than merely responding to them after they occur.

Seeing the whole picture

Adopting the adversary's mindset necessitates we see the whole picture and understand the context of an organization's vulnerabilities. Security professionals often grapple with a fragmented view of their organization's security landscape. This fragmented perspective can be attributed to time constraints and the complexity of large-scale IT infrastructures. Existing tools often only give visibility into specific areas, such as the cloud. While the findings in that area may be in-depth, they often lack the context of the business flow or the integration or interaction of other IT assets, which limits their actual value.

On the other hand, attackers meticulously analyze the business context and operational flow to pinpoint areas most susceptible to impactful attacks or deeper system penetration. This approach goes beyond mere technological vulnerabilities; it encompasses a comprehensive evaluation of business processes, data flow, and human elements that could be potential targets.

Getting a holistic view leverages the information gained through a risk assessment that extends beyond the conventional technology stack. This may seem overwhelming initially, but it does not have to be done all at once. By prioritizing and phasing the assessment process, the task can be broken up into digestible pieces that eventually account for all organizational assets.

The asset inventory is our foothold in this phased process. Knowing what we have, we can make a game plan for implementing the risk assessments. The inventory ensures that when we scope the risk assessment, we include all the assets of our most critical or vulnerable areas, such as key data assets and essential workflows.

We might start with our cloud infrastructure, or if that is too broad, we can narrow it to just a specific set of our e-commerce systems. By breaking it down this way, resources can be better planned and allocated. Hence, ASM is a systematic process rather than a sprint toward a monolithic goal, which would almost certainly end in failure.

The risk assessment will eventually encompass all facets of the business, including operational workflows, data management practices, and the roles of human actors within the system. Of course, this is part of the end game because such an all-encompassing approach gives us the full visibility to understand how different components interact and potentially create risk.

This interaction is seen when mapping out potential attack pathways. Viewing how disparate IT systems interface, less obvious vulnerabilities emerge where sensitive information might be exposed, or exploitable entry points may exist. By thoroughly mapping these pathways, organizations can gain valuable insights into their security posture, allowing them to preemptively address and fortify areas that an attacker might exploit. A proactive approach like this is vital for transitioning from a reactive to an aggressive stance in cybersecurity defense.

At a glance, it might seem that the visibility necessary for security teams also leads to an overreach in access and breaking segregation of duties. This problem can be addressed by implementing stringent governance mechanisms. These should include comprehensive logging infrastructure, regular audits, role-based access controls, incident management system, and strict oversight to maintain checks and balances.

By adopting an iterative process that respects the principles of least privilege and privacy, organizations can gradually expand their understanding of the attack surface in a controlled and secure manner, thus avoiding the pitfalls of an overly broad or intrusive approach.

Spotting easy targets

Cybercriminals often employ strategies akin to natural predators, seeking out the weakest and most vulnerable targets first. This efficient approach to hunting allows them to exploit the most accessible vulnerabilities with minimal effort. These "easy targets" often include people, outdated systems, predictable passwords, hardcoded secrets, and other overlooked security gaps within an IT environment. Cybercriminals view these weaknesses as low-hanging fruit, making them the first point of attack in their strategy.

However, a focus on easily exploitable vulnerabilities does not preclude them from attempting more complex and esoteric attacks. Understanding this predatory behavior is required for effective attack surface management, which stresses the importance of identifying and securing apparent yet often neglected vulnerabilities. Organizations can prioritize these weaknesses to prevent threat actors from gaining an easy foothold within their systems.

Recognizing and addressing common vulnerabilities forms the cornerstone of the proactive defense approach. Vigilance is indispensable in identifying weaknesses that cybercriminals often exploit, including unpatched software, systems with default configurations, and weak authentication mechanisms.

Regular vulnerability scans and security assessments become foundational tools in the arsenal of ASM. These scans and assessments allow organizations to stay one step ahead, identifying and mitigating these "easy targets" before attackers can leverage them. The threat landscape is continuously evolving. The constant vigilance of feeding vulnerabilities back into the attack surface evaluation process is indispensable for ensuring the ongoing security and resilience of an organization's IT infrastructure against new and emerging threats.

Keep your eyes on the prize

The process of *asset criticality analysis* plays a significant role in this strategic approach. It thoroughly evaluates which assets are integral to the organization's core functions and operations. This analysis considers factors such as the importance of the asset to business operations, the sensitivity of the data it holds, and the potential impact on the organization should the asset be compromised. It also factors in which devices represent the most risk or could cause the most damage if misused, accounting for insider threats of all varieties.

Once the high-priority assets are identified, it is imperative to implement a layered defense strategy, or defense in depth, around them. An example is using a combination of firewalls and an intrusion detection system to generate alerts if someone bypasses the firewall. The goal is to use multiple security measures to protect these assets so that even if one defense layer is breached, others are in place to continue the protection.

It is important to note that critical or mission-critical systems are not the only things addressed. An approach like that would be akin to placing all the guards at a castle's front door while leaving the cellar door unattended. It's more that they are prioritized, giving them more of the limited resources available.

Across the organization, baseline standards will still need to be upheld, and these help reduce the attack surface holistically. Each door to the outside may have locks and a guard, but the front gate will also have reinforcements. By taking this approach there is still some security in place, but our focus is on the most likely targets.

Adapt and overcome

The landscape of cyberthreats constantly evolves, with bad actors continually crafting new tactics and strategies to breach defenses. We need to do the same as defenders. In this environment, vigilance becomes more than a practice; it is necessary. ASM is fundamentally about maintaining an ongoing state of alertness, closely monitoring for emerging vulnerabilities, and being prepared to adapt defense mechanisms to mitigate novel attacks rapidly. This continuous adaptation process is beneficial and essential for avoiding potential threats. It involves an understanding that what works today may not be effective tomorrow.

Adapting to evolving threats requires a twofold approach: staying informed on the threat landscape and developing a flexible and agile security posture. Staying informed means keeping abreast of the latest threat intelligence, which can shed light on emerging threat vectors and the tactics, techniques, and procedures used by attackers. This knowledge is invaluable for anticipating potential attack scenarios and preparing defenses accordingly.

On the other hand, developing a flexible and agile security posture is about building a security strategy that can quickly and efficiently adapt to new information about potential threats and vulnerabilities. This includes having the capability to swiftly reconfigure systems, implement new security controls, and adjust policies as the threat environment changes. It's about creating a security framework that is not rigid but is robust enough to withstand current threats while being adaptable enough to evolve with future challenges.

Proactive Strategy: Playing Attacker

Adopting a threat actor's mindset involves asking, "What would I do if I were the adversary?" This approach allows security professionals to anticipate potential attack methods, think creatively about vulnerabilities, and develop more effective defense strategies. By understanding the adversary's logic and potential targets, ASM transforms the approach to cybersecurity from reactive to proactive, ensuring that defenses are robust and strategically focused on the most probable threats.

ASM reframes cybersecurity strategy by combining defensive tactics with an offensive mindset. This perspective empowers organizations to think like attackers, anticipate their moves, and build more resilient and proactive defense systems, ultimately leading to a more secure and robust IT environment.

Threat-hunting strategies such as Atomic Red Team and the M.O.R.D.O.R. project build on using the attacker's mindset. These valuable tools enable organizations to proactively identify and mitigate potential security vulnerabilities. Atomic Red Team lets security teams execute specific, targeted attacks (atomics) against their systems to test and improve the effectiveness of their defensive mechanisms in real time. This helps ensure that security measures are robust enough to thwart attack scenarios.

Similarly, the M.O.R.D.O.R. project provides prerecorded, realistic attack scenarios based on observed threats, allowing organizations to simulate complete attack life cycles. This not only tests the resilience of current security postures but also aids in effectively training security teams to recognize and respond to complex, multistage threats.

ASM Use Cases and Security Challenges

Attack surface management is a multifaceted solution to various organizational challenges, addressing multiple use cases through a single, robust program. By implementing ASM, organizations can simultaneously tackle various issues that pertain to their cybersecurity posture. This includes enhancing the visibility of network assets, identifying and mitigating vulnerabilities, ensuring compliance with regulatory standards, and improving overall security resilience. ASM's comprehensive approach not only streamlines the process of managing the security of an organization's network but also ensures that multiple problems, such as weak points in the network, compliance risks, and potential attack vectors, are addressed concurrently. Modern infrastructure is too large and scales too rapidly for traditional security practices to be effective. Attack surface management is designed to help organizations gain control of these environments and effectively manage risk with the teams' existing staffing, not the ones they want or wish they could afford.

Visibility Challenges

One of the most significant challenges addressed by attack surface management is visibility challenges due to the complexity of modern infrastructures. Gone are the days when an organization's infrastructure was confined to a data center. The widespread adoption of cloud infrastructure, containerization, virtualization, and SaaS products has dispersed data across various platforms, often outside the organization's direct control. This dispersion reduces control over data and often comes with inadequate native tools for visibility.

Traditional tools designed for on-premises environments struggle to adapt to these new, dispersed environments. Moreover, even when a tool performs well outside the traditional data center in a specific environment, it often cannot interoperate with other tools to create a unified view of all organizational assets and data. The result is a fragmented and incomplete picture of the organization's attack surface, leaving dangerous gaps in visibility and increasing the risk of security breaches.

ASM practices help organizations surpass the limitations of traditional tools, offering capabilities tailored to manage the complexities of modern distributed infrastructures. By integrating various data sources and providing insights across different environments—whether on-premises, in the cloud, or a hybrid of both—ASM helps bridge the gap in visibility. They enable organizations to map out and understand their entire attack surface, regardless of where their data and assets are located. This comprehensive visibility is necessary for identifying hidden vulnerabilities, monitoring emerging threats, and ensuring consistent security practices across all segments of the IT infrastructure.

Asset Management

One practice ASM is intrinsically linked to is *asset management*. Asset management leverages the processes of *continuous asset discovery* and *change awareness* to regularly identify and track new and existing assets within an organization's network. They ensure that the inventory of assets is constantly up-to-date, allowing security management to be more responsive to the ever-evolving IT landscape.

The categorization and monitoring of assets within ASM is a vital step involving classifying assets based on their type, importance, and potential risk. Categorization is key to prioritizing security efforts effectively and allocating resources where they are most needed. ASM also encompasses dynamic risk assessment and prioritization, a process that continuously evaluates and ranks assets based on their susceptibility to threats and their significance to business operations. Lastly, vulnerability identification is a cornerstone of ASM, focusing on systematically detecting weaknesses or flaws in assets that could be targeted for cyberthreats.

Asset Intelligence

In *asset intelligence*, ASM extends and enhances traditional asset management approaches. With ASM, asset intelligence goes beyond mere discovery and monitoring; it involves integrating contextual information about each asset within an organization's network. This includes understanding an asset's role, its configuration settings, how it connects and interacts with other assets, and its dependencies within the broader network architecture. By incorporating these layers of context, ASM provides a deeper, more nuanced understanding of each asset, enabling more precise and effective management of the attack surface. This approach is vital for identifying potential vulnerabilities and interdependencies that might not be apparent in a standard asset management framework.

Shadow IT

One of the major challenges that organizations face with their IT infrastructure is tracking the numerous assets that were not purchased and set up as a part of the standard IT process. In some cases these assets are temporary systems created to facilitate a project but not disposed of properly, leaving behind residual tech debt to address at a later time. This "zombie IT," if it persists for long periods unmanaged, creates easy attack surfaces. Alternatively, it might come as rogue IT such as SaaS solutions purchased and run by a department on their own.

No matter what the variety is, shadow IT creates attack surfaces that are not tracked or managed, leaving the organization exposed for extended periods of time. In many cases, this exposure can last well through an incident, with the company only finding out about a breach after being notified by a third party.

In discovering exposures, ASM is particularly valuable in identifying and managing risks associated with shadow IT (which we will discuss in more detail in Chapter 4), legacy systems, and dynamic cloud environments. With ASM, discovering exposure involves locating unmanaged, outdated, or abandoned systems within a network that may pose significant security risks due to their lack of regular maintenance and monitoring.

Cloud environments are a frequent location for shadow IT, making ASM instrumental in maintaining visibility in these dynamic environments. By providing comprehensive coverage and continuous monitoring of these environments, ASM ensures that all assets, regardless of location or complexity, are accounted for and secured.

This thorough approach to discovering and managing exposure is vital for organizations to maintain a robust and resilient cybersecurity posture, especially to handle the increasingly diverse and distributed IT infrastructures.

Managing Risk

ASM helps organizations effectively reduce and understand cybersecurity risks. It provides a contextual risk understanding, allowing organizations to evaluate risks based on their relevance and potential impact on business operations. The assessment is pivotal in discerning which risks pose the greatest threat to the organization's assets and objectives. ASM's focus on significant risks involves prioritizing various security alerts and information to help concentrate efforts on mitigating the most impactful threats, thereby optimizing resource allocation and response efficacy.

Further enhancing risk management is the use of proactive threat detection in ASM. It leverages strategies and tools to identify potential threats before they evolve into full-scale attacks. The proactive approach in ASM ensures that organizations are not just reactive to threats but are steps ahead in anticipating and neutralizing potential cybersecurity risks.

Keeping pace with a dynamic threat landscape

The rapid pace of change in contemporary IT environments is significantly accelerated by widespread cloud adoption. Over the last few years, the speed at which developers can create and implement new software functionality has drastically increased. Changes that once took weeks or months can now be executed in a matter of days. The accelerated pace of development and implementation, while advantageous in terms of efficiency and innovation, often surpasses the capabilities of traditional application security measures. Existing security processes, designed for slower development cycles, struggle to keep up with this rapid pace, leaving potential security gaps as new software is deployed or updated.

ASM plays a crucial role in enabling organizations to adapt to this accelerated pace of change. By providing a comprehensive and up-to-date view of the attack surface, ASM helps organizations identify and target the areas most impacted by the rapid changes. This focus is imperative, as these are the areas where vulnerabilities are most likely to arise and have the highest impact. ASM equips organizations with the agility to swiftly identify and address these emerging vulnerabilities, ensuring that security measures evolve with the IT environment.

Prioritization of risks

ASM is a significant benefit in the complex task of risk prioritization, especially in the modern landscape of advanced security tooling. These tools empower organizations to detect various vulnerabilities across their networks, systems, and applications, offering an unparalleled breadth of cybersecurity insight. While the enhanced detection capability results in a substantial influx of data and potential security risks, ASM turns this challenge into an advantage. It equips security teams with the ability to efficiently sift through a deluge of alerts, enabling them to identify and prioritize the most dangerous vulnerabilities effectively. The prioritization is foundational, as it ensures that the most significant threats are addressed first and with the appropriate resources, thereby optimizing the organization's response to potential security incidents.

Prioritizing risks has become an increasingly complex yet necessary task, particularly in light of the advancements in security tooling. These advanced tools enable organizations to detect a vast and varied array of vulnerabilities across their networks, systems, and applications. While this heightened detection capability is undeniably beneficial, it also brings a deluge of data concerning potential security risks. This influx can often be overwhelming, leading to an environment where security teams are inundated with alerts. The scenario poses a significant challenge: discerning which vulnerabilities represent the most substantial threat and determining the order in which they should be addressed.

The sheer volume of detected vulnerabilities can lead to more serious threats being lost in the noise of less significant issues. As a result, the ability to effectively prioritize risks is paramount. It requires an understanding of the technical aspects of each vulnerability and a keen awareness of their potential impact on the organization's broader operations and objectives. This prioritization ensures that the most impactful vulnerabilities are addressed promptly, mitigating the risk of significant breaches or disruptions to the organization's core functions. Consequently, the role of security teams evolves from merely responding to alerts to strategically managing risk based on a comprehensive understanding of the cyberthreat landscape and the organization's unique vulnerabilities.

With all these discovered vulnerabilities, organizations face a bigger challenge of managing prioritization based on risk, which we will delve into deeper in Chapter 5. Effective prioritization of risks is not only about identifying the most significant threats but also about aligning the response to these threats with the organization's available resources. This includes considering the availability of technical staff, understanding budgetary limitations, and assessing the feasibility of implementing specific security measures. By prioritizing risks in the context of these constraints, organizations can ensure a more efficient allocation of their limited resources. Such a strategic approach ensures that the most critical vulnerabilities are addressed promptly and with the appropriate level of urgency, thereby maximizing the impact of the organization's cybersecurity efforts within the bounds of its operational capabilities.

An underlying issue is contextualizing vulnerabilities within the business operations framework to drive this prioritization. An in-depth understanding of the business context for each vulnerability is essential. This process evaluates how a specific vulnerability can affect the IT infrastructure and the broader business operations and objectives. At a high level, the fundamental factors in this assessment include:

- The criticality of the affected system to essential business functions
- The type of data at risk (personal, financial, or sensitive corporate information)
- The potential repercussions of a security breach on the organization's reputation and legal standing

By contextualizing these elements, organizations can categorize vulnerabilities more accurately based on their potential impact on business operations. Doing so enables a more strategic and focused response, ensuring that resources and efforts are directed toward mitigating risks that pose the most significant threat to the organization's core objectives and functions.

Risks associated with mergers and acquisitions

ASM provides significant benefits by addressing the complexities associated with the rapid expansion of the attack surface. When an organization acquires another, it gains new assets and inherits associated security risks. ASM plays a vital role in systematically assessing the security posture and potential vulnerabilities of the newly combined entity. It enables comprehensive visibility of all assets, including hardware, software, digital assets, user accounts, and data repositories, which is essential for understanding the full scope of the expanded attack surface.

ASM does not operate based on assumed open trust between enterprises. Instead, a critical preliminary step involves rigorous attack surface validation to ensure that all assets, vulnerabilities, and threats are accurately identified and assessed. This validation is essential to establish a reliable foundation for ASM. Once validated, ASM can be systematically applied to manage and mitigate risks associated with the attack surface. Establishing stringent standards for attack surface validation ensures that ASM strategies are based on accurate data and can effectively protect the organization against potential security breaches.

Using ASM effectively navigates the challenges posed by differences in security infrastructure and the presence of previously unknown or unmanaged assets. By providing a clear and thorough assessment of the new, combined attack surface, ASM facilitates informed decision-making and strategic security planning, ensuring the organization's expanded digital environment is secure and resilient.

Incident Response and Prioritization

ASM excels in enhancing incident response and prioritization efforts. Through ASM, there is an enhanced visibility of asset usage, allowing for a more precise and comprehensive understanding of how network assets are utilized. This visibility is crucial in spotting anomalies swiftly, which could indicate potential security threats or breaches.

Additionally, ASM aids in rapid anomaly detection, enabling organizations to quickly identify and respond to unusual activities that might signal a security breach. Rapid detection is essential for minimizing the impact of such incidents. ASM utilizes automated alerting and efficient resolution mechanisms. These systems are designed to automatically alert security teams of potential threats and streamline the response and resolution process. The automation speeds up the response time and ensures a more organized and practical approach to managing security incidents.

Improved incident response

Attack surface management significantly enhances incident response by providing a detailed mapping of all potential points of ingress within an organization's network. This comprehensive mapping includes the obvious and less apparent entry points that cybercriminals could exploit. ASM enables organizations to implement proactive defense measures by identifying these potential vulnerabilities. These measures might involve reinforcing firewalls, applying stricter access controls, and continuously monitoring entry points for unusual activities.

In the event of a breach, ASM's detailed understanding of ingress points facilitates rapid identification of the breach's origin. The swift pinpointing of the attack's starting point is crucial for a quick and effective response, which is vital in limiting the breach's spread and reducing its overall impact.

ASM tools provide visibility into the actions taken by threat actors once they have penetrated a system. They enable organizations to track attackers' movements within their networks and identify which data or assets have been accessed or compromised. The tracking is pivotal in assessing the full scope of an incident. With ASM, organizations can more accurately determine the severity of a breach and the necessary steps for containment and remediation.

The insights gained from observing attacker behavior and understanding the impact of their actions are invaluable for future security planning. These insights allow organizations to refine their ASM strategies, adapting them to better anticipate and counter future threats by understanding the motivations and methods behind attacks on specific areas of their network.

Resource allocation

ASM offers a significant benefit in terms of resource allocation, despite the inherent challenges posed by limited resources. ASM's advantage lies in its ability to facilitate strategic planning and optimize these resources. By effectively identifying and prioritizing potential risks and vulnerabilities within an organization's IT environment, ASM enables a more focused and efficient allocation of resources. This targeted approach ensures that the most critical areas of the attack surface receive the attention and resources they require, enhancing the overall security posture with optimal resource utilization.

Investments in infosec need to be meticulously strategized, as all budgets are inherently limited. Selecting tools and technologies that offer quantifiable value and demonstrate versatility is essential. An example is tools that are capable of scanning vulnerability in diverse environments like cloud and on-premises rather than being confined to just one area. This approach not only ensures efficiency but also maximizes the return on investment. Additionally, infosec teams often find themselves in a competitive scenario, vying for funding against other departments. This necessitates articulating security investments' tangible value and importance to senior leadership to secure the necessary resources.

The security team's continuous training and skill development also play a pivotal role in resource allocation. Keeping up with the latest technologies and threats requires ongoing training, which demands investment of already limited resources. The advent of cloud computing is a prime example of how a lack of skills in new technologies can lead to significant security breaches, such as those resulting from misconfigured cloud services. Numerous breaches due to misconfigured S3 buckets exposing sensitive data are a stark reminder of this problem.

Security teams are constantly grappling with balancing operational security and implementing new, more robust security controls. Directing resources toward one area inevitably reduces the availability of others. This is compounded by team members' limited weekly working hours, which must be judiciously allocated between maintaining daily operations and pursuing proactive security measures. Achieving this balance is crucial, as both aspects are integral to maintaining a secure and resilient organization.

Policy Enforcement

ASM is vital in policy enforcement, particularly in ensuring regulatory and compliance alignment within organizations. With the complexities of modern cybersecurity, adhering to various legal and regulatory standards is not just mandatory but essential for maintaining organizational integrity and trust. ASM facilitates this alignment by providing a framework through which organizations can ensure that their operations, particularly IT and cybersecurity, comply with the necessary legal and regulatory requirements.

Compliance and Regulatory Pressures

Effective ASM helps the organization align with legal, regulatory, and internal data handling and protection rules. Compliance and regulatory requirements are about adhering to laws and protecting the organization from potential breaches and their consequences. ASM gives organizations visibility and understanding of how their data is exposed, allowing them to tailor controls to meet a wide range of industry and governmental requirements:

Internal governance
   In the context of cybersecurity, this refers to the set of policies, procedures, and controls an organization establishes to effectively manage its operations and associated risks. This aspect of governance is crucial in determining how cybersecurity risks are identified, assessed, and mitigated. Effective internal governance requires a clear understanding of the organization's risk appetite, which guides the development of robust cybersecurity policies.

External regulations
   Compliance with external regulations is critical to an organization's cybersecurity strategy. Laws such as the Health Insurance Portability and Accountability Act (HIPAA), the Sarbanes-Oxley Act (SOX), and the General Data Protection Regulation (GDPR) set specific cybersecurity requirements for organizations. HIPAA, for instance, is focused on safeguarding patient health information. At the same time, SOX is concerned with the integrity of financial data, and GDPR emphasizes protecting personal data rights within the European Union. Compliance with these regulations is mandatory, and failure to adhere can lead to significant monetary penalties, legal consequences, and reputational damage. Understanding the nuances of each law that applies to your organization helps in tailoring your cybersecurity strategies to ensure compliance and avoid the potential ramifications of noncompliance.

Industry mandates
   In addition to general regulatory requirements, certain industries are subject to specific mandates that dictate cybersecurity standards. For instance, the Payment Card Industry Data Security Standard (PCI DSS) is crucial for organizations handling credit card transactions. Service Organization Control 2 (SOC 2) is pertinent for service providers, and the ISO 27001 standard is vital for information security management. These industry mandates offer a structured framework for cybersecurity best practices and typically require organizations to undergo regular reporting and compliance audits. Adhering to the mandates is about more than just meeting regulatory requirements; it also plays a significant role

in building and maintaining trust with customers and partners. Demonstrating a commitment to rigorous cybersecurity standards through compliance with the industry-specific mandates reflects an organization's dedication to protecting its own data and that of its clients and stakeholders.

Compliance is further strengthened by ASM's role in improving reporting and documentation. By maintaining detailed records and generating comprehensive reports, ASM supports transparency and accountability in cybersecurity practices. These records and reports are crucial for demonstrating compliance during audits and reviews, and they also serve as invaluable resources for the continual improvement of security practices.

Summary

After reading this chapter, you should now have a better understanding of attack surface management and the fundamental role it plays in cybersecurity. Starting with a clear definition of ASM, we explored the comprehensive nature of an organization's attack surface, which includes physical hardware, software systems, and human elements that interact with these technologies.

As organizations increasingly incorporate advanced technologies like cloud computing, IoT, and AI into their infrastructures, the complexity and scope of their attack surfaces expand, introducing unique security challenges. ASM is your ongoing proactive defense against emerging threats, adapting as technology and risks change to preemptively address threats before attackers can exploit these surfaces.

Next, let's dive a bit deeper, exploring more on the specific types of attack surfaces. We'll discuss how the attack surfaces have evolved from traditional environments to today's modern and expanding IT ecosystem. We'll dig into how each component, from legacy systems to advanced cloud solutions, contributes to the organizational attack surface, and how that has given rise to a need for tailored security strategies that address the unique challenges posed by these diverse elements. By understanding the specifics of each type of attack surface, you will be better prepared to tackle the security complexities within your organization's environment.

CHAPTER 2

Types of Attack Surfaces

The transformation of IT infrastructure over the years has led to a multifaceted and complex landscape of attack surfaces, blending traditional elements like servers, workstations, and legacy systems with advanced technologies such as cloud computing, IoT devices, AI, and virtualization. This evolution has expanded the scope of IT beyond physical data centers to include virtualized environments, mobile and interconnected devices, and a vast array of cloud-based services and applications.

While this change has enhanced operational flexibility and efficiency, each component introduces unique security challenges and management complexities. This has created a need for new ways to manage security without overloading existing teams or technologies. By understanding these surfaces, we can learn how to find a balance in getting the benefits of these new technologies without applying so much security friction that keeping them safe eliminates their benefits.

The Ever-Expanding Organizational Attack Surface

When we start looking at attack surfaces, it's no longer as simple as it was in the early days of IT and the internet. We still have all of the traditional components of IT that keep businesses running, including workstations, networks, and servers, but IT is so much more now.

IT and how we do business has expanded to include a wider variety of technologies that are just as integral to business operations as the traditional components. Mobile devices keep employees who are on the go connected to work, no matter where they do business. Hosted applications and websites provide data and services to a remote workforce regardless of where they are geographically, but this also creates new targets for attackers.

In response to this transition, IT has evolved how it handles everything, including how we authenticate into systems and where our data is stored. Cloud technologies provide unprecedented availability and agility but significantly increase our exposure by shifting technology outside offices and often into someone else's data center. Even emerging technologies such as generative AI are helping facilitate faster, more agile business processes. However, they also create additional risks and security challenges that many businesses have yet to address. Figure 2-1 illustrates many attack surfaces organizations must manage.

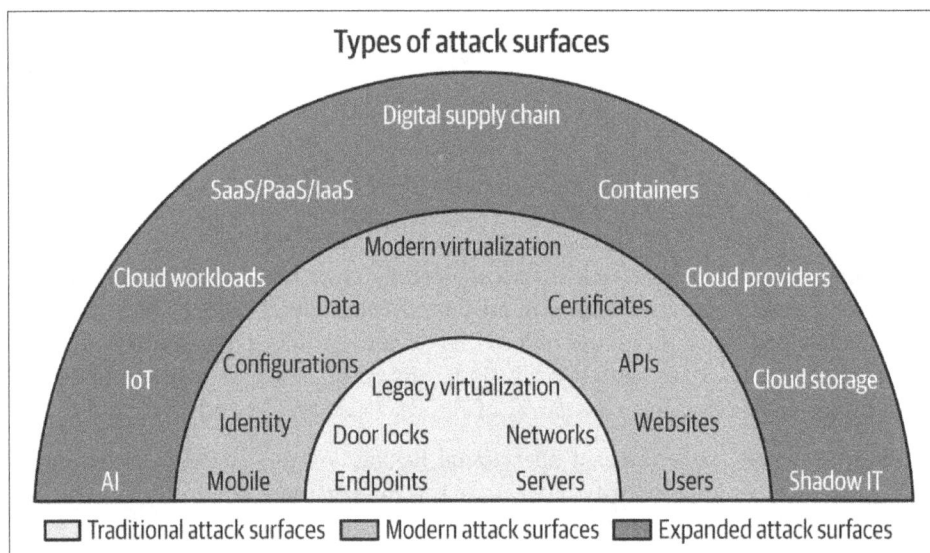

Types of attack surfaces

Digital supply chain

SaaS/PaaS/IaaS — Containers

Modern virtualization

Cloud workloads — Cloud providers

Data — Certificates

Configurations — APIs

IoT — Legacy virtualization — Cloud storage

Identity — Door locks — Networks — Websites

AI — Mobile — Endpoints — Servers — Users — Shadow IT

☐ Traditional attack surfaces ▨ Modern attack surfaces ■ Expanded attack surfaces

Figure 2-1. Organizations have evolved their view of attack surfaces over the years. Traditional attack surfaces were originally all that was in scope for IT and security. As IT has evolved, so has the view of attack surfaces and how they must be managed.

Each attack surface comes with its own security challenges. In this chapter, you'll learn how to identify and classify each, making you better equipped to identify your organization's attack surfaces. After all, you can't manage what you don't know exists. This chapter is all about understanding these complex surfaces so we can tackle their security challenges head-on.

Traditional IT Components

In traditional IT infrastructure, data centers form the nucleus, housing an array of standard technologies crucial for the day-to-day functioning of an organization. This array typically includes physical servers, workstations, and various networking equipment. Each component ensures the organization's IT operations run smoothly and efficiently. Physical servers, for instance, are the bedrock of enterprise data processing and storage, while workstations provide the necessary interface for employee inter-action and productivity. Networking equipment, comprising routers, switches, and firewalls, knits these elements together, facilitating communication and data exchange both within the organization and with the external world.

However, the prevalence of legacy systems is an often overlooked aspect of these traditional IT setups. Many organizations continue to rely on older technologies implemented years, if not decades, ago. They may use legacy code built on legacy languages or unpatched open-source code, creating an attack surface rife with vulner-abilities that cybercriminals love to see.

These legacy systems frequently present a unique challenge, as the staff who origi-nally installed and managed them have often moved on, taking their intricate knowl-edge and expertise with them. This generational knowledge gap leaves current IT staff grappling with fully understanding and effectively operating and maintaining these older systems. The inherent complexity of legacy systems and lack of expertise among the existing staff leads to inefficiencies and increased vulnerability to security risks.

Compounding the challenge is the issue of maintenance and documentation for all IT systems. While many organizations may start with complete documentation for new infrastructure, daily operations keep staff busy, making it challenging to keep all documentation up to date.

Regular maintenance of IT infrastructure is critical to ensure operational efficiency and security. However, maintaining them becomes daunting without thorough docu-mentation or a comprehensive understanding of existing systems. When the existing documentation is outdated or incomplete, current staff fall back to trial and error or external expertise. This hampers the effective maintenance of these systems and poses significant risks such as system failures, data loss, and security breaches. The prob-lem is compounded when infrastructure changes, incorporating poorly documented systems. An additional risk is created as these systems integrate with new systems and services but carry undocumented functionality or features, introducing potential vulnerabilities.

Technical debt is also better managed through regular maintenance. If regular updates and maintenance are neglected, organizations accumulate technical debt as systems evolve and technologies age. This debt manifests as increased costs and risks over time, especially when systems become outdated or are no longer compatible with new technologies.

Maintaining accurate documentation and a comprehensive understanding of existing systems is essential to avoid falling into costly trial-and-error cycles or reliance on external expertise.

It is essential to recognize that all IT systems have a life cycle. Mindful management of this life cycle includes planning for the eventual retirement of systems once they have served their useful lifespan. This planned obsolescence is necessary to mitigate the risks of aging technology and ensure a smooth transition to more modern and secure systems. The final stage of life cycle management is a well-structured plan to retire outdated systems, which helps reduce technical debt and align IT infrastructure with current technological standards and business needs.

Legacy Virtualization

Virtualization was one of the first significant evolutions in the design and management of IT infrastructures. It led to the shift from traditional physical setups to more flexible and scalable virtual environments. This was one of the first steps in moving from traditional IT infrastructure to more modern components.

Adopting virtualization has many benefits, including increased agility in deploying and scaling IT resources and cost efficiencies through better hardware utilization. In virtualized systems, the familiar endpoints and servers of conventional IT are transformed into virtual equivalents. These can include virtual machines replicating physical servers' functionality, virtual networks mirroring the complexities of physical networking infrastructure, and virtual storage solutions offering scalable and efficient data storage options.

One of the key advantages of a virtualized environment is its enhanced visibility and ease of management. Unlike physical systems, where the complexities of physical space can obscure unmanaged or underutilized resources, virtual assets are clearly listed in digital management systems, serverless code snippets, or virtual infrastructure lists. The transparency makes it much simpler to identify and address resources that have fallen out of active management, streamlining and maintaining an up-to-date and efficient IT infrastructure. This visibility is crucial not only for operational efficiency but also for ensuring that all elements of the IT environment are secured and compliant with organizational policies.

It's important to note that the visibility gained over virtual infrastructure does not always give us a clear picture of what is running on the asset. The centralized hosting lets us know that it exists and requires management, but there is still risk involved. The infrastructure's operational teams cannot always see what is running on them, who is running it, and why. These teams must know who owns the underlying asset so that they can be properly assessed for risk and validated for proper management.

Efficient utilization of virtual resources requires a balance between taking advantage of the flexibility and scalability of virtual environments and maintaining rigorous oversight to ensure these assets remain secure and aligned with IT management and security protocols. Without effective governance, virtualization leads to sprawl, where the ease of creating new virtual assets leads to an uncontrolled increase in virtual machines, networks, and storage resources, overwhelming IT management capabilities.

Modern IT Components

Over time, the IT infrastructure evolved, shifting from a traditional focus on servers and core network infrastructure to a more holistic approach. The new perspective encompassed not just the essential servers and networks but all connected devices, websites, and supporting technologies. This evolution was driven by the operational needs of modern organizations and the expanding scope of IT responsibilities.

Modern Virtualization

When virtualization first emerged as a technology, it was generally treated as just another server. The same level of management and oversight was applied to it, much like physical infrastructure. Users were given remote access to machines through RDP or SSH; as far as they were concerned, it was just another server.

However, this view was very shortsighted and ignored many of the challenges of maintaining isolation between virtual machines (VMs) and securing the hypervisor. These areas increased the attack surface beyond just being another server to viewing it as a complex ecosystem, one hosting numerous systems interconnected by a management backplane that is hidden from end users.

Virtualization by design is meant to maintain a level of isolation between VMs sharing physical hosts. On the surface, that appears to be the case. Still, when delving deeper into the architecture, it must be acknowledged that they all share memory space, CPU time, and sometimes storage, opening up a risk of breaking the virtual walls between them. Cross-VM attacks attempt to circumvent the isolation by targeting shared system components like the CPU cache or hypervisor to influence or attack another VM. This might allow the unintentional leakage of sensitive information between tenants, posing significant risks in environments that handle sensitive or regulated data.

Attackers may also target the underlying hypervisor, which creates and runs the virtual machines. By targeting the software that allows administrators to manage virtual environments, they aim to gain control over all hosted VMs. They may leverage escalation of privileges to exploit vulnerabilities in the hypervisor and access other VMs or the entire host. Alternatively, they may target the administrators with tailored malware in spear-phishing campaigns to hijack credentials and overtake infrastructure.

Improperly configured virtualized systems also risk adding new VMs without appropriate governance oversight. In some cases, anyone with hypervisor access could create and operate their own VM, bypassing security guardrails. This common path can lead to significant amounts of shadow IT, further broadening the attack surface.

For the modern attack surface, administrators must shift the paradigm beyond the individual hosted assets and focus on the holistic environment encompassing the virtualized infrastructure.

IoT

One of the first drivers of modern IT infrastructure was the prevalence of IoT devices across modern networks. This changed how digital environments needed to be structured and managed. These devices, which range from smart door management systems to HVAC monitors, play crucial roles in automating and optimizing various operational functions. Their integration into network infrastructures has become increasingly common, offering enhanced efficiency and advanced control mechanisms.

However, the widespread incorporation of IoT devices brings unique challenges and complexities. Their functionality, often critical to daily operations, makes them indispensable, yet their interconnectedness with other network components requires careful management to ensure overall system integrity and security.

Despite their utility, IoT devices frequently face significant management challenges. A primary concern is manufacturers' lack of ongoing support, which often manifests in infrequent or nonexistent updates and patches. This negligence can leave devices vulnerable to security breaches, as they may not be equipped to defend against the latest cyberthreats. The absence of regular firmware updates and security patches means that many IoT devices operate with outdated defenses, making them easy targets for cyberattackers. The situation is exacerbated by IoT devices often being deployed and forgotten, with little to no active management or monitoring, further increasing the risk of compromise.

The inherent risk associated with IoT devices stems from their connectivity to networks. Being networked exposes them to many cyberthreats, and their compromise can have far-reaching consequences. If an IoT device is breached, it can serve as a staging ground for more extensive network attacks, allowing cybercriminals unauthorized access to other critical parts of the network. For instance, a compromised IoT device can be used as a point of entry to deploy malware or to gain access to sensitive data. The high risk of compromise requires a holistic protection strategy in managing the IoT device and ensuring that communications to and from it are scoped to reduce the risk.

Websites

Websites are the digital signpost for most organizations and are often a central focus of their IT infrastructure. Whether public-facing or internal, they deliver services and disseminate information. From complex e-commerce platforms to simple informational pages, the sites facilitate engagement with external customers and support internal operations and communications. Their functionality extends beyond information sharing, often encompassing critical business processes and data handling. This central role in external outreach and internal functionality makes websites indispensable elements of modern organizational infrastructure.

However, the very features that make websites indispensable expose them to various security vulnerabilities. Misconfigurations of web servers can create enormous risks, opening the doors for cyberthreats that use the sites to pivot deeper into the organization. Compromised web servers may provide access to internal databases or allow server-side request forgery (SSRF) attacks, which enables internal calls to be made on behalf of the trusted web server to other resources. This leads to the exposure of sensitive data or organizational disruptions.

Website threats are well documented and often fall into common categories. OWASP has a top 10 list of typical attack vectors, targeting websites, APIs, and LLMs, including SQL injections and cross-site scripting. Most of these attacks are due to misconfigurations or lack of validation on website input or output. The attacks can allow direct theft and manipulation of backend databases or execute commands on behalf of regular users.

Public-facing websites are most likely to face frequent attacks due to high visibility; yet assuming that internal-facing servers are without risk is dangerous. No matter the organizational size, internal accounts will be compromised at some point, or a threat will gain inside access, allowing visibility to these systems. Stopping threats requires a defense-in-depth approach using secure coding practices, ongoing monitoring, and protective measures like web application firewalls to prevent attacks.

Certificates

Certificates help round out the modern IT infrastructure, ensuring private and secure communications over untrusted networks. Digital certificates are cryptographic assets generated for extremely large coprime integers that are related to form public and private keys. The client and server each have their own pair of public and private keys, and using a complex handshake algorithm, they create a secure and secret channel to transfer data without the unauthorized entities intercepting it, even if they can see both sets of public keys.

This process is used in various protocols, including SSL/TLS, for secure web browsing. Servers have their public key on their website, and clients viewing the site negotiate a secure channel when they browse there. By creating this protected tunnel, clients can safely view sensitive data, such as financial information or personal data, without fear of it being intercepted, even if they are on an insecure network such as public WiFi. As an added benefit, this process also maintains the integrity of the data in transit, allowing all parties to feel secure that no data was manipulated in transit. (Changes to the encrypted data would mangle the data, making it unreadable.)

Certificates go beyond security; they also play an integral role in authentication and digital trust. By verifying the legitimacy of the entities involved in a communication, certificates help organizations authenticate their network traffic. The verification process ensures that the data is sent to and received from trusted sources and not intercepted or manipulated by external, potentially malicious entities. This is extremely important for preventing phishing, as attackers commonly use adjacent DNS names such as Amazn.com instead of Amazon.com in typo squatting attacks to trick users into going to a site that is controlled by bad actors. Using certificates, users can verify site ownership and ensure their data goes where they trust. Protecting the certificate chain is crucial, as failure can lead to cybercriminals using the certificate on their fake sites, allowing them to masquerade as a trusted system.

Cloud

Beyond traditional and modern computing, cloud computing has dramatically changed how organizations handle IT. Cloud has transformed existing models, moving resources outside of locally controlled data centers into hosting managed by providers such as Amazon Web Services (AWS), Microsoft Azure, or Google Cloud. Rather than buying fixed resources, which requires significant financial outlay, they allow organizations to pay for resources such as servers and databases as they are used. With benefits such as dynamic scaling for load and fast provisioning, companies have shifted how they develop and manage their IT infrastructure, with most companies leveraging some cloud in their IT stack.

While similar to traditional IT, there are distinct differences in how resources are utilized and managed. It requires a skill set beyond traditional server administration to properly configure and leverage. As it is publicly hosted, it also creates a broader attack surface for cybercriminals to target.

Cloud Providers

Cloud providers are the backbone of the cloud system, providing various services for organizations to purchase on demand. AWS, Azure, and Google Cloud are the most prominent players in this area, offering similar services and technologies, ranging from fundamental computing power and storage to more specialized offerings like machine learning tools, big data analytics, and IoT services. While the services are similar in operations, they all have different names, costs, and management inter-faces, adding to the complexity of operations.

The financial model of cloud computing, often appealing due to its lack of substantial up-front costs, can nonetheless lead to unexpectedly high expenses for customers not well-versed in managing cloud resources. This situation typically arises from the inherent complexity of cloud services. Without careful planning and a solid understanding of how cloud pricing models work, customers may find themselves entangled in larger or more resource-intensive configurations than they actually need. Poor designs, such as over-provisioning resources or not optimizing cloud services, can result in running more nodes or using more bandwidth and storage than necessary. Criminals can also run attacks spamming a costly AWS service or S3 bucket in a "denial of wallet" attack, leading to a dramatic cost increase, counteracting one of the primary benefits of cloud computing—cost-efficiency.

The risks aren't limited to higher-than-anticipated costs, though. Another pitfall of cloud computing is the shared responsibility model between cloud providers and users. The provider and the user each play a role in the overall security of the cloud and the data stored in it. The cloud provider focuses on the underlying infrastructure, such as the hardware, software, networking, and facilities that run the services. They do this to provide a secure foundation from which users of the platform can build.

The client has a more complex role as they are responsible for securing the data they store and process in the cloud. Doing this requires managing their application security, controlling resource access, encrypting sensitive data, and maintaining com-pliance with relevant governance and regulatory requirements. And that takes a complex and specialized skill set that many organizations rarely have in its entirety among their current staff. Often, some staff members only have portions of the skill set. This problem has led to numerous data breaches and disclosures due to misconfiguration or mismanagement.

Cloud Workloads

Cloud workloads shift away from the legacy dedicated server model of traditional computing. With cloud workloads, the cloud system is just a resource, providing processing, networking, and storage for the job required. Organizations leverage these workloads to host web servers, store data, run complex analytics, provide email services, support virtual desktop environments, and facilitate software development and testing.

Workloads bring dynamic scalability and flexibility to companies using them. As needs require, more capacity can dynamically be allocated, and when the demand decreases, companies can scale back on what they are using, reducing costs. This is an excellent benefit for processing large data sets, hosting high-traffic websites, and developing new software without the baseline investment in physical servers and data centers.

Workloads not only shift how organizations handle data but also come with security changes. Legacy models would have administrators' security servers in their entirety; for workloads, the storage service and any supporting aspects, such as access control or encryption, must be configured. This is especially important for organizations hosting sensitive or critical business data in the cloud, even if temporarily, as it moves outside of traditional security perimeters, increasing its exposure.

Compounding this concern is the availability aspect of cloud services. As cloud services are accessible from anywhere, limiting access to data and services is crucial for secure operations. This objective encompasses everything from limiting who can sign into the cloud environment to scoping the APIs and interfaces that interact with cloud services. Failing to do so allows attackers to manipulate these interfaces directly, gaining unauthorized access or disrupting services.

Containers

As part of the transition from traditional IT infrastructure, containers have emerged as a lightweight form of application virtualization. Rather than running a complete virtual platform, containerization encapsulates dependencies and applications into a self-contained unit. This method allows containers to be leveraged across different cloud platforms without worrying about the underlying provider or their architecture. The portability and flexibility make containers especially attractive for cloud-based applications, facilitating easier development, testing, and deployment processes.

Docker, Kubernetes Pods, and Amazon ECS (Elastic Container Service) tasks have emerged as industry leaders in this field. Each approaches the containerization challenge differently, providing unique creation and management features. Docker focuses on simplifying containers' creation and management, making them more accessible. On the other hand, Kubernetes offers robust orchestration capabilities for managing large-scale container deployments. While not being cross-platform-friendly, Amazon ECS integrates with AWS services, providing a seamless container management experience in the AWS ecosystem.

As with other cloud technologies, containers come with security exposures and challenges. Insecure or outdated container images bring vulnerabilities in dependencies that attackers exploit. These may allow escalations of privileges or remote code execution attacks, exposing sensitive data within containers, such as API keys and credentials.

Similarly, escape attacks allow attackers to exploit vulnerabilities, breaking out of a container and gaining unauthorized access to the host system. These same attacks can also exploit inadequate isolation between containers, resulting in cross-container data breaches, where a compromised container may affect others on the same host. By leaving the container sandbox, sensitive data can be exposed, or attackers may gain control of the containers themselves.

Cloud-Based Applications

Part of shifting to the cloud is moving software solutions away from traditional, internally hosted applications in data centers to more dynamic, cloud-hosted environments. By making this transition, companies can attain an unlimited scalability advantage with hosted solutions rather than adding more hardware to accommodate the increased load. The cloud allows automatic scaling to increase the usage during the hours needed most and then scale back when the load decreases. This benefits organizations with variable workloads or rapid growth, such as startups.

Applications that take advantage of cloud benefits include web-based email services, customer relationship management (CRM) systems, enterprise resource planning (ERP) solutions, and various SaaS applications. By hosting in the cloud, they also offer remote accessibility, enabling organizations with a highly mobile or remote workforce to leverage the software without having the overhead of a VPN solution to contend with.

As with all cloud services, there are also security concerns that stem from cloud-based hosting. The first is the need for increased accessibility, which is an advantage to staff but increases the attack surface. These applications lack the traditional security perimeter of hosting in a local data center, allowing them to more easily be targeted by external threats. Cybercriminals can more easily experiment with credential-based attacks, such as testing credentials stolen from phishing or purchased off the dark web.

Data

Storage has also made enormous adjustments in the transition to the cloud. It's not simply an add-on to workloads and servers but offers numerous capabilities to fit various business needs. It can deliver rapid data access for AI, data analytics, and real-time processing to power decision-making and operational strategies. It can also provide slower, high-capacity needs to enable backup and recovery operations. Of course, it offers many variations in between, allowing organizations to balance the speed and volume required to meet their budgetary needs.

What makes the cloud unique isn't just that it offers all of these storage variations; so is the flexibility that comes with it. Organizations pay for a combination of the storage used and retrieval. So rather than buying large storage area networks (SANs) or network attached storage (NAS), which may never get fully used to capacity and require periodic hardware refreshes, cloud solutions extract the cost as they are used.

This is far more economical than investing in hardware for dynamic workloads that don't require persistent storage but may need volume bursts.

Cloud storage has been at the heart of many security incidents in the past, though. AWS S3 buckets have been noted in numerous data breaches due not to weaknesses in the technology but instead to failures of the users to configure it properly. S3 and similar solutions require a combination of access controls, data encryption, and regular security audits to keep data private and reduce the risk of inappropriate access. Some providers, such as Amazon, have added controls to help users make the right choices in protecting their data. These controls may include policies restricting access to resources by default, forcing users to explicitly grant access, or enabling encryption by default, preventing them from inadvertently exposing data to everyone.

Configuration Management

As has been mentioned previously, proper configuration is crucial for secure cloud services. One of the ways this is partially mitigated is through configuration management, which allows organizations to create reusable files to base new infrastructure on a golden image rather than creating a build every time. Configuration-as-code also allows for a reusable script to help configure systems on the fly, using modules as building blocks that can be offered to the organization via a self-service catalog. The modules already have security configurations built into them and are preapproved by security, ensuring controls are installed by default.

These approaches reduce the risk of new errors being introduced every time a new instance is created. For organizations using cloud horizontal scalability to launch multiple instances of identical nodes, a fixed configuration is necessary to launch exact copies automatically.

There are multiple security challenges with these files. First is ensuring that configuration file changes are managed and controlled. Limiting changes reduces the risk of dangerous changes, such as including vulnerable versions of supporting software or modifying network rules that could make the new node more accessible or eliminate access altogether.

Another challenge you may encounter when using fixed configuration files is ensuring a hardened configuration. As these files will be reused for some time, they must be hardened to ensure they follow best practices. As with most cloud components, failures in configuration will lead to security breaches and vulnerabilities. Ensuring a hardened configuration from the outset means establishing robust security protocols, such as encrypting sensitive data, implementing strong access controls, and defining clear data handling and storage policies.

Finally, maintaining a proper configuration also means ensuring that it remains up to date. Over time, existing dependencies such as software versions and libraries must

---

be replaced as vulnerabilities are discovered or new versions are released, and as creators no longer support the old ones. Configurations must be regularly reviewed and updated to keep pace with these changes. The continuous updating process is essential to maintaining the security and functionality of the cloud infrastructure. It involves updating software and libraries and adapting to new security standards and compliance requirements.

SaaS

SaaS has dramatically changed how companies do business in the cloud. Rather than organizations hosting all of the underlying infrastructure, a provider runs SaaS applications, and customers gain access to the interface (often by paying per user) to utilize it. This approach eliminates the burdens of installing and maintaining the software on individual computer endpoints or a centralized server, reducing management overhead. Even licensing is dramatically simplified as key management goes away; the provider tracks available seats or assigned accounts, often allowing organizations to scale the licenses they pay for accordingly.

SaaS applications come with challenges for customers, as there is an inherent risk in turning data over to a third party and leveraging a service you don't fully control. While many providers include a service level agreement (SLA) stating expected performance metrics, customers can do little if an outage happens or the provider has poor security controls. The very nature of SaaS abstracts out the backend visibility, preventing customers from seeing how the provider is performing. That does not mean customers lack control, but their visibility and ability to make configurations are limited to what the SaaS provider grants them.

SaaS Management

Reduced management efforts do not mean there is no work for the SaaS customer. Generally, the most critical area for customers to control is setting up user access and permissions, which is crucial for controlling who can access specific data and features inside the application. This is done to limit access to sensitive data or administrative-level features where users could grant themselves elevated privileges, allowing them to self-grant access to sensitive or restricted data.

However, the management challenges for customers do not stop here. For more advanced SaaS software, there is the ability to integrate with other technologies in the IT stack. The SaaS software may either be ingesting data from customer assets or providing a data feed for the customer to integrate with existing technologies. Generally, the SaaS provider is not responsible for integrating existing technologies but may provide APIs to simplify the process for the customer. The actual work of leveraging the APIs or provided interface falls to the customer and their IT staff.

As these communication channels may contain sensitive information, the process of securing it belongs to the customer's team.

As mentioned, the management of a SaaS solution mainly falls on the provider's side. It starts with ensuring basic access control by providing authentication or integration for customers' authentication via OAuth and multifactor authentication. As they are housing customer data, they are also responsible for maintaining encryption to prevent data theft and implementing backup and recovery procedures to reduce the risk of data loss. They also provide management interfaces, monitoring or reporting features, setting up alerts and notifications for critical events, and scheduling regular updates and maintenance.

Many SaaS providers go the extra mile in this process and gain certifications in ISO 27001, SOC 2 Type II, or other industry standards. By attaining these certifications, they demonstrate to customers that they are committed to maintaining robust security and operational excellence, which is necessary for those storing sensitive data or in highly regulated industries. These certifications do not guarantee that no breach will happen, but a third-party certification provides validation that the provider generally follows best practices for information security, data protection, and risk management.

Beyond these certifications, providers often engage in continuous security assessments and improvements, ensuring their infrastructure and services stay ahead of evolving cyberthreats. Many also include auditing and security reporting requirements in contractual agreements. This ensures that the SaaS provider regularly offers detailed security audits and compliance reports, allowing organizations to verify that the provider meets all agreed-upon security standards and practices. These tools create a comprehensive approach to management and security by the SaaS provider, securing the data and services, building trust with customers, and reinforcing the provider's reputation as a reliable and secure choice for cloud-based software solutions.

Identity

Identity and access management are crucial for cloud and on-premises computing. Knowing who has access to what resources sounds like a simple issue, but it has numerous challenges. Not all resources are tied to a single management platform, creating a proliferation of different accounts where a single individual may have multiple accounts across the organization or even for a single resource. Tying this information together to get a holistic view of what a user can access, and maintaining it throughout their life cycle with the organization, is daunting, even for a small organization. Managing the identity and access landscape for a large organization becomes incredibly complex without leveraging centralized authentication and additional tooling to pull this data into a singular location.

One tool for accomplishing this is privileged access management (PAM), which involves controlling and monitoring the credentials of administrators and other highly privileged accounts, which, if compromised, could pose significant risks to the entire IT infrastructure. Implementing PAM strategies helps secure these powerful credentials against unauthorized access and misuse. This includes enforcing strong authentication measures, regularly updating and rotating credentials, and monitoring the activities of privileged accounts to detect and respond to suspicious behaviors promptly.

Users

One of the significant changes that came with cloud computing was altering the concept of what a user is. There was a shift from users being only individuals to including machine and service accounts that facilitate access to various resources in the cloud environment. This expanded the number of identities that had to be managed, increasing the workload for maintaining the environment. Each identity needs to have an appropriate level of access maintained at all times, but must also be disabled when it is no longer needed, such as when an employee leaves the organization.

This task becomes even more complex as most organizations blend cloud, multi-cloud, and on-premises resources. As a result, access needs to be maintained across multiple locations, with changes to access and permissions being updated across all environments. Technologies like active directory and role-based access control provide frameworks to simplify identity management across multiple environments. However, they bring their own challenges, especially regarding integration and scalability across diverse and distributed environments.

These technologies help to ensure that not every identity ends up with the same level of permissions, especially when dealing with sensitive data. Breaking users into groups and assigning permissions to groups rather than individuals simplifies permissions management. Though group management simplifies the process, its misuse, such as creating an "everyone group" and giving broad rights to it, can overly genericize permissions and inadvertently undermine the system's intent. Instead, organizations should use the principle of least privilege as their guide, only assigning the minimum necessary access to users and roles to allow them to do their jobs. While this sounds good on paper, the implementation is challenging, as doing it requires understanding each identity's roles and responsibilities to tailor access appropriately.

Data Access Across Platforms

The widespread availability of data in cloud environments, accessible across a broad spectrum of platforms, services, and systems, significantly advances how information is stored and accessed. Cross-platform access means that data is no longer confined to a single system or network, allowing for greater flexibility and efficiency in operations.

However, ease of access comes with its own challenges in service integration, where data is shared or transferred between different cloud services. This enhances operational flexibility but adds complexity in managing and securing this data. The key challenge here lies in maintaining data integrity and security across diverse platforms, as there is no simple way to ensure security measures and data policies remain consistent. Each platform has unique interfaces and access protocols, so creating consistency requires third-party tooling or manual efforts.

Further complicating this effort is the mix of authentication methods for identity and access management across cloud platforms. Standardized protocols such as OAuth, LDAP, and SAML provide a unified framework for authenticating users, delivering consistency and security in granting access. However, some cloud services opt for custom account management systems, which might not integrate seamlessly with standard protocols. This divergence creates complex scenarios where integrating multiple authentication methods becomes a juggling act for IT teams, who must ensure that all systems communicate effectively without compromising security or user experience.

Adding another wrinkle to the identity challenge in the cloud is that individuals may have multiple user accounts across various services. The management task becomes exponentially more complicated as the number of accounts each individual has grows, making it more likely that errors and oversights will occur. Individuals may have combinations of account access that appear harmless on their own but, when used together, allow for access beyond what they should have.

The situation is further complicated by the lack of centralized oversight, often leading to challenges in maintaining a clear view of who has access to specific resources. Without proper visibility, mistakes may occur, opening the door to unauthorized access, data breaches, and noncompliance situations. Many organizations must turn to centralized identity governance and administration solutions to help sort the tangled web of access rights.

Identity and Access Management Challenges

As with any IT environment, the user population is never static, so managing user transitions such as onboarding, role changes, and offboarding becomes crucial for maintaining security.

The onboarding process must be efficient and secure, granting new employees access only to the necessary resources and applications needed to perform their jobs. Any delay in granting access prevents employees from becoming productive and increases frustration, creating a bad first impression.

Similarly, the offboarding process is equally essential; when employees leave the company, their access to all cloud and local resources must be promptly and wholly revoked to prevent unauthorized access. Any delay in removing this access creates a window of opportunity for misuse and attack, especially for those who did not leave the organization on good terms.

Role changes within the company add another layer of complexity, as access rights need to be updated to reflect the employee's new responsibilities. Assuming that a role change is only an addition of access is dangerous, as this also creates the potential for misuse. Old access that is no longer necessary must be eliminated to prevent accidental or deliberate over-access. This is especially important in areas where sensitive data is present, as merely having excessive access could be a compliance issue.

While these access management challenges sound like common sense on the surface, their implementation is complex. Other than in the smallest companies, a single individual or team rarely understands appropriate access for every individual in an organization. There are often numerous resources managed by different teams. These resource owners understand who should have access to their materials, but not holistically for the organization, leading to a significant management challenge. Resource owners need to be a part of the review and validation process of access changes, and their information needs to trickle back to centralized management.

It's important to remember that customer access also requires appropriate management. Given the prevalent risk of credential stuffing attacks, where stolen account credentials are used to gain unauthorized access, robust measures must be in place to protect customer interfaces. Implementing strong authentication methods, such as multifactor authentication, monitoring login behaviors for anomalies, and educating customers about secure password practices, is critical. These measures help safeguard against unauthorized access, protecting the customer's data.

Handling complex access management is challenging, requiring more than just a single solution. It starts with regular reviews of user access rights to identify and remove permissions that are no longer necessary, especially for those belonging to former employees or those who have changed roles. Automated systems such as automatic deprovisioning play a key role as they can remove access immediately when user status changes occur, such as employment termination or job role changes.

Supply Chain

No single organization is large enough to accommodate every IT need entirely in-house. Organizations rely on numerous third-party services, including software- and hardware-related services, for their daily operations. Any vulnerabilities within parts of the supply chain trickle back, introducing risks to the entire network.

An example of such a vulnerability is the SolarWinds breach, where the infrastructure of a well-known software provider was compromised. The compromise allowed attackers to insert vulnerabilities via software updates, granting them access to the networks of thousands of SolarWinds customers, leading to widespread data breaches and system compromises.

Similarly, the widespread Log4j vulnerability exposed numerous organizations to potential risks. Log4j, a common Java logging library used by numerous applications and considered safe, had a critical flaw that could allow attackers to execute remote code on a server, emphasizing the need for rigorous security measures and prompt patch management in third-party components.

Additionally, breaches in third-party services like the MoveIt data transfer tool show the cascade effect in supply chain security. Such breaches can enable unauthorized access to sensitive data across multiple platforms and services, and they can have far-reaching effects without being the customer's fault.

Software Development

Most organizations develop software in some capacity, whether a full-blown application or a simple web page. Rather than developing all capabilities from the ground up, especially for standard functionalities, developers frequently use third-party libraries. Open source or commercially purchased libraries are crucial in accelerating development processes and adding complex functionalities to the software without building everything from scratch.

However, this dependency also introduces risks, as the security of these libraries is in the hands of external parties. When third-party libraries contain vulnerabilities, they can be transferred to the application that incorporates them. The challenge is compounded by the sheer volume of libraries and components used in modern software development. A single application may have hundreds of different libraries incorporated directly, with each library having its own set of dependencies, creating a giant tree of dependencies for a single application.

A Software Bill of Materials (SBOM) is an inventory that lists all components, libraries, and dependencies included in a software product, enhancing transparency in software compositions and making tracking easier. SBOMs are crucial for identifying vulnerabilities, ensuring compliance with cybersecurity regulations, and improving risk management by providing a detailed overview of third-party software components. They enable quicker security responses and more efficient audits, helping organizations mitigate risks associated with the software supply chain.

Never updating libraries is not the solution, as most vulnerabilities are not maliciously inserted but instead are discovered. They have been there all along, and at some point security researchers or malicious actors discover a flaw, making the vulnerability known. Researchers do this so it can be remediated, while malicious actors do this so it can be exploited.

Instead, this attack surface must be managed through a more comprehensive application security approach. Libraries incorporated into software must be periodically checked against vulnerability databases to discover known risks. Additionally, they should be reviewed with static application security testing tools, which look for flaws in the source code. This step helps to catch unknown vulnerabilities, allowing organizations to proactively stop threats rather than relying on external resources.

Applications

Supply chain vulnerabilities extend beyond software libraries to include third-party applications that provide services to organizations. External parties manage and maintain these applications and form a significant part of an organization's operational infrastructure. However, any lapses in the security of these applications can have direct implications for the organizations using them.

The SolarWinds incident is a prime example of an application supply chain attack. It highlights the cascading nature of this style, where a single vulnerability in a widely used application can lead to multiple victims. These attacks are incredibly tempting to cybercriminals as they bypass the security of the victim organization, which is often far more restrictive than the supplier's.

Managing the application supply chain risk is challenging since many applications automatically update, push, and install new patches. From an administrative standpoint, this reduces management overhead, but from a security standpoint, it creates an opportunity for a supply chain attack. To fully mitigate the risk, organizations must remove the automated update process when possible and review the software before it is installed or updated in the enterprise. However, not every organization has the tools and expertise to validate every application, requiring other controls to help mitigate the risk.

Certificates

When considering the supply chain for organizations, it is easy to overlook certificates. Even though many organizations generate their own, the certificate management process all rolls up to third-party certificate authorities (CAs). The entire certificate system works off of a hierarchy, with the CAs at the top providing the authoritative sign-off on all certificates and subordinate CAs further down the chain. They validate business information to create trust in information about an organization provided by the certificate. When users see a certificate signed off by a reputable CA, they trust that they know they are interacting with the legitimate company the certificate claims to represent.

However, all of this trust relies on the security of the CA. Any breach in the CA system could allow malicious attackers to generate any number of certificates in a spoofing attack, letting them masquerade as legitimate companies, potentially deceiving users and other businesses. In supply chain attacks, compromised certificates can be used to distribute malicious software or operate a website under the guise of a trusted provider.

BYOD and Mobile

BYOD and mobile devices have become commonplace in the workplace, creating substantial challenges for organizations striving to secure digital environments. These devices significantly broaden the organizational attack surface because they often exist outside the traditional controls and security measures governing corporate equipment. Being introduced and managed by end users, BYOD and mobile devices can easily bypass standard security protocols designed for in-house technology, such as network firewalls and antivirus systems. This situation leaves organizations vulnerable to various security threats, including data leakage, unauthorized access, and malware infiltration from these devices.

The diverse range of operating systems and applications on personal devices introduces significant complexities when implementing unified security policies and measures across an organization. This variability means that security solutions and policies suitable for one type of device or operating system may not be applicable or effective on another. For instance, Android devices' security controls and software updates are incompatible with iOS systems and vice versa.

Moreover, these devices frequently connect to insecure networks, such as public WiFi, increasing the risk of interception and data theft. A common tactic is to use a rogue access point to mimic a legitimate network, allowing attackers immediate man-in-the-middle access. As users browse business data, the attacker intercepts and steals it. Targeted attacks like this can occur at coffee shops and restaurants near a business, hoping to catch specific users from a company nearby.

Drive-by compromises also target these devices, which occur when users unknowingly trigger malware downloads by simply visiting a compromised website, with no further interaction required. This stealthy method leverages vulnerabilities in web browsers and can install various malicious software, posing a significant security risk without any visible signs to the user.

There is no easy answer for organizations attempting to secure these devices. Solutions may include enforcing strong authentication, sandboxing, secure connection protocols, and continuously monitoring device activities. Additionally, educating employees about the risks and best practices for securing their personal devices is critical in mitigating these threats and protecting the broader organizational network.

In some cases, the cost of security is too high, so the organization simply blocks all BYOD from any network access and forbids employees from using noncontrolled devices for work.

Artificial Intelligence

AI has recently become a core component of technology and business operations, creating a unique attack surface to manage. As a newer attack surface, AI has numerous vectors by which it can be attacked, everything from manipulating the training information to creative attempts to extract data.

AI Models and Neural Network Architecture

AI models and neural network architectures are complex computational structures designed to replicate human brain functions. They enable machines to learn from data, interpret it, and make decisions or predictions based on that learning. They train on massive volumes of data, creating intricate interconnections focused on specific areas of knowledge or expertise. The effectiveness and reliability of AI models depend heavily on the quality and integrity of the data on which they are trained.

Their reliance on quality data for learning makes the training data a prime target for criminals. These methods include adversarial attacks, where subtly modified inputs deceive AI models into making incorrect predictions, and data poisoning, where the training data is manipulated to corrupt the model's learning process. Each of these attacks, which modify the data ingested, leads to incorrect outputs down the line.

Targeting the training data disrupts the foundation of the AI; other methods focus on the output. Many AI models have controls to prevent them from generating dangerous output, such as the code for malware. Evasion attacks query the model in ways that appear benign, such as asking for code that does something similar to a virus in a very roundabout way, which tricks it into generating the dangerous output. For public AI models, users share these tricks on social media, increasing the speed at which they are abused.

Malicious users also target the output to steal hidden data from the training set. In the training process, sensitive information, such as individual addresses, activities, and associations, may be ingested and used in doxing attacks. This data is usually hidden behind layers of protection to prevent end users from directly querying it. Model inversion and membership inference attacks work like evasion attacks, circumventing controls in the interface to request sensitive or training data. All of this information is dangerous, allowing threat actors to harm individuals directly or reuse it to gain inference and further data that allows the criminals to reverse-engineer the model and create an unauthorized duplicate.

AI Pipelines and Infrastructure

The model and architecture are only part of the overall AI attack surface. AI pipelines and infrastructure interconnect systems and processes necessary for the entire AI model life cycle. The infrastructure includes mechanisms for collecting, processing, and analyzing vast amounts of data and the required resources for training, deploying, and maintaining these models efficiently and at scale.

As these pipelines are a direct pathway into the core of the AI model, failures in protecting the ingress/egress path complicate the entire model. The paths create a direct route by which the training process can be compromised, allowing mass ingestion of corrupted or manipulated data, which can poison the model. Since the pipelines go both ways, they are also a more direct path to extracting sensitive information, bypassing the controls implemented by the frontend.

Mitigating the infrastructure's threats is relatively complex and requires multiple layers of controls. It must start with robust access control, limiting access to only the users and processes directly interacting with the system. This reduces the potential scope of attackers and risks from compromised accounts. From here, continuous monitoring and anomaly detection will be added to identify when changes in utilization, such as users increasing data sent or changing locations, could signify a potential attack. Catching attacks against the infrastructure early significantly reduces the potential damage and allows for the potential of rolling back improper training without destroying the entire model.

AI User Interfaces and APIs

With functional AI models, there are also direct interfaces via user interfaces (UIs) and APIs. APIs offer functionality similar to the UI but are machine-formatted rather than providing a visual interface. This allows for faster throughput of information and necessitates implementing any controls that may exist in the UI on the server side.

A robust authentication mechanism for both interfaces prevents unauthorized users from gaining access and tracking activity. To be effective, though, it must be coupled with adequately configured access controls to restrict user or system access, preventing unauthorized manipulation or access to AI functionalities. These restrictions may be in place via user roles, limiting the information that can be presented and preventing the insertion of dangerous input, such as code snippets. While some AI models can leverage code and even create their own, it is also likely that input code is used as an attack for cross-site scripting and cross-site request forgery attacks and must be appropriately sandboxed to prevent this. These attacks exploit a lack of input validation to allow attackers to execute scripts or launch malicious requests in the context of a user's session. By effectively sandboxing environments and employing rigorous input validation measures, organizations can safeguard against these vulnerabilities and ensure that AI models process inputs securely without inadvertently facilitating security breaches.

Summary

As we wrap up this chapter, we've examined how old and new IT components make up today's complex attack surfaces. We've looked at everything from traditional servers and networking gear to modern technologies like cloud services and IoT devices. Each element, despite its benefits, brings unique security challenges. Managing these—whether they're outdated legacy systems or cutting-edge applications—is crucial for keeping data safe and systems secure.

In the next chapter, we will dive into the process of identifying and classifying these assets. This step is key for building a detailed asset inventory, which is vital for effective ASM. By understanding each asset's role, its business context, and how it impacts the organizational IT ecosystem, we can better prioritize security efforts and manage resources. We'll also continue reviewing the strategies and best practices of ASM that strengthen your organization's cyber defenses.

CHAPTER 3

How the Attack Surface Relates to Risk

Understanding the relationship between an organization's attack surface and risk exposure is foundational for protecting valuable assets. This chapter explores the essential role of risk management in cybersecurity, guiding professionals through the various methods of identifying, measuring, and managing risks that endanger their organizations.

Together, we discuss qualitative and quantitative risk assessments and analyze widely used frameworks published by NIST and ISO. We'll look at practical insights into selecting the right approach for different environments. We'll dive into prioritizing risks based on impact and likelihood, ensuring that the most consequential vulnerabilities are addressed first. This information will equip you with the tools necessary to translate technical risks into actionable business strategies that non-technical business units can understand and act on.

Measuring Risk

Let's begin with the concept of measuring risk. A threat is anything that has the potential to cause harm to an organization's assets, including cyberattacks, natural disasters, internal access abuse or unintentional mistakes. Risk, on the other hand, is the possibility that a threat will exploit a vulnerability to harm an asset. Essentially, risk arises from the intersection of threats and vulnerabilities.

In ASM, we need to identify and classify assets, and then understand the various risks each one faces and the best methods to manage them. The choice of risk management strategy is influenced by the nature of the asset, the potential threats, and the organization's tolerance for risk. This strategic selection ensures that resources are allocated efficiently and protective measures are tailored to actual needs, enhancing the overall security posture. The following strategies each can be leveraged in varying degrees, which all affect the security posture relative to the threats they are facing:

Avoidance

This involves eliminating the risk by changing plans or strategies. For instance, if a specific software poses a high risk, avoiding its use altogether might be a sensible option. Imagine an organization considering the deployment of a new cloud service that has known security issues. By choosing not to use this service, the organization effectively avoids the associated risks.

Mitigation

This focuses on reducing the likelihood or impact of a risk through controls or processes. Implementing security measures like firewalls, intrusion detection systems, or regular software updates can help mitigate risks. For example, an organization might implement multifactor authentication to reduce the risk of unauthorized access, thereby mitigating potential security breaches.

Acceptance

This is sometimes the easiest up-front approach, especially if the cost of mitigation is higher than the potential damage. That means acknowledging the risk and choosing to accept its potential impact without taking action. For instance, a small business might accept the risk of a low-probability cyberattack because the cost of advanced security measures exceeds the potential financial impact of such an attack.

Transference

This shifts the risk to a third party, such as through insurance or outsourcing, so another entity bears the responsibility and potential impact. For example, an organization might transfer the risk of data breaches by outsourcing its data storage to a third-party cloud provider that specializes in security.

Enhancement

This involves increasing the probability or positive impact of an opportunity. The method is used to capitalize on beneficial risks. For instance, a company might enhance the impact of a successful product launch by increasing marketing efforts to maximize reach and customer engagement.

Sharing

This is about collaborating with others to share the benefits and responsibilities of the risk. It can be particularly effective in joint ventures or partnerships. For example, two companies might collaborate on a new technology project, sharing both the risks and the potential rewards.

The diversity of risk management methods reflects the complex nature of modern organizational environments. Each method provides a unique approach to managing different types of risks associated with various assets. Organizations can ensure that their ASM efforts are effective and efficient by understanding the specific implications of each risk and the most applicable management strategy.

Incorporating these varied strategies into the ASM process allows organizations to defend against potential threats and make strategic decisions that align with their business goals and risk appetite. This holistic approach to risk management within ASM ensures that organizations are protected and poised to capitalize on opportunities that risks sometimes present.

When crafting a risk management strategy within the ASM framework, we consider interrelated factors that influence the selection of an appropriate response to potential threats. These factors, detailed in the following list, should guide the strategy and ensure that it aligns with the organization's broader objectives and capacities.

The top factors to consider in that influence our response include:

Risk appetite
This is the amount of risk an organization is willing to accept. Organizations with a low risk tolerance might prefer avoidance. Conversely, organizations with a higher tolerance for risk might opt for acceptance or exploitation.

Impact and probability
These play a crucial role in deciding how to manage risks. If a risk has a high probability of occurring and severe consequences, mitigation or transference might be necessary. On the other hand, low-impact or low-probability risks might be more cost-effectively managed through acceptance.

Cost-benefit analysis
This is essential. The cost of implementing a risk strategy, like mitigation or transference, should be weighed against the potential benefit or loss from the risk itself. Doing so ensures that resources are used efficiently.

Resource availability
This also dictates which risk management strategies are feasible. The availability of financial, human, and technological resources can determine whether a risk can be mitigated, transferred, or must be accepted.

Strategic goals
This can influence risk management decisions. Some risks might align with strategic goals or provide opportunities that can be exploited or enhanced to benefit the organization.

Compliance

This can force organizations to adopt specific risk responses like avoidance or mitigation to meet legal or industry standards. However, it isn't always as rigid as it seems. Many organizations still apply a cost-benefit analysis here, and if the cost of compliance or the penalty for noncompliance isn't significant, they may choose to accept the risk.

Considering these diverse factors helps organizations tailor their risk management strategies to their unique circumstances, enhancing effectiveness and efficiency. Doing so also acknowledges that not all organizations possess the resources or face the same threats, thus allowing for a flexible, context-driven approach. That holistic view is vital because it facilitates a deeper understanding of how various risks interact with the organization's operational reality and strategic vision, enabling more informed and strategic decision making.

Incorporating all these variables into your ASM process doesn't just protect against threats; it turns risk management into a strategic tool that can aid in achieving broader business objectives. This comprehensive approach ensures that decisions made at the tactical level of risk management resonate with and support the organization's overarching goals, maximizing resource allocation and strategic alignment.

Qualitative Risk

Qualitative risk assessment is a method that involves evaluating risks based on their characteristics and potential impacts rather than relying on numerical data. It's more of an art than a science, relying heavily on the experience and judgment of those conducting the assessment. Qualitative assessments are more descriptive and subjective than quantitative methods, which produce precise numerical values.

Think of qualitative risk in terms of a cuisine. Imagine you're a chef tasting a dish and deciding whether it needs more salt. You don't measure the exact amount of salt already in the dish; you use your experience and taste to make a judgment. Similarly, in qualitative risk assessment, you evaluate the potential impact and likelihood of risks based on available information and expert insights.

Qualitative risk assessments can be particularly effective in dynamic environments, such as cloud computing or rapidly evolving technologies, or in any environment where detailed numerical data may not be available. They are useful for organizations of all sizes and budgets because they are generally less expensive, require less resources, and are quicker to implement than quantitative methods.

Examples

To better understand qualitative risk assessment, let's explore some practical examples that illustrate its application in cybersecurity and attack surface management.

Prime factors that weigh in the assessment are:

Understanding vulnerabilities and risks

It's essential to differentiate between vulnerabilities and risk. Vulnerabilities are weaknesses that can be exploited, such as a software bug that allows unauthorized access. A risk, however, quantifies how likely it is that a vulnerability will be exploited and the extent of the damage if it is. This combined view helps prioritize which vulnerabilities need immediate attention.

Risk assessment formula

The formula Risk = Impact × Likelihood helps quantify risk, even in qualitative assessments. For instance, the risk of a volcanic eruption in Florida is extremely low, but the impact would be catastrophic if it occurred near a data center. Conversely, a broom closet with the passcode "1234" might be frequently accessed, making the likelihood of access high, but since the closet is empty, the impact is negligible.

Let's consider a SQL database accessible via the internet that contains sensitive customer data. It's frequently targeted by known threat actors, making it a potential vulnerability. In a qualitative assessment, we evaluate both the likelihood of exploitation and the potential impact:

Likelihood

Given the frequent targeting by threat actors, we might rate the likelihood of exploitation as "Possible."

Impact

Since the database contains sensitive customer data, a breach could have severe consequences, so we rate the impact as "Major."

Using a risk matrix, we can visualize this assessment in Table 3-1.

Table 3-1. Example risk matrix

	Minor	Moderate	Major	Catastrophic
Almost certain	Medium	High	High	Extreme
Likely	Low	Medium	Medium	High
Possible	Low	Medium	Medium	High
Unlikely	Low	Medium	Medium	Medium
Rare	Low	Low	Medium	Medium

In this case, the risk of the SQL database being exploited is rated as "Medium." This qualitative assessment provides a clear picture of the potential risk, helping the organization decide on appropriate mitigation strategies.

Benefits

Qualitative risk assessments are particularly valuable for organizations aiming to manage security threats efficiently and cost-effectively. These assessments stand out because they don't require costly tools or lengthy processes, making them quickly accessible and implementable across various budget constraints. Their straightforward results are easy for stakeholders at all levels to understand, holistically enhancing decision-making capabilities.

These assessments draw on professionals' expert judgment and experience to uncover and evaluate risks, blending technical analysis with human insight. This approach brings depth to the assessment and fosters active engagement from various organizational sectors, ensuring a comprehensive evaluation of potential vulnerabilities.

The inherent flexibility of qualitative assessments allows them to be swiftly adapted to meet the needs of rapidly changing environments, using available data or well-grounded estimations. This will enable them to maintain relevance and effectiveness in dynamic settings such as cloud environments.

Challenges

Despite their many benefits, qualitative risk assessments face significant challenges that stem primarily from their reliance on subjective judgments. The subjectivity can lead to inconsistencies and biases, where two professionals might evaluate the same risk differently based on personal experience, potentially skewing risk management strategies. The result can be a lack of precision, making the assessments less accurate than quantitative methods and complicating the objective comparison and prioritization of risks.

Whenever a staff shortage or a skills gap exists, there is an increased potential to overlook or entirely misevaluate a risk, leaving organizations overly exposed without their knowledge.

Organizations may choose to address these issues by maintaining consistent risk assessment criteria across various departments or locations. This approach then demands additional labor to standardize the assessment framework and train team members. All of this is very resource-intensive, especially for larger organizations, where the labor may be spread out more.

Quantitative Risk

Quantitative risk assessment uses numerical data to measure risk levels, offering a more precise and objective approach than qualitative methods. This type of assessment relies on statistical methods, models, and historical data to evaluate the likelihood and impact of risks. The process involves gathering reliable data, analyzing it through various models, and generating numerical outputs that help in making informed decisions.

In a quantitative risk assessment, data drives the entire process. For instance, historical data on past security incidents, costs of those incidents, and the frequency of attacks are all analyzed to calculate the potential risk of future occurrences. This method allows organizations to tie risk management directly to business metrics, making it easier to prioritize resources and make strategic decisions.

Examples

To better understand quantitative risk assessment, let's look at some practical examples that illustrate its application in cybersecurity and attack surface management.

Earlier, we discussed risk on a higher level by determining the likelihood and impact based on broad categories such as high, medium, and low. Now, we'll delve into quantifying risk, which involves looking at values and assessing likelihood based on actual incidents. This approach matters because hard numbers help tie everything back to business, allowing for better-informed decision making and asset prioritization. It addresses the problem of "When everything is a critical issue, what do we address first?"

For established organizations with historical data, this process is more straightforward. Historical data helps formulate accurate impacts and likelihoods. Not every organization will have this data, but when available, it is highly valuable for accurate prioritization.

Walkthrough: Practical Application of Quantifying Risk

Start with impact. Consider three core systems in an organization: a web server, an email server, and a Salesforce server. Here's a simple exercise to illustrate quantifying risk:

- Web server: Generates $1 million per month, totaling $12 million annually.

- Email server: Services 1,000 employees with an average salary of $50,000 each, supporting $50 million in employee productivity annually.

- Salesforce server: Supports 30 sales personnel who each generate $80,000 per month, contributing to $28.8 million in annual sales.

From these figures, it's clear that the email server's downtime impacts the business more than the web server or Salesforce outages, because the $50 million annual impact of the email server is almost twice as high as the Salesforce server's $28.8 million, and more than four times as high as the web server's $12 million. Even though the email server doesn't generate revenue directly, its outage affects productivity, making it critical to business operations.

Calculate risk

Next, we use the formula Risk = Impact × Likelihood to calculate risk:

Web server risk calculation
- Average 3.65 outages per year
- Each outage costs $1,369.83
- Annual risk cost: $1,369.83 × 3.65 = ~$5,000

Email account compromised risk calculation
- 10,000 attacks per year with a 18.25% success rate, resulting in 1,825 successful attacks annually
- Each incident costs $136.99
- Annual risk cost: $136.99 × 1,825 = ~$250,000

Salesforce account compromised risk calculation
- Estimated 12 incidents per year
- Each incident costs $18,461
- Annual risk cost: $18,461 × 12 = ~$221,532

Comparing these, the risks to the email and Salesforce systems are similar, at around $250,000 and $221,532, making email more significant. Both are much higher than the web server's $5,000 annual risk cost. This example shows that even though the web server directly generates revenue, its risk cost is lower than Salesforce or the email system, illustrating that IT components' business value and security cost are not always obvious.

Determine per-incident cost

To further understand the impact of individual incidents, consider the following:

Web server incident impact
- Generates $12 million annually
- 8,760 hours in a year
- Loss per hour: $12 million / 8,760 hours = ~$1,369 per incident

Email account compromised impact
- Each employee earns $50,000 annually
- 365 days in a year
- Loss per day per employee: $50,000 / 365 days = ~$136 per incident

Salesforce account compromised impact
- Each salesperson generates $80,000 in monthly revenue or $960,000 annually
- 52 weeks in a year
- Loss per week per salesperson: $960,000 / 52 weeks = ~$18,461 per incident

These calculations only account for lost productivity and do not include other costs like remediation expenses or potential fines for noncompliance. By focusing on both impact and likelihood, organizations can gain a clearer picture of their risk landscape and make more-informed decisions.

Benefits

Quantitative risk assessments use numerical data to manage organizational risks with high precision and objectivity. These assessments allow for exact measurements of risk levels, facilitating easier comparisons across different areas of the organization and enabling the tracking of risk changes over time. They also employ statistical models and modern tools like machine learning to predict potential future threats, thus preparing organizations to address these risks proactively. The precision supports objective decision making, reducing subjectivity and bias by basing evaluations on historical data rather than solely on expert opinions.

These risk assessments enhance organizational efficiency by strategically allocating resources to the areas of greatest need. Organizations can target their preventive measures more effectively by quantifying and ranking risks based on their potential impact and probability. This data-driven approach ensures that the most critical vulnerabilities are addressed first, optimizing financial and human resources use. Consequently, organizations can allocate their efforts and investments more effectively, focusing on mitigating high-priority risks that pose the greatest threat to operational stability and security.

Challenges

While offering precision in evaluating organizational risks, quantitative risk assessments confront significant challenges that can hinder their effectiveness. Ensuring access to reliable and comprehensive data is a major hurdle, especially for startups and less mature organizations that may lack adequate historical data. This issue is compounded by data often being in proprietary or inconsistent formats, complicating analysis.

Creating accurate models that reflect real-world scenarios requires a deep understanding of the statistical methods and the specific context in which they are applied. For example, modeling the risk of a cyberattack on a cloud infrastructure might require detailed knowledge of cloud security practices and the ability to interpret large data sets accurately.

As the scope of the assessment expands, models become increasingly complex, requiring more intricate calibration and validation. Integrating diverse data sources from various parts of a growing organization can be challenging, particularly when maintaining data consistency and quality. Larger data sets and more complex models demand higher computational power, which can become a limiting factor in timely risk assessments and consume expensive CPU time.

Organizations often balance quantitative assessments with qualitative insights to achieve the best of both worlds, sacrificing a little in quality to offset the cost and complexity of quantitative evaluation.

Determining the Right Fit

Choosing between quantitative and qualitative risk assessment methods depends on several factors, including the nature of the data available, the complexity of the risks, the resources and capabilities of the organization, and the specific needs of stakeholders. Let's explore these considerations to help you determine which approach is best suited for your situation.

Data and Complexity Considerations

The type of data you have access to plays an integral role in deciding which method to use. If your data is more anecdotal or harder to quantify, qualitative methods might be more appropriate. For example, if your organization relies on expert opinions and subjective judgments about potential threats, qualitative assessments can still provide valuable insights. This approach is useful when dealing with new or emerging risks where numerical data is scarce or nonexistent.

Alternatively, quantitative methods are ideal when detailed numerical data is available and precision is crucial. For instance, if you have extensive historical data on past security incidents, their costs, and their frequencies, a quantitative approach will provide a more accurate assessment. This method involves crunching numbers and generating precise metrics that can inform decision making and resource allocation.

The complexity of the risks you're assessing also influences your choice. Quantitative assessments can provide more nuanced insights into complex risks that involve multiple variables and potential outcomes. For instance, evaluating the risk of a sophisticated cyberattack that could exploit several different vulnerabilities requires detailed statistical analysis and modeling.

However, for less complex risks, qualitative assessments may be sufficient. For example, assessing the risk of a single known vulnerability in a small, well-defined system might not require the depth of a quantitative approach. Qualitative methods can quickly identify and categorize such risks, allowing for prompt and straightforward mitigation strategies.

Resource and Capability Considerations

Qualitative methods are generally less resource-intensive and can be performed by teams with a broader range of skills.

Quantitative assessments require more resources and specialized skills. They involve gathering and analyzing large data sets, which can be time-consuming and expensive. Additionally, they often require expertise in statistical methods and data analysis. If your organization has limited resources, opting for a qualitative assessment might be more practical.

Quantitative risk assessments also involve significant technological and processing requirements. Here are some key considerations:

Hardware requirements
Running sophisticated statistical software and simulations often requires powerful servers and computing systems. If your organization lacks the necessary hardware, investing in it can be costly.

Software requirements
Advanced statistical analysis and modeling software are essential for handling large data sets and complex algorithms. Ensuring you have the right software tools is necessary for effective quantitative assessments.

Data processing
The ability to manage and analyze big data sets efficiently often requires robust data storage and fast processing capabilities. Without these, quantitative risk assessments can become slow and less effective.

Purpose and Stakeholder Considerations

The specific goals of your risk assessment will also influence your choice. Qualitative assessments might suffice for broader risk evaluations or when dealing with unknown variables. For instance, if you're exploring potential risks associated with a new technology that hasn't been widely adopted yet, qualitative methods can help identify and categorize these risks without needing extensive numerical data.

In contrast, quantitative methods are ideal for detailed financial risk analysis or situations where precision is needed. For example, if you're conducting a cost-benefit analysis to determine the ROI of different security investments, quantitative assessments will provide the precise metrics needed for accurate calculations.

Consider what type of information your stakeholders require. Quantitative data might be necessary for external stakeholders like investors, who often need precise numerical information to make informed decisions. For example, presenting a detailed quantitative risk analysis can help justify security investments to your board of directors or potential investors.

Internal management might prefer the broader overview provided by qualitative data. Qualitative assessments can highlight key risks and vulnerabilities in a more narrative format, making it easier for managers to understand the potential impacts and necessary actions without getting bogged down in numbers.

Should I Use a Mix?

In some situations, employing both quantitative and qualitative methods can be beneficial. Here are some questions to help determine when a mixed approach might be appropriate:

Comprehensive analysis
Do you need a broad understanding of risks combined with precise data-driven insights? Using both methods can provide a holistic view, allowing you to capture the nuances of complex risks while also generating specific metrics for informed decision making.

Diverse stakeholder needs
Are different stakeholders requiring both narrative explanations and numerical evidence? A mixed approach ensures that all stakeholders, from technical teams to executive management, receive the information they need in a format that is most useful to them.

Complex decision making
Does the decision-making process benefit from both strategic overviews and detailed risk quantifications? Combining methods can help balance the big picture with detailed analysis, leading to more robust and well-rounded decisions.

Resource flexibility
Do you have the resources to manage and integrate both methods effectively? While quantitative assessments require more specialized skills and tools, qualitative assessments are generally less resource-intensive. If your organization can support both, a mixed approach can leverage the strengths of each method.

Regulatory compliance
Are there regulatory requirements that necessitate both qualitative narratives and quantitative validations? Some industries and regulations may require detailed quantitative data for compliance, while also benefiting from the broader perspective provided by qualitative assessments.

Example: Choosing the Right Method

Imagine you're the CISO of a mid-size company, and you need to assess the risk of migrating to a new cloud service. Here's how you might decide between qualitative and quantitative methods:

1. Assess the data and complexity

If you have detailed historical data on cloud service incidents, such as downtime costs, security breaches, and their frequencies, a quantitative approach will allow you to generate precise risk metrics. This data-driven analysis can help you compare different cloud service providers based on their risk profiles.

However, if the cloud service is new and you lack specific numerical data, a qualitative assessment might be more appropriate. You can gather expert opinions, industry reports, and anecdotal evidence to evaluate the potential risks and make an informed decision based on this broader qualitative information.

2. Determine resources and capabilities

Conducting a quantitative assessment might require specialized skills in data analysis and access to advanced statistical software. If your team lacks these resources, a qualitative assessment could be a more feasible option. You can still gather valuable insights by consulting with internal and external experts and using more straightforward risk-assessment tools.

3. Assess the purpose and stakeholder needs

If you need to present your findings to external stakeholders, such as investors or a board of directors, they might expect precise, numerical data. A quantitative assessment would meet this need by providing detailed risk metrics and financial impact analyses.

For internal discussions, especially with nontechnical managers, a qualitative approach might be more effective. You can present the risks in a narrative format, highlighting key concerns and potential impacts in a way that's easy to understand and act on.

By carefully considering these factors, you can choose the risk assessment method that best fits your organization's needs, resources, and objectives. Whether you opt for a quantitative, qualitative, or mixed approach, the goal remains the same: to identify and manage risks effectively, ensuring the security and resilience of your organization's assets.

Risk Frameworks

As we transition from understanding the relationship between Attack Surface Management and risk management, it is valuable to delve deeper into specific risk frameworks that can guide our strategies. Each framework offers a structured approach to identifying, analyzing, and mitigating risks tailored to different organizational needs and environments. In the following sections, we will explore various risk frameworks

It can be complicated to determine which risk framework is best for your organization. The reference chart in Table 3-2 will serve as a quick reference guide, covering the pros and cons, so you can determine which frameworks might best align with your organization's unique challenges and goals in managing its attack surface effectively.

Table 3-2. Brief risk framework reference

Framework	Benefits	Challenges	Best environments
NIST RMF	Structured approach to risk management, enhancing overall cybersecurity posture through comprehensive policies and practices that align with regulatory compliance	Complex and resource-intensive to implement, potentially challenging for organizations with limited cybersecurity expertise	Organizations requiring rigorous compliance with federal regulations, such as government agencies and contractors, health care providers, and financial institutions
ISO 31000	Enhances risk awareness and management through structured identification and proactive mitigation of risks, supporting global compliance and operational resilience	Resource-intensive, requiring significant expertise and adjustment to integrate with existing organizational processes	Ideal for large or complex organizations in heavily regulated industries such as finance and health care, where comprehensive risk management is essential for compliance and strategic operations
ITIL	Enhances service continuity and quality by improving the reliability and standard of IT services, aligning closely with business objectives to support informed decision making	Complex and resource-intensive, often requiring substantial change management and extensive training to integrate effectively with existing processes	Organizations where IT services are core operations, such as data centers and large IT departments, particularly in dynamic environments where frequent updates are common
COSO ERM	Enhances strategic risk management by integrating risk considerations into organizational decision making, improving governance and compliance oversight	Complex and demanding, requiring substantial changes in organizational culture and processes	Ideal for large, complex organizations in regulated industries such as finance, health care, and energy, which benefit from a structured approach to comprehensive risk management
OCTAVE	Enhances organizational control over cybersecurity by enabling self-assessment of threats and vulnerabilities, focusing on the unique business context and operational risks	Time-consuming and relies heavily on the expertise of internal teams, which may challenge organizations with limited cybersecurity resources	Well-suited for medium-size organizations that can dedicate the necessary time and have the capacity to engage deeply without being overwhelmed by the complexity of larger systems

NIST

The NIST Risk Management Framework offers a structured methodology for managing cybersecurity risks to protect information systems while aligning with organizational goals and compliance demands. Here's a brief breakdown of its key steps:

Categorization
> Systems are categorized based on their risk levels.

Control selection
> Appropriate security controls are chosen and tailored to the categorized risks.

Implementation
> These controls are then implemented across systems.

Assessment
> The effectiveness of the controls is regularly assessed.

Authorization
> Systems are authorized for operation based on their risk assessments.

Continuous monitoring
> Ongoing monitoring tracks any changes in risk profiles.

This framework helps organizations systematically manage the security and privacy of their information systems.

Benefits

NIST RMF not only fortifies an organization's security posture but also streamlines risk management. The systematic approach aids significantly in identifying, assessing, and managing cybersecurity risks, ensuring a robust defense mechanism is in place. Additionally, it enhances vulnerability management, enabling organizations to pinpoint and mitigate potential security weaknesses effectively.

NIST excels in regulatory compliance, aligning with various legal requirements and regulatory standards. The framework facilitates compliance by ensuring that organizations can meet their obligations under different regulatory frameworks, effectively reducing legal risks. Additionally, the framework enhances audit readiness by preparing organizations with thorough documentation and proper control implementations. The comprehensive documentation aids in smoother audit processes, providing easily available evidence that auditors require.

The NIST framework is very flexible. It easily adapts to various organization sizes and types, allowing for customization to meet specific needs. The adaptability ensures that organizations can implement robust cybersecurity practices effectively regardless of their scale or industry.

As a strategic benefit, stakeholders are often more confident in risk assessments like NIST due to the level of comprehensive analysis that takes place. The level of documentation and investigation required creates a significant volume of artifacts and evidence that many stakeholders associate with quality.

Challenges

While the NIST framework offers substantial benefits, it also presents notable challenges in its implementation. The process can be resource-intensive, requiring significant time, expertise, and financial investment from organizations. Similarly, integrating the NIST framework with existing processes or systems can be complex and often necessitates substantial adjustments. This complexity can pose a barrier to organizations with limited resources or those with entrenched systems and processes that are difficult to modify.

Adapting to the comprehensive demands of the NIST framework poses significant challenges, particularly for organizations with limited cybersecurity expertise. Many organizations look at the numerous aspects of the framework and become over-whelmed. There are so many layers to investigate that they become lost in the details. The problem becomes even worse as organizations become larger and have more complex systems that may each encompass multiple layers to assess, further complicating and prolonging assessments.

Based on these issues, some might assume that smaller organizations would have an easier time dealing with the NIST framework. Unfortunately, this is not the case, but for different reasons. Smaller organizations often find the scope and scale of the framework excessive for their operations, making risk assessments too complex.

What also makes NIST difficult is its long-term commitment to continuous monitoring and regular updates, which can be resource-intensive and draining for organizations. Organizations must continuously update their assessments to incorporate changes to their IT and operations; otherwise, the risk findings and recommendations from before will no longer be effective and relevant. Similarly, as the threat landscape changes and novel threats are detected, organizations will need to update their assessments with controls that effectively address them.

Best environments

NIST is often the go-to standard in the US, where regulatory compliance is a necessity. Government agencies and contractors use NIST by default. Still, other industries with stringent data protection standards, like health care and finance, also find NIST useful due to how comprehensive the assessments are. With NIST, organizations can show in-depth risk assessment and due diligence, which is necessary for proving compliance in audits.

It also helps that NIST thrives in larger complex IT infrastructures. The framework's scalability and customizability fit well into these organizations, allowing it to be effectively integrated with existing processes and systems, making it an ideal choice for these settings.

NIST's structured approach also helps enhance ASM efforts. It emphasizes the crucial step of identifying and categorizing all IT assets, which is foundational in ASM for understanding what needs protection. By implementing the security controls recommended by NIST, organizations can effectively mitigate vulnerabilities within their attack surfaces. Both NIST and ASM advocate for continuous monitoring of systems to detect changes in the attack surface and identify emerging security threats, ensuring that defenses remain relevant and effective against evolving risks.

ISO

The ISO 31000 risk management framework provides a comprehensive set of guidelines designed for organizations of any size, industry, or sector. It outlines a clear process for managing risk, which includes risk assessment, monitoring and review, and communication and consultation. This structured approach helps organizations achieve consistency in risk management, improve decision making, and enhance overall resilience.

The risk assessment process has multiple steps. It starts with an identification step that pinpoints the specific risks that could impact the organization, including their sources and potential consequences. Using this information, an analysis step determines the nature of the identified risks and evaluates their likelihood and impact. This helps in understanding how these risks could affect organizational objectives.

Once the analysis is done, the framework evaluates the risks by comparing the analyzed risks against risk criteria set by the organization to prioritize them. This step involves making decisions about which risks need treatment and in what priority.

Benefits

The ISO 31000 framework offers significant benefits in enhancing risk awareness and management within organizations. It supports a structured approach to risk identification, facilitating systematic assessment and pinpointing of risks. The structured identification helps organizations recognize potential vulnerabilities proactively. Additionally, the framework promotes proactive risk mitigation strategies, enabling businesses to implement preventive measures effectively. These capabilities together foster a well-prepared environment that can respond to and mitigate risks before they manifest into significant threats, enhancing overall organizational resilience.

The framework also significantly enhances organizational resilience by increasing adaptability and enhancing recovery capabilities. It equips organizations to better adapt to changes and challenges, thereby improving overall resilience. And it aids in developing strategies that enable quicker and more effective recovery from incidents. This not only helps minimize the impact of disruptions but also ensures that the organization can maintain continuity and restore normal operations swiftly, further solidifying its resilience in the face of adversity.

From a regulatory and compliance perspective, ISO 31000 offers significant benefits for global business operations as it is aligned with internationally recognized standards. This ensures that organizations can maintain a consistent approach to risk management across different countries and regulatory environments. The framework provides robust support for meeting various legal requirements, helping organizations navigate complex compliance landscapes efficiently and effectively. This global recognition and compliance support is necessary for businesses operating internationally, enhancing their credibility and operational stability.

Challenges

Implementing the ISO 31000 framework presents certain challenges, particularly in terms of resource and skill requirements. It necessitates a deep understanding of risk management principles, making expertise dependency a significant hurdle. Moreover, the implementation of this framework can be quite resource-intensive, demanding considerable time and personnel. These challenges require organizations to invest in training and possibly increase staffing, which can be a substantial commitment, especially for smaller organizations or those with limited resources.

While comprehensive, ISO 31000 presents integration and application challenges that can impact its effectiveness across different organizations. One major challenge is organizational alignment, as integrating the framework into existing processes can be difficult, requiring adjustments that may disrupt established workflows. Additionally, the framework's broad applicability means it often needs significant customization to meet the specific needs of various industries or sectors. This generic nature can complicate implementation, demanding tailored solutions to ensure the framework delivers value in diverse operational contexts.

Implementing the ISO framework, much like NIST, is not a one-and-done undertaking. ISO 31000 requires an ongoing commitment to continuous improvement and monitoring to remain relevant. Organizations must engage in persistent monitoring and regular updates of their risk management practices to ensure they remain effective. Additionally, the dynamic nature of the risk landscape poses a significant challenge, as staying abreast of evolving risks and adapting the framework accordingly can be complex and resource-intensive. Without taking a proactive approach to risk management, ISO can rapidly lose its relevance and effectiveness, rendering findings and recommendations useless.

Best environments

Much like NIST, the ISO 31000 framework is particularly well-suited to environments with complex regulatory needs, such as the finance, health care, and energy industries, which require stringent risk management to adhere to legal standards. The framework's depth of coverage provides necessary insights for properly securing these organizations while meeting required standards.

ISO 31000 is a valuable choice for multinational corporations that need a consistent risk management approach across varied geographical and regulatory landscapes. Many larger organizations are multinational, so they also benefit from ISO's structured methods, which allow them to comprehensively identify, assess, and manage risks. However, any organization, regardless of size or sector, seeking to improve its systematic risk management can adapt and utilize this framework effectively.

There is one caveat here: small companies may still become overwhelmed with ISO 31000 due to its broad scope and the need for customization to fit specific organizational contexts. However, it may still be a better fit than NIST because ISO 31000 is designed with flexibility in mind. The flexibility allows smaller organizations to adopt portions of the framework that are most relevant and manageable for their operations. The key for small businesses is to focus on the fundamental principles of ISO 31000 and implement risk management practices that align with their specific capacities and needs.

For those using ASM, the ISO 31000 framework fits well into their efforts due to its structured approach to risk management. It aligns with ASM by emphasizing the identification and assessment of vulnerabilities within an organization's IT infrastructure, promoting a comprehensive understanding of potential threats. Much like ASM, it also encourages continuous improvement and regular updates to security strategies, essential for adapting to emerging threats that could impact the attack surface. This fits well with the cyclical nature of ASM as a process.

The collaborative nature of ISO also benefits ASM. By its design, the ISO framework fosters enhanced stakeholder communication. This communication helps ensure interdepartmental efforts are collaborative rather than siloed, allowing teams to manage risks more effectively.

ITIL v4

Risk management is a key component of ITIL (Information Technology Infrastructure Library), which provides best practice guidelines for effective IT service management. This framework emphasizes identifying, assessing, and controlling risks to ensure the effective and efficient delivery of IT services. Key components include risk identification, which pinpoints potential issues in IT services; risk assessment and analysis, which evaluate the likelihood and impact of these risks; and risk mitigation, which involves implementing measures to manage and reduce risks. Additionally, ITIL advocates for continuous monitoring to adapt risk management practices in response to changes in the IT environment. This integrated approach enhances operational stability and minimizes service disruptions, aligning closely with an organization's overall service management strategy.

Benefits

The ITIL risk management framework significantly bolsters service continuity and quality within organizations. By reducing the frequency and impact of service disruptions, ITIL enhances service reliability, ensuring smoother operations. It promotes enhanced service quality by enabling proactive risk management, which helps maintain consistent, high-quality IT services. This strategic approach not only stabilizes operations but also boosts customer satisfaction by delivering dependable and efficient IT services.

It also helps align IT services with broader business objectives, ensuring that IT operations are in sync with an organization's overall goals and risk tolerance. The strategic alignment is required for making informed decisions about IT investments and priorities, as it provides a structured approach to evaluate and manage risks associated with IT services. By doing so, ITIL not only supports optimal resource allocation but also enhances decision-making processes, leading to more effective and strategic IT service management.

ITIL's emphasis on resource optimization and process improvement significantly enhances operational efficiency. By prioritizing the effective use of IT resources based on risk assessments, ITIL ensures that resources are allocated where they are most needed, thereby increasing operational effectiveness. The framework encourages continuous process improvements through regular risk evaluations, fostering a culture of constant enhancement and adaptation within IT operations.

Challenges

Implementing the ITIL risk management framework can present several challenges. One significant hurdle is the resource intensity required for effective implementation, which includes substantial time, effort, and expertise. Additionally, organizations often encounter difficulties integrating ITIL practices with their existing processes and systems. This challenge can lead to complexities in aligning new ITIL guidelines with current operational procedures, potentially disrupting established workflows and requiring extensive adjustments to ensure compatibility and effectiveness.

The implementation process may also encounter cultural and organizational challenges. One significant barrier is change management, as resistance to change can significantly hinder the adoption of ITIL principles. This resistance can stem from discomfort with new procedures or skepticism about the new system's benefits. Some of this resistance may also stem from the need for training, which is required to ensure that staff understand and can effectively apply ITIL practices. The requirement can be resource-intensive and necessitates a commitment to ongoing education to build proficiency across the organization.

Rapid advancements in technology may also cause friction with ITIL, as they often outpace updates to ITIL standards. The misalignment can make it difficult for ITIL to remain relevant and effective in dynamic tech environments. Additionally, ITIL can sometimes exhibit rigidity, making it challenging to tailor the practices to fit specific organizational needs or unique risk environments. The lack of flexibility can hinder the practical application of ITIL in diverse or rapidly evolving operational contexts.

Best environments

The ITIL framework is particularly well-suited to environments where IT service management is at the core of business operations, such as data centers, large IT departments, and service-oriented companies. It excels in organizations with complex IT systems that require structured management and ongoing maintenance.

ITIL is also advantageous for organizations aiming to improve IT governance, service reliability, and customer satisfaction through standardized practices. It is highly effective in dynamic environments that undergo frequent updates and changes, ensuring that risk management processes are continuously up-to-date and relevant.

The framework significantly enhances ASM through its structured approach to managing IT services. By emphasizing the identification and analysis of all potential threats and vulnerabilities within IT systems, ITIL aligns closely with ASM's goal to minimize the attack surface. Its iterative process of continuous improvement ensures that new vulnerabilities are promptly addressed, maintaining an effective ASM. Moreover, ITIL integrates risk management within the life cycle of IT services, embedding security considerations into the infrastructure and thus reducing the overall attack surface. This focus on service management under ITIL supports better security practices and proactive risk management within IT operations, bolstering the effectiveness of ASM.

COSO ERM

The COSO ERM (Committee of Sponsoring Organizations of the Treadway Commission Enterprise Risk Management) framework is designed to guide organizations in managing risks comprehensively to achieve strategic objectives. It integrates risk management into the organization's overall strategy and operations, promoting a structured approach to risk identification, assessment, response, and monitoring. The framework also emphasizes the importance of governance and culture, ensuring that risk awareness and effective management practices are deeply embedded throughout the organization, enhancing the overall risk governance structure.

Benefits

The COSO ERM framework offers significant benefits by aligning risk management with strategic objectives, which enhances organizational decision making. It integrates risk management processes directly with strategic planning and decision making, ensuring that all levels of the organization are focused on common goals. This structured approach helps in evaluating risks in the context of strategic objectives, facilitating more informed decisions. By aligning risk management practices with organizational strategy, COSO ERM ensures that decisions are both strategic and risk-aware, improving overall organizational effectiveness.

The framework also significantly boosts operational efficiency by promoting proactive risk identification and standardized risk management practices. Early identification and mitigation of risks enhance operational resilience by preventing disruptions and enabling smoother operations. Additionally, the framework encourages the standardization of risk management processes across the organization, leading to more streamlined operations and consistent handling of risk exposures. This not only reduces redundancy but also ensures a unified approach to risk across all departments.

COSO's framework enhances governance and compliance. It strengthens governance structures by clearly defining risk management roles and responsibilities and ensuring that all levels of the organization are engaged and accountable. The framework also supports regulatory compliance by providing a comprehensive methodology for documenting and managing risks. The systematic approach not only helps meet various regulatory requirements but also improves the overall reliability and integrity of risk management practices within the organization.

Challenges

While many risk management frameworks present challenges for organizations with limited resources, the COSO ERM framework can be particularly demanding due to its depth and breadth. Like others, it requires time, training, and skilled personnel—but COSO's emphasis on integrating risk management into strategic decision making and performance measurement sets it apart. This comprehensive approach, while valuable, also increases implementation complexity. As a result, smaller organizations or those new to structured risk practices may find COSO ERM especially difficult to adopt without significant adaptation or external support.

Adapting an organization's culture and processes to align with the principles of COSO ERM requires careful change management and can be particularly challenging. It requires gaining and maintaining stakeholder buy-in, which is crucial and often difficult, as it takes convincing various levels of the organization of the framework's benefits. Ensuring that all stakeholders understand and support the implementation is essential for the successful adoption of COSO ERM.

This framework may also be difficult to integrate with existing risk management practices and systems, and differences in principles and methodologies can lead to conflicts. The integration challenge requires careful alignment and potential overhauls of current practices.

Achieving consistent application of any enterprise risk management framework across departments and business units is a common challenge. However, COSO ERM's integrated and principle-based structure can make uniform implementation particularly demanding. Its emphasis on aligning risk with strategy and performance requires not only coordination but a shared understanding of risk at all organizational levels. This complexity can amplify integration challenges, especially in organizations with diverse operations or decentralized governance.

Best environments

The COSO ERM framework will be especially valuable to organizations that demand a very structured approach to managing risk. These organizations may include financial, health care, energy, or technology companies, which often have stringent regulatory requirements and need a comprehensive method for managing risks that is required for compliance. Similarly, organizations aiming to align their risk management strategies with their strategic objectives and governance structures will find the COSO ERM framework instrumental in achieving these goals.

It is particularly advantageous for large or complex organizations that face diverse risks across various operations. Smaller entities, though, might find the framework's comprehensive requirements somewhat overwhelming, especially if they lack the personnel or expertise to manage a detailed risk management system. However, COSO ERM can still be tailored to fit smaller scales by focusing on the most relevant elements that directly impact the organization's operations, allowing these entities to benefit from structured risk management practices aligned with their capacities.

The COSO ERM framework also works well with ASM through its structured approach to managing organizational risks. It promotes holistic risk identification for pinpointing vulnerabilities within the attack surface. By integrating risk management with strategic planning, COSO ERM ensures that ASM aligns with broader organizational goals. Furthermore, its emphasis on continuous monitoring and improvement is vital for adapting ASM strategies in response to evolving threats and maintaining the effectiveness and relevance of risk management practices within the dynamic landscape of cybersecurity.

OCTAVE

The OCTAVE (Operationally Critical Threat, Asset, and Vulnerability Evaluation) risk framework is a set of tools and techniques developed by Carnegie Mellon University for managing information security risks. It emphasizes self-directed assessments by operational teams, focusing on the integration of organizational and technological aspects. While many frameworks aim to align risk management with business objectives, OCTAVE stands out by empowering internal staff—rather than external auditors or centralized risk teams—to drive the assessment process. This bottom-up approach makes it especially well-suited for organizations looking to tailor risk priorities to their specific operational realities and foster greater internal ownership of security practices.

Benefits

The OCTAVE framework significantly empowers organizations through its focus on self-assessment and customization. Encouraging operational teams to conduct their own security assessments promotes a sense of ownership and fosters a deeper understanding of the specific security risks they face. The empowerment is further enhanced by the framework's flexibility, allowing organizations to tailor the assessments to align precisely with their unique needs and business processes. This approach not only ensures relevancy but also enhances the effectiveness of the risk management process.

The framework also provides a comprehensive risk analysis by integrating both technological and operational aspects, offering a holistic view of organizational risks. This approach ensures a thorough understanding of the entire risk landscape. OCTAVE emphasizes the importance of focusing on operationally critical assets, helping organizations identify and prioritize risks based on their potential impact. The targeted approach facilitates effective risk management by concentrating resources on areas that are crucial to the organization's continuity and success.

The OCTAVE framework enhances strategic decision making by providing detailed insights into vulnerabilities and their potential impacts on organizational operations. This informed perspective facilitates strategic risk management decisions, ensuring that efforts are directed where they are most needed. Additionally, OCTAVE aids in the efficient allocation of resources by helping organizations focus on managing the most significant risks and optimizing the use of both financial and human resources to safeguard critical assets and ensure operational continuity.

Challenges

One of the biggest challenges with OCTAVE is related to staffing resources and skills during implementation. OCTAVE requires a strong understanding of organizational processes and risk management, often requiring specific training for team members involved in the self-assessment process. This self-assessment can be time-consuming, demanding a significant time investment from operational teams. These factors can pose barriers to effective and efficient implementation, particularly in organizations with limited resources or expertise in these areas.

Other OCTAVE challenges are related to scalability and adaptation. Its detailed and hands-on approach may become cumbersome in very large or complex organizations, potentially slowing down the risk assessment process. These environments may have trouble maintaining the framework's effectiveness due to their rapidly changing technological environments, as continual updates and adaptations are necessary to keep pace with new threats and evolving IT landscapes. These factors can make OCTAVE less feasible for certain organizations without dedicated resources for frequent framework updates.

OCTAVE implementations may also find issues with consistency and integration because ensuring uniform application across various departments can be difficult, as different parts of the organization may have varying levels of risk exposure and management capabilities. Additionally, integrating the OCTAVE framework with existing risk management or IT systems poses challenges due to potential overlaps or gaps. Achieving a seamless integration requires careful planning and coordination to ensure that the framework complements rather than conflicts with existing processes.

Best environments

The OCTAVE framework is particularly well-suited to environments that encourage organizational involvement across various levels. Its success hinges on the ability of different operational teams to conduct thorough self-assessments, making it ideal for organizations that can facilitate this broad participation. OCTAVE's flexible implementation also makes it a good fit for organizations needing a customizable framework to align closely with specific operational needs and risk profiles.

It is especially effective in medium-size organizations, where its comprehensive approach can be deeply integrated without the complexities often encountered in larger enterprises.

The OCTAVE framework effectively complements ASM efforts through its asset-focused assessments and holistic risk evaluation. It emphasizes the identification of critical information assets, aligning with ASM's goal to reduce and manage the attack surface, particularly focusing on the most valuable or vulnerable parts of the IT infrastructure. This approach not only pinpoints potential security gaps that could expand the attack surface but also encourages strategic, proactive management of risks. Consequently, organizations are better equipped to strategize and prioritize their security efforts, effectively protecting the most valuable assets and minimizing their attack surface.

Communicating Risk to Your Business Team

Effective communication of risk to business teams is essential in ensuring that risks are understood and acted on appropriately. To illustrate, consider a scenario where you have to explain a hurricane to someone visiting Florida from the Midwest of the

US who has never experienced one. A native Floridian might try to explain it to the Midwesterner in terms of hurricane categories, as they are already familiar with the intensity differences between a CAT 1 and a CAT 5 hurricane. To the Midwesterner, these categories mean very little, possibly that one is bigger than the other.

Due to their experience, Floridians inherently understand the significance of the different categories regarding wind speeds, rain, damage, and possible flooding. To the Midwesterner, the different categories are very nebulous and don't fully convey the problem. In order to overcome this, the Floridian needs to break down the explanation, perhaps explicitly stating just how bad the winds of a certain storm may be and what that might do to a building. This gives the explanation meaning that matters to the Midwesterner, increasing the likelihood of their taking appropriate actions to protect themselves.

This example directly correlates to how security professionals need to discuss risk with stakeholders. Using vague industry terminology, such as Common Vulnerability Scoring System (CVSS) scores, is too vague. The stakeholders may understand a 10 is far bigger than a 1, but it has no context in their world. Just how bad the difference is may be lost on them.

Instead, if the security professional steps back and reframes the problem in terms they relate to, the message resonates. For example, explaining the risk of a SQL injection with a CVSS score of 8 needs to be reframed to matter. If the target stakeholder is the web programmer, the problem can be explained as the vulnerability allowing remote threat actors to steal or modify data through your web interface—then the problem has context they understand. By fixing the interface, they prevent an attacker from damaging the core infrastructure that drives their product.

While doing this sounds simple, we need to strategically frame the discussion by relating risks to their potential impact on business objectives. That connects the concept of risk with concrete outcomes that affect the company's bottom line, emphasizing the relevance of risk management to overall corporate strategy. This is done by tailoring your messaging to address the unique concerns and understanding levels of different stakeholder groups within the organization. Customization of the communication style and content ensures that the message resonates with each audience, making the information more relatable and compelling.

Incorporating data visualization tools such as graphs, heat maps, and dashboards to present complex data in an easily digestible format may help this process. Visual aids can significantly enhance comprehension for nontechnical stakeholders, making the data not only accessible but also actionable.

However, establishing communication with stakeholders requires more than just clearly delivering information; it needs to be consistent. This can be done by establishing a regular schedule for communicating risks to ensure that stakeholders are consistently informed about emerging risks and the status of ongoing mitigation efforts. Regular updates help maintain a continuous dialogue about risk management and reinforce the importance of vigilance and proactive measures.

As a part of these communications, they must always be paired with actionable recommendations, otherwise teams dismiss them as purely informative. Provide clear, practical steps to mitigate risks, prioritizing actions based on the level of risk and potential impact. This approach not only informs but also empowers stakeholders to take necessary actions promptly.

Know Your Audience

Understanding your audience is critical when communicating risk within an organization. It is essential to tailor the presentation of risk information to align with the specific roles and responsibilities of the audience. That means customizing the communication to ensure it resonates and drives action based on the unique functions of each role within the company. Additionally, conducting an impact analysis to highlight how risks affect the day-to-day operations and long-term goals of different departments can make the information more relevant and compelling. Such an approach ensures that risk communication is not only informative but also actionable across various levels of the organization.

Adjusting communication techniques based on your audience's background is crucial. Using professional jargon that is familiar to the audience can significantly enhance their comprehension of the risks discussed. Furthermore, it's essential to practice cultural sensitivity, particularly in international organizations where diverse cultural backgrounds can influence how information is perceived and acted on. That approach not only ensures the clarity and relevance of the message but also fosters a respectful and inclusive communication environment.

Incorporating interactive communication is pivotal too. Establishing robust feedback mechanisms is essential, as they allow you to verify that the audience has understood the communicated risks and address any concerns they may have. This interactive process not only clarifies understanding but also informs improvements in future risk communications, ensuring that the information remains relevant and effectively drives action across all organizational levels.

Technical Jargon Confuses Business Teams

Effective communication within organizations, especially regarding technical subjects, hinges on the comprehensibility of the message. Simple, clear language is essential to making technical risk assessments accessible and actionable for nontechnical stakeholders. Employing analogies and metaphors can further demystify complex technical issues by relating them to familiar business or real-world scenarios, aiding in bridging the gap between technical and business teams.

Incorporating educational components into communications can significantly enhance understanding. Brief segments explaining key technical terms or concepts can gradually increase the business team's familiarity with IT language, thus improving their grasp over time. Moreover, interactive communication methods such as Q&A sessions, workshops, or webinars encourage active participation and allow for real-time clarification of technical terms, further enhancing comprehension.

The use of collaborative communication tools plays a crucial role. Tools that facilitate easy dialogue and interaction can help business teams ask pertinent questions about technical terms and risks, promoting a clearer understanding. These tools not only support ongoing education but also foster a collaborative environment where technical and business teams can engage more productively.

How to Translate Technical Risk to Business Language

Translating technical risk into business language involves a structured approach that ensures the information is both meaningful and comprehensible to nontechnical stakeholders. Here's how to break it down into repeatable steps for any given risk:

Identify key risks
Begin by pinpointing the technical risks that are most pertinent to the business objectives.

Simplify terminology
Translate complex technical terms into simpler language that nontechnical stakeholders can easily understand.

Assess impact
Define how each risk affects business operations, emphasizing potential disruptions or financial consequences.

Prioritize risks
Order the risks based on their potential impact and likelihood to highlight which issues need immediate attention.

Develop actionable recommendations
Propose clear, practical steps for mitigating or managing each identified risk.

Prepare visual aids
Use visual aids like charts and graphs to effectively convey the risks and their impacts.

Review and refine
Before presenting, review the material with someone from a nontechnical background to ensure the message is clear and understandable.

This process helps ensure that risk communication is targeted, clear, and actionable, bridging the gap between technical and business perspectives.

Managing Excuses for Poor Communication

To effectively counter common excuses for not simplifying technical communication, a structured response can ensure clarity and reinforce the importance of adapting the message for all stakeholders:

Excuse: "They are also in security."
Response: Even within security, specializations can vary significantly. Simplifying communication ensures that all professionals, regardless of their area of expertise, fully understand the risks and their implications.

Excuse: "They are also technical."
Response: Technical proficiency varies among stakeholders. Clear, simplified communication ensures alignment and effective action across different technical domains.

Excuse: "They might think I am not technical enough."
Response: Translating complex technical issues into strategic business impacts demonstrates a higher level of understanding and professional maturity, fundamental to leadership and collaboration.

Excuse: "It's too time-consuming to simplify."
Response: Investing time to clarify technical risks in business terms saves time later by facilitating quicker decision making and efficient resource allocation.

Excuse: "They should learn the technical terms."
Response: Effective communication is tailored to the audience's expertise. Simplifying information ensures it is accessible and enhances understanding across departments.

Excuse: "It dilutes the urgency or importance."
Response: Articulating risks in clear business terms can actually emphasize their urgency and importance by linking them directly to operational impacts and strategic objectives.

Excuse: "Business teams don't care about the details."
Response: Business stakeholders are responsible for risk oversight and need a comprehensive understanding of technical risks to make informed decisions.

These example responses should give you the tools to help mitigate other potential excuses from team members. By restructuring your teams' communication, you will make it easier for stakeholders to understand the full scale of the risks they are facing, which often increases their willingness to address them in a timely manner.

Summary

In this chapter we've outlined the critical connection between managing an organization's attack surface and effectively mitigating risks. Having explored both qualitative and quantitative approaches to risk assessment, you are now equipped to choose the most appropriate method for your organization's unique needs, ensuring that resources are allocated to the most pressing vulnerabilities. We've looked at the risk management frameworks, such as NIST, ISO, and ITIL, and offered practical guidance for selecting and implementing the right structure for various organizational environments. You should now understand the importance of clear communication with nontechnical stakeholders. Translating technical risks into business terms is key to driving informed decision making and securing organizational buy-in from all stakeholders.

As we transition to Part II, we will dive into initial steps in ASM by guiding you through the processes of identifying and classifying assets within an organization.

PART II

Identification and Classification

Now that we've covered the basics, it's time to dive into identification and classification. These topics are arguably the backbone of effective ASM, and they focus on understanding and managing your assets. Whether you're dealing with sprawling networks or a growing list of cloud services, asset discovery is vital to controlling your organization's attack surface. In this section, we'll focus on how to pinpoint every asset your organization relies on, from hardware to software, and even those tricky-to-spot shadow IT systems.

But here's the game-changer: automation. Tracking everything manually is a daunting, never-ending task that leaves plenty of room for error. That's where automation comes in, giving you a clear, up-to-date picture of all your assets without the headache. We'll walk through how automated tools make the job easier, faster, and way more accurate—so you're not just managing your assets but staying ahead of risks as they evolve.

By the end of Part II, you'll understand how automating asset discovery transforms ASM from a tedious task into a strategic advantage. With the right tools, you'll be able to see the big picture, catch those hidden risks, and keep your security efforts focused where they matter most. Let's get started!

CHAPTER 4

Identification and Classification of Assets

The first step for any organization implementing ASM is the identification and classification of assets. This is an integral step because many organizations don't have a complete understanding of them, leaving unidentified risks that skew their perception of their overall security posture. Throughout the chapter we'll cover this topic in-depth, offering a detailed, business-centric approach to discerning various assets, their business roles, and their importance within an organizational context. While we'll address many important variables, the primary goal of this step is to accurately categorize assets to inform and enhance ASM practices.

As you'll learn, we emphasize the development of a comprehensive *asset inventory* utilizing *asset enrichment*. These are vital for understanding the full scope of your organization's attack surface. By accurately identifying and classifying assets, from hardware and software to data and human resources, we lay the groundwork for ASM.

This process is not just about listing assets. A detailed inventory and classification of assets enables us to better understand the potential vulnerabilities and security gaps that each one may introduce. Understanding all of their interconnections, dependencies, and the possible risks they pose allows you to prioritize security measures and allocate resources effectively.

Identification

Before you can start managing your attack surface, it is important to understand precisely what makes up your organization's unique attack surface. This is more than a cursory inventory assessment; instead, it is an in-depth and systematic process to uncover and document all assets in your organization.

Identification is a far-reaching process that helps uncover all attack surfaces in an organization. It covers assets, people, processes, and communications, as well as untracked elements commonly referred to as shadow IT or business-led IT.

The identification process assesses all elements that may be exposed to potential threats. These threats may be externally facing, such as external websites and cloud infrastructure. They may also be segmented on internal networks, such as workstations, database servers, or printers. Clearly identifying and understanding all components within your organizational ecosystem will help inform decision making around attack surface management to effectively create targeted security measures and precisely allocate resources.

Asset Inventory

Prior to classifying assets, we must broaden our understanding of what constitutes an asset within an organization's information system. Traditionally, an asset is defined as any valuable component that supports organizational operations. The category includes physical devices like servers, computers, and networking equipment, as well as software assets such as applications, operating systems, containers, IoT devices, and databases. Data assets are another critical category, encompassing stored corporate information, financial data, intellectual property, and personal data of employees and customers.

Moreover, assets also encompass virtual components like virtual machines, cloud services, and digital certificates. We must also consider a range of intangible assets that, while lacking physical form, significantly contribute to the organization's value and operational efficacy. They include established workflows, processes, patents, copyrights, trademarks, goodwill, and digital assets like software or cryptocurrency.

When it comes to managing your attack surface, including intangible assets is essential as they often interact with or result in creating digital data, which can be an attack vector. For example, the documentation of patents, the code underlying digital assets, or the systems supporting the management of trademarks all represent potential security risks if not properly managed. While these intangible assets might not traditionally be viewed as part of an organization's attack surface, their digital traces and the systems supporting them must be secured. This approach must be comprehensive to ensure that every facet of an organization's asset portfolio is considered.

An asset is any valuable resource in an organization, including hardware, software, data, and any other technology-related component that contributes to business operations and security.

Assets are not just relegated to IT elements; individuals with access to an organization's systems or network are counted as part of an attack surface and must be considered. These include employees, contractors, vendors, customers, and other guests who may access IT resources in any manner. They can all potentially be exploited by threat actors—or *be* the threat actors—making them part of your overall attack surface. While we may not inventory them like we do IT assets, we do need to track their identities and access. We'll cover this in Chapter 6, where we delve deeper into risk.

Why Maintaining Inventory Is Foundational in ASM

The saying "you can't protect what you don't know you have" has been bantered around IT circles for years. It is a lighthearted phrase to remind each other that there is no practical way to build defenses for assets that you don't know exist. The adage underscores a foundational truth in cybersecurity: the first step in securing an organization's digital environment is getting a comprehensive awareness of all of its assets. Security efforts may be misdirected or inadequate without an accurate inventory and a clear understanding of which resources need protection, leaving unseen vulnerabilities wide open for attackers to exploit.

Building on that established truth, we must also recognize that every asset carries its own unique value and associated risks, primarily due to the distinct attack surfaces each presents. This understanding helps set the stage for classification, categorization, and accurate attack surface assessment.

In asset management, classification and categorization serve distinct but complementary purposes. Classification involves assessing each asset's characteristics, such as the type of data it stores, its role in core business operations, and its significance in customer interactions. For instance, an application that tracks customer information containing sensitive personal data would be classified as high value due to the critical nature of the data it handles. We'll cover classification in greater detail later in this chapter.

Once assets are classified, they can then be categorized, which involves prioritizing them based on the urgency and importance of the required protection. While classification assesses their characteristics and value, categorization ranks them based on their importance to the organization's operational integrity and cybersecurity posture. It is crucial to recognize that an asset can be of high value but vary in importance depending on its role in immediate business functions or its impact on service delivery.

For example, a classified high-value asset like a customer tracking application is undoubtedly important due to its data sensitivity and operational necessity. It would be categorized as high priority or mission-critical, necessitating stringent protective measures. However, other assets, such as a backup data server, might also be classified as high value. While its day-to-day operational importance might be lower, its criticality in disaster recovery scenarios categorizes it differently, focusing on long-term rather than immediate impacts.

The categorization process leads directly into attack surface identification, where each asset category is analyzed to identify potential vulnerabilities and how attackers might exploit them. This analysis acknowledges the varied nature of categorized assets—hardware, software, SaaS solutions, and data stores—which, despite their differences, may all fall under a mission-critical category. This nuanced understanding allows for a more targeted and effective cybersecurity strategy tailored to the specific risks associated with each category of assets.

Distinguishing between classification and categorization ensures a two-tiered approach to asset management. This allows us to address our cybersecurity infrastructure's urgent and important needs, ensuring that all assets, regardless of their type, receive the appropriate level of attention based on their classified value and categorized importance.

Identifying Asset Inventory Solutions

There are many methods available for tracking inventory. They range from basic lists of assets to more complex agent-driven solutions that automatically track assets throughout their life cycle. While manual efforts are a good starting point for this process, it's important to note that they are out of date from the moment they are completed, making them a poor choice for organizations adopting ASM.

Most organizations start with spreadsheets, like the basic example shown in Figure 4-1, for asset management. Most organizations will want to track significantly more information if they use the spreadsheet for any asset enrichment beyond inventory.

Name	Hostname	Environment	Operating system	Installed software
Ron's MacBook	eddings-mbp	Internal	macOS Ventura 13.4	Chrome (120.0.8) Zoom (5.16)
MJ laptop	mj-kauf-win-10	BYOD	-	-
Prod web app	asm-training.co	aws-prod	Amazon Linux 2	gcc (14.0.3) npm (8.9.4)

Figure 4-1. Manual asset tracking can be as simple as a spreadsheet listing assets and information about them.

A spreadsheet is accessible and familiar to most, fulfilling the basic requirements of gathering all the asset data in one location. While this is a sufficient solution for very small organizations, it comes with several challenges that make it unsuitable as your company grows. Notably, spreadsheets rely on manual data entry, making them subject to human error—and making it challenging to consider them a single source of truth for inventory data.

Also, spreadsheets cannot incorporate real-time updates without using additional software to collect and push the updates. At this point, the spreadsheet becomes a light database for the software that is doing the heavy lifting.

Even with additional software managing the spreadsheet, its nature and design make it unsuitable for large inventories or complex asset tracking. Spreadsheets have limited capacity for showing relationships and interdependencies between assets, which is vital for attack surface management. While it is true that spreadsheets can do some linking between cells, it rapidly makes the spreadsheet challenging to read and search.

Part of what makes spreadsheets a poor choice as a database substitute is that they lack the security features that ensure a database cannot be inappropriately modified. Databases allow credentials for multiple users, permitting logging of what each user does and the ability to limit access as necessary. On the other hand, spreadsheets are limited by a single password, which restricts access, letting anyone with the password modify the spreadsheet as necessary. This is especially problematic as we start tracking more sensitive asset data, such as the CEO's laptop name and IP, allowing it to be directly targeted by attackers.

Instead of spreadsheets, consider more advanced solutions to manage your inventory needs. Here are a few questions to consider before settling on any solution:

- What is the size of your organization?
- Do all IT assets reside in one location?
- Do you use cloud technologies?
- Do you have remote or mobile workers? Will you in the future?
- How sensitive is the data your organization handles?
- Do you need third-party vendors or contractors to collect or handle inventory information?
- Do you already have software with inventory tracking features you are not using? Why?
- What level of customization does the solution offer to fit your specific business needs?

- Can the solution integrate with your existing IT infrastructure and other business systems?

- What are the scalability options as your organization grows or evolves?

- How does the solution handle data security and comply with relevant regulations?

- What is the learning curve for using the new system, and does it offer user training?

- Does the solution provide analytics and reporting capabilities to aid in decision making?

- How does the vendor provide support and updates for the solution?

Answering these questions will help narrow down the possible solutions to effectively manage your inventory. Possible solutions include IT asset management (ITAM) software, configuration management database (CMDB) tools, cloud-based asset management tools, or some form of custom solution. Let's explore each of these categories in a bit more detail.

ITAM solutions are purpose-built for asset management, providing functionality to track assets throughout their life cycle. They provide a centralized system for tracking and managing hardware, software, and other IT assets. To help with this process, they leverage automated processes for reporting and analytics to drive decision making. However, ITAM solutions are not always the best option as they are often complex, making initial setup and long-term operations challenging, especially for teams that lack time, special expertise, or resources.

While purpose-built for inventory, CMDB tools go further as centralized repositories that allow for storing information about IT assets and their configurations. These solutions excel at providing detailed insights into the relationships and dependencies between different IT assets. This information is used as a part of attack surface management to help determine prioritization for core dependencies for systems. Much like ITAM, these systems are complex and don't always have automated processes to update information as assets change.

Cloud-based asset management tools may behave similarly to ITAM or CMDB solutions but only gather data for cloud assets. This functionality is important as cloud environments are highly dynamic, with new instances continuously being created and destroyed, making cloud assets more challenging and in some cases impossible to track with solutions that are not cloud-focused. While these solutions are highly effective for monitoring cloud data, they are not always backward compatible with on-premises IT, meaning a complementary solution that works in tandem will likely be necessary to get a complete view of the inventory.

Discovery of Assets

To create an accurate inventory, we need to look under rocks and in dark and long-abandoned digital caves (or data centers) to create a complete inventory. Many of these go well beyond the basic identification we just covered, to taking a more holistic view of what an organization owns and manages.

This process is not limited to physical assets like hardware, equipment, and real estate; it encompasses digital assets, including software, data, and various network elements. The scope of discovery is comprehensive, ensuring every asset is accounted for—from core systems vital to the organization's operations to peripheral devices that may seem less significant.

Asset discovery is the process of identifying and cataloging all digital and physical assets within an organization, including hardware, software, and networked devices, to ensure their security and management.

Considering the diverse and dynamic nature of assets in modern organizations, it likely comes as no surprise that asset discovery spans various locations and environments. Since assets range from traditional physical items to increasingly prevalent digital and virtual ones, they can be located on-premises, utilized remotely, and exist in cloud infrastructures.

The discovery process lays the groundwork for robust asset management, serving as a core element in attack surface management as it connects to cybersecurity, compliance, and risk management strategies. Building a complete asset inventory is achieved through a comprehensive discovery process. In this process, the organization will discover not only what assets it possesses but also how they are utilized. This knowledge is instrumental in informed decision making across various domains, including budget allocation, strategic planning, security posture enhancement, and operational efficiency optimization.

The asset discovery process helps create a clear, up-to-date picture of an organization's resources, enabling it to safeguard assets, comply with regulations, manage risks effectively, and fully capitalize on its investments.

Manual asset discovery

When it comes to asset discovery, manual efforts are often the only way a business can manage the discovery process. This may be fine for smaller businesses, as there are fewer assets to track. However, as a company grows, tracking assets can become unwieldy and complex.

Manual asset discovery involves a meticulous process of physical inspections, where personnel systematically examine an organization's premises to account for all tangible hardware assets, from servers and workstations to mobile devices. This method often encompasses conducting surveys and interviews with employees across various departments, aiming to unearth assets that might not be immediately visible through this process. Complementing these physical checks are network scanning exercises, which involve manually reviewing network infrastructures to pinpoint and catalog networked devices and systems.

Manual asset discovery is far from optimal, but it becomes necessary when automated tools are either unsuitable or unavailable. While this method creates a foundational understanding of the asset landscape, operationalizing and maintaining an accurate inventory of assets is hard.

One significant hurdle is the extensive time investment required; this method demands considerable human effort and hours for thorough execution. It involves employee cooperation and knowledge sharing to identify all assets. Manual assessments are time-consuming, tedious, and reliant on fallible human efforts; there is an inherent risk of error, from overlooked assets to inaccuracies in documentation. Correcting these errors is difficult and may require physical inventory audits, extending the process. Also, assets are rarely static, so physical inventories will become out of date the moment the software is updated or a system is moved, such as someone taking a laptop home or moving a server to a different rack. It's a never-ending treadmill of management rather than a one-and-done effort.

It is also important to note that a manual approach generally only identifies physically tangible assets. Digital assets like software licenses, cloud services, and online resources often escape the net of manual discovery methods due to their nonphysical nature. Without leveraging supplementary strategies, overlooked assets will likely lead to undiscovered and untracked vulnerabilities in the attack surface.

Shadow IT and untracked assets

We've discussed the importance of tracking asset inventory because you can't manage an attack surface you don't know exists. *Shadow IT* is that attack surface. The rise in the use of SaaS applications has contributed to the proliferation of shadow IT, but a wide range of untracked IT assets might exist within your organization. Here are a few of the more common examples:

Unauthorized software/applications
Unapproved software may be used for tasks like file sharing, collaboration, or project management (e.g., Dropbox, Trello).

Personal devices
Employees may use their personal laptops, tablets, or smartphones for work purposes without IT approval.

Cloud services
Utilization of cloud storage or computing services may not be sanctioned by the IT department (e.g., Google Drive, AWS).

Legacy systems
Outdated hardware or software could still be operational but not actively managed or tracked.

Orphaned devices
Devices could be left connected to the network but no longer be in active use or monitored (e.g., old printers, unused servers).

Undocumented network devices
Network devices like switches, routers, or WiFi access points are added without IT's knowledge. Even physical devices such as servers or Next Unit of Computing devices can be plugged into the network without authorization, expanding the attack surface.

Unregistered virtual machines
VMs created for testing or temporary projects could remain on the network unnoticed after they are no longer needed.

This is further facilitated by the widespread availability of cloud-based services, which can be quickly adopted without technical expertise; we will dive a bit deeper into these in Chapter 5. A significant factor contributing to the rise of shadow IT is the mindset that when officially sanctioned IT solutions do not adequately meet the needs or expectations of users (whether in terms of functionality, ease of use, or agility), it is acceptable to circumvent official channels and create or acquire a solution unofficially. The mismatch between the offerings of organizational IT and the needs of its users creates a fertile ground for shadow IT to flourish.

Shadow IT can manifest in various organizational forms, ranging from seemingly innocuous to critically risky. One common form is using unauthorized software, which employees might install on company devices to facilitate work or improve efficiency. For example, an employee can download unsupported videoconferencing software on their computer to meet with a third-party vendor. After using it, there is no need to use it again, so it remains installed without any company-supplied updates, leaving the network vulnerable.

The software doesn't have to be videoconferencing; it can be anything from open source applications to those purchased outside the standard procurement pipelines. But it can become a problem when the software has discovered vulnerabilities, especially when these vulnerabilities are not promptly addressed due to the lack of oversight from the IT department. This situation poses a significant security risk as unmonitored software may become a gateway for cyberthreats such as malware or data breaches.

Trouble also emerges when shadow IT comes as cloud services for storage and collaboration. Many consumer-grade solutions, such as Dropbox and Google Drive, offer convenience and ease of access but often sidestep the stringent security measures and compliance standards mandated in corporate environments. Using these solutions without corporate governance creates enormous operational and compliance risks.

Problems start with the siloing of data. Operating independently from organizational solutions, this siloed data exists unmanaged and is only usable to the teams who own it. This limits the service's value, reducing others' ability to access and analyze the data, which may be useful for their projects. In many cases, silos like this happen repeatedly throughout the organization, with many teams operating the exact same solutions unbeknownst to each other, duplicating efforts, creating conflicting data, and wasting resources.

Security concerns are amplified when sensitive data is placed outside organizational control, with little tracking of how it is secured and who has access to it. As individuals or teams own the service rather than central IT, the service is unlikely to be configured in alignment with established organizational standards. It may allow weak passwords, lack multifactor authentication, or have open access controls, allowing everyone using it to have full access. This creates a perfect storm where valuable data is poorly protected and easily targeted by attackers, increasing the risk of an incident. Depending on the data, it can result in significant fines or legal penalties, even if the organization is unaware of it having happened.

Similarly, external storage devices, such as USB drives, fall into this category when used without proper oversight or encryption, posing significant data security risks. If these devices are lost or stolen, it can be categorized as a data breach. This happened to Coplin Health Systems in 2013 when the data of 43,000 patients was lost due to a stolen, unencrypted device (*https://oreil.ly/PfHtP*).

Shadow IT may also come from IT infrastructure that was never meant to persist, such as a demo system for a product or a temporary database to transform data for a new schema. These systems weren't intended to be permanent but remained beyond their usefulness because the team moved on rapidly to other projects, intending to decommission them later. Forgotten and orphaned, they sit on the network, unmaintained, creating an easily exploitable hidden attack surface.

Exacerbating the security concerns related to untracked assets is the increasing trend of employees using personal devices for work purposes, a practice known as BYOD, which further blurs the lines between personal and professional IT use. Users often see no issue using these devices to store or process business data. This leads to organizational data falling outside the company's control and creating another unmonitored, often unknown attack surface.

While solving immediate productivity challenges, these various forms of shadow IT and untracked assets increase the attack surface and inadvertently expose organizations to a heightened risk of data breaches and compliance issues. Discovering them through manual discovery is difficult at best. Automated tooling and discovery is the only appropriate, consistent, and thorough way to find these potential risks.

Automation of asset discovery

Automated asset discovery helps overcome the challenges of manual discovery and the existence of shadow IT. While this section offers a preliminary overview, the topic will be explored in greater depth throughout the rest of this chapter. The automated approach uses technology to systematically identify, track, and manage physical and digital assets, providing speed, efficiency, and consistency enhancements that manual methods cannot match.

It overcomes the manual challenges of being labor-intensive and prone to inaccuracies by utilizing sophisticated software to scan networks, monitor hardware and software installations, and maintain an up-to-date inventory of all assets. The shift from manual to automated processes streamlines the discovery phase and ensures a more accurate and comprehensive asset registry. By automating the tedious and repetitive aspects of asset management, organizations can allocate their human resources to more strategic tasks, optimizing overall operational efficiency.

Automated systems offer enhanced visibility and control over tangible and intangible assets, facilitating better asset utilization and efficient management. This heightened control is crucial in ensuring compliance with various industry regulations, as organizations can more easily monitor and report on their asset status.

Automation also enables a proactive approach to asset management. By providing real-time, up-to-date information, these systems allow for timely preventive maintenance, early detection of potential issues, and swift response to security threats. Staying ahead of risks and efficiently managing resources can be the difference between smooth operations and disruptive setbacks.

Classification for Asset Enrichment

Asset enrichment is built from information gathered in asset discovery and is designed to help comprehensively understand an organization's assets. This process goes beyond a mere inventory, involving systematically gathering, analyzing, and effectively utilizing data related to these assets. Additionally, it encompasses a spectrum of information, from fundamental inventory details such as type, quantity, and location of assets to more intricate and insightful aspects. These aspects include the usage patterns of assets, their interdependencies within the organizational infrastructure, and their life cycle stages.

By understanding these dimensions, organizations classify their assets into logical groupings based on business risks and data types. Doing so allows them to unlock more profound insights into how assets contribute to operational effectiveness, identify potential risks and inefficiencies, and strategically manage their resources. This holistic approach to asset enrichment enhances day-to-day operational decision making and feeds into long-term strategic planning and risk management endeavors.

Several data points need to be gathered to create a comprehensive understanding of each asset. It starts with understanding what type of assets we have and how they are configured. Then, we build on this by collecting an in-depth view of how the asset is used and what variety of data it handles to help understand the risks involved. The data is augmented with information about what other assets it depends on and how they are secured. The goal is to understand the complex nature of an asset to see how it fits into the organizational attack surface.

Asset Type Details

The bedrock of an effective tracking system lies in the meticulous documentation of crucial asset details. It is imperative to understand each asset's essential characteristics—such as its type, hardware, software, network device, model, serial number, and specifications.

This fundamental information forms the backbone of asset tracking, equipping organizations with the necessary tools to maintain a clear and detailed inventory. The significance of this data extends beyond recordkeeping; it is instrumental in ensuring that every asset is accurately accounted for and can be easily identified. This level of detailed knowledge about each asset is not just a matter of administrative convenience but of strategic value, enabling organizations to swiftly locate and deploy resources as needed and respond effectively to any operational challenges.

By having precise details of each asset, organizations can maintain an accurate and exceptionally organized inventory. Knowing the exact specifications of assets aids in categorizing them effectively, thereby streamlining inventory processes. This detailed categorization is not a trivial matter; it has significant implications for managing asset quantities, ensuring adequate resources are available to meet operational demands, and preventing both surplus and shortage.

Comprehensive information is crucial for strategic planning, particularly in forecasting future inventory needs. Whether planning for procurement, allocating resources for maintenance, or strategizing for upgrades, the clarity provided by a well-maintained inventory based on detailed asset information is invaluable in making informed, proactive decisions that keep an organization's operations running smoothly.

Configuration Data

Configuration data is the detailed settings and characteristics of each asset within an organization. This data encompasses a wide array of information, from software versions installed on devices to operating system settings, network configurations, and the suite of applications each asset operates with.

The nature of configuration data is both dynamic and complex, as it varies significantly across different assets. In hardware, for instance, it may include settings pertinent to the device's operation and connectivity capabilities. For software assets, configuration data encompasses version details, custom settings tailored to specific operational needs, and any additional plug-ins or extensions that might be in use.

Configuration data profoundly impacts an asset's functionality, security, and ability to integrate seamlessly with other systems within the organizational network. For example, information about the software version is not a trivial detail; it is critical to determine how well the software will work with other systems and to assess the asset's vulnerability to potential security threats. These versions can be tied back to known CVEs (common vulnerabilities and exposures) that outline the details of issues such as affected software versions and exploitation paths.

The network configurations describe how each device connects and communicates within the broader network, which is necessary to maintain network integrity and optimal performance. An accurate understanding of these configurations is indispensable in pinpointing potential network bottlenecks or security vulnerabilities, preempting operational issues, and enhancing overall system resilience.

Configuration data is about more than security. It is also intricately linked to compliance management. Regulatory standards in sectors like finance and health care often dictate strict adherence to specific configuration settings, especially concerning data protection and encryption, making regular audits and reviews of configuration data essential practices.

Data Classification

Data classification involves categorizing data stored or processed by an asset based on its level of sensitivity, proprietary nature, or compliance with regulatory requirements. This categorization is pivotal as it dictates the level of protection and specific handling protocols each data type requires.

The data classification process is not a one-size-fits-all solution; instead, it is highly subjective and tailored to meet the specific needs of each organization, influenced by its business and revenue models. While a basic framework might segment data into public, internal, confidential, or highly confidential categories, the specific criteria for these categories depend on multiple factors. These factors include the potential impact of a data breach, the legal or regulatory obligations tied to the data, and the organization's unique operational needs.

For example, a company's public marketing materials are generally classified as public since they are intended for broad dissemination. In contrast, financial records or employee information typically fall under confidential or highly confidential categories due to their sensitivity and the severe consequences of unauthorized access.

Organizations may also look to established guidelines from entities such as the National Security Agency or the Department of Defense, which use well-defined classification levels to protect national security. These levels include Top Secret, Secret, and Confidential, which clearly delineate the sensitivity of information and the extent of measures required to protect it. The designation of Controlled Unclassified Information addresses sensitive but unclassified data that still requires safeguarding, ensuring that important information remains secure even when it doesn't meet higher classification thresholds.

Additionally, compliance with regulatory bodies such as the Securities and Exchange Commission may dictate specific classification standards and handling requirements, particularly for financial data. This regulatory influence ensures that data handling aligns with legal mandates, further emphasizing the need for a tailored approach to data classification within each organization.

Data classification guides organizations to apply appropriate and effective security measures. Data that is sensitive or under regulatory purview, such as personally identifiable information, financial records, or health-related information, necessitates stricter security protocols to comply with privacy laws or industry-specific legal frameworks. Proper classification of data aids organizations in creating effective data handling policies, determining who has access to various data types, and implementing encryption standards to protect data integrity and confidentiality.

It all comes down to a holistic understanding of the data, from where it is to what it is, to help determine risk. This information influences how it is stored, transmitted, and shared outside the organization so that data handling practices align with data security and privacy policies.

The classification of data that an asset holds or processes is instrumental in defining the security requirements of that asset. In the context of ASM, assets that handle highly sensitive or regulated data are central to operational integrity and represent significant potential vulnerabilities within the attack surface. To effectively manage these risks, ASM requires implementing stringent security measures tailored to the data's sensitivity.

Usage Information

Usage information offers a wide array of metrics that provide insights into an asset's operational patterns because it includes data on how an asset is utilized within an organization. For instance, in the case of hardware devices, usage information might include metrics such as operational hours, intensity of usage, and the specific types of tasks the device is performing. High CPU or memory usage might indicate a vulnerability to resource exhaustion attacks like DDoS, which can be critical for managing the attack surface.

Similarly, observing data creation and modification patterns and analyzing user interaction statistics for software or digital assets can reveal anomalies that suggest security threats, such as unauthorized access or potential data breaches. This information is instrumental in identifying areas where an asset may be underperforming or where opportunities for optimization directly relate to security.

Furthermore, usage information helps manage the longevity and relevance of an asset's life cycle in the context of ASM. By understanding how frequently and intensely assets are used, organizations can plan maintenance and upgrades to enhance operational efficiency and anticipate security risks. For example, suppose an asset runs close to its storage capacity. In that case, it might impact performance and pose risks such as system crashes that could take down mission-critical applications during peak operations.

Through a detailed analysis of usage patterns, organizations can predict when an asset might reach the end of its useful life or require significant maintenance, and how these factors might expose it to security vulnerabilities. Usage trends thus inform strategic decisions about resource allocation, system upgrades, and security enhancements, ensuring a proactive approach to asset management and attack surface management.

Location and Environmental Data

Location and environmental data encompass the details about where an asset is physically or virtually located and the conditions of its operational environment. For physical assets, this means their geographic location, whether in an office, in a data center, or at a remote site. For virtual assets, such as cloud-based services or virtual machines, location data refers to their specific positioning within the network infrastructure, like their assigned network segment or presence in a particular cloud environment.

Environmental data includes factors like temperature, humidity, or exposure to potential hazards, which are especially crucial for sensitive equipment requiring specific environmental conditions to function optimally.

The physical location of an asset is intimately tied to its security. Knowledge of an asset's geographic location is part of implementing the appropriate security measures. Assets located in high-risk areas or accessible public spaces might necessitate extra layers of security, such as advanced surveillance systems or robust physical barriers.

Understanding who is responsible for or "owns" the asset is also valuable in this process. Asset ownership is essential for determining who has the authority to make decisions regarding each asset's risk management and security protocols. This accountability ensures that risks are managed and that the asset complies with organizational security policies.

Additionally, understanding an asset's geographic location helps assess its risk of exposure to natural disasters, such as floods, earthquakes, or other local threats. This information is instrumental in crafting effective disaster recovery strategies and developing comprehensive business continuity plans. While this attack surface does not originate from a digital location, it is still a legitimate concern and must factor into the overall ASM assessment.

Beyond operational considerations, assets' physical and network locations can also have significant compliance and regulatory implications, particularly for those handling sensitive data. Certain assets are subject to stringent regulatory requirements that dictate how they should be managed and where they should be located. For instance, data sovereignty laws in various jurisdictions may mandate that data be stored in specific geographic locations, directly influencing decisions about where to house data centers and cloud services.

Interdependencies

Interdependencies represent the relationships and connections between various assets within an organization's infrastructure. This concept challenges the traditional view of assets as isolated entities, recognizing instead that they are integral components of a more extensive, interconnected system. These interdependencies can occur between diverse types of assets, such as the reliance of a software application on specific hardware, or among similar assets, like network devices that are linked within the same infrastructure.

Understanding these connections allows for the recognition of how changes or issues in one asset can ripple through and impact others. For example, updating the software on one system might inadvertently affect the functionality of interconnected applications, or a malfunction in a network device could disrupt the entire network's services. Mapping these relationships is a key step toward a holistic understanding of the asset ecosystem, providing vital insights for troubleshooting, risk management, and planning future changes or upgrades.

By understanding the interconnected nature of assets, organizations gain the ability to identify potential points of failure and vulnerabilities within their infrastructure. This understanding is indispensable in developing targeted risk mitigation strategies, including implementing redundancy systems or enhancing specific security measures. When contemplating asset changes or upgrades, an awareness of these interdependencies ensures that all potential impacts are thoroughly considered. This foresight is critical in preventing unintended consequences, where a modification in one part of the system might inadvertently affect another. For example, upgrading security protocols on a network could necessitate concurrent updates on connected devices to maintain overall network integrity and functionality.

Security Posture

An asset's security posture encompasses a comprehensive assessment of its current security status and ability to resist cyberattacks. This assessment includes a review of the security tools installed on the asset, an evaluation of any existing vulnerabilities, an analysis of the asset's history regarding security incidents, and a verification of its compliance with established organizational security policies and standards.

The specific aspects of security posture vary depending on the type of asset. For example, for network devices, it involves analyzing firewall settings and intrusion detection systems. It focuses on the presence of the latest security patches and antivirus software for software applications. For data assets, crucial factors include the robustness of encryption methods and the effectiveness of access control mechanisms.

Compliance with security policies and industry regulations is also part of an asset's security posture. Adherence to internal security governance and compliance with external regulatory requirements are essential for maintaining the integrity and security of assets. These external requirements can vary from general data protection laws, like the GDPR, to more specific industry standards, depending on the nature of the asset and the data it handles.

Regular audits and assessments of the security posture help ensure continuous compliance and identify areas where assets might not meet the necessary standards. Through these regular reviews, organizations can address any compliance gaps and reinforce their overall security posture.

Life Cycle Status

Understanding an asset's life cycle status is the final piece of asset data to be gathered. It encompasses an asset's entire range of stages, shown in Figure 4-2, from planning to disposal. This life cycle typically includes procurement or acquisition, where the asset is acquired; deployment, where it is set up and integrated into the operational environment; active operation, where it serves its intended function; regular maintenance, to ensure its ongoing efficiency and reliability; periodic upgrades, to enhance its functionality or security; and finally, its disposal or retirement, when it is no longer viable or cost-effective to maintain.

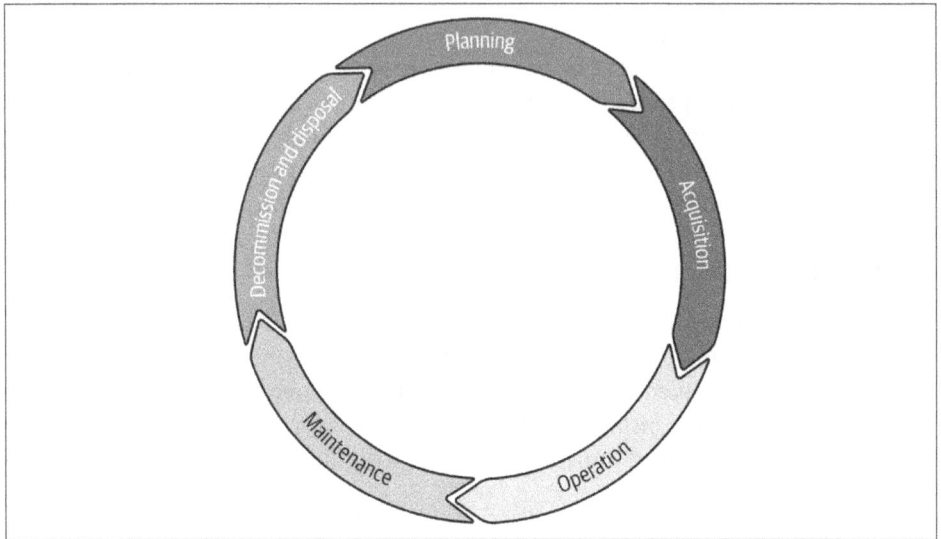

Figure 4-2. A complete asset life cycle takes the asset from the planning stages through its disposal.

By effectively managing the life cycle, organizations can properly track and manage assets to reduce security risks during their operations and ensure that no sensitive data is left behind after it is no longer needed.

Tracking an asset's position within this life cycle informs maintenance schedules, ensures assets are kept in optimal condition, aids in determining the most opportune times for upgrades based on technological advancements or wear and tear, and helps in deciding when an asset should be retired, a decision often driven by cost-effectiveness, efficiency, and evolving organizational needs. This tracking is fundamental for effective budget management and for determining when an asset is close to no longer being supported by the manufacturer. At this stage, it will no longer receive security patches when vulnerabilities are discovered, increasing the risk that comes with the asset.

Integrating Asset Enrichment with Business Strategy

Integrating asset enrichment into business strategy significantly shifts how organizations view and manage their assets and is necessary for effective attack surface management. Asset enrichment encompasses a comprehensive understanding of an organization's assets, capabilities, usage patterns, life cycle stages, and interdependencies.

Integrating this wealth of information with the broader business strategy means aligning the management and optimization of these assets with the organization's overarching goals and objectives. It transforms asset management from a mere operational function to a strategic one, leveraging the insights gathered from asset data to inform critical decision making. This ensures that assets are managed for efficiency and longevity and are strategically employed to foster business growth and enhance competitiveness.

Strategic alignment and decision making are at the heart of integrating asset enrichment with business strategy. This approach is needed in ASM as it allows for more informed and proactive decision making when determining how vulnerabilities affect the business. For instance, analyzing usage patterns and interdependencies through asset enrichment enables organizations to identify systems that are vulnerable and business-critical. This shifts vulnerability management from a reactive checklist exercise to a prioritized, impact-driven strategy. Instead of treating all vulnerabilities equally, businesses can focus their remediation efforts where disruption would be most costly, improving efficiency and protection.

Achieving this level of targeted insight isn't just about having more data. It's about activating it through collaboration and strategic alignment. It often requires breaking down silos between security, operations, and leadership teams to ensure asset intelligence informs not just security posture but business planning.

Moreover, this integration elevates risk management from routine assessment to dynamic resilience planning. Organizations gain the ability to anticipate and prepare for cascading effects of failures, whether from cyberattacks, system outages, or supply chain issues. By understanding how flexible or fragile each asset is in different scenarios, companies can design responses that are not only swift but adaptive, sustaining momentum even when unexpected disruptions occur.

A comprehensive view of an organization's assets is valuable to effective management and strategic decision making. It lays the foundation for prioritization and effective risk management in later stages of attack surface management.

Better Prioritization

A clear, comprehensive asset view enables organizations to assess which systems are truly mission-critical to daily operations. Identifying these high-value assets, such as servers running core business applications, allows for smarter allocation of protection, maintenance, and investment efforts. Rather than treating all assets equally, teams can prioritize based on business impact, ensuring operational continuity where it matters most. This approach isn't just about asset protection. It's about sustaining the essential functions that keep the business running.

This prioritization is often risk-based, helping organizations focus on assets most susceptible to cyber threats, physical damage, or technological failure. With a clear understanding of these risks, teams can direct their efforts where they'll have the greatest impact—such as strengthening security around servers that handle sensitive data, rather than dispersing resources evenly across all systems.

That said, prioritization doesn't mean ignoring lower-risk assets. It's about applying protection proportionately. Like reinforcing the structural beams of a building while still inspecting the foundation and roof, organizations must ensure that less obvious vulnerabilities don't become points of failure. A well-rounded, risk-informed approach offers resilience without overcommitting to one threat at the expense of others.

Consider a financial institution prioritizing its customer database as a high-value asset and dedicating significant security resources to protect it. While this asset deserves a higher level of protection, the institution must also ensure that supporting systems—like those managing employee access, transactional logs, or third-party integrations—receive appropriate safeguards. Overlooking these "back door" systems could provide attackers with indirect paths to high-value data, undermining the security of even the most protected assets.

When organizations clearly understand the role and importance of each asset, they can allocate their resources—including funds, staffing, skills, and time—more effectively. The focused allocation ensures that high-priority assets, crucial for business continuity and growth, receive the necessary support and upgrades. By doing so, organizations can optimize the performance of these key assets, maximizing their return on investment and minimizing wasted resources on less critical assets.

Accurate Inventory

A comprehensive asset view enhances visibility and control over an organization's assets, contributing significantly to maintaining an accurate inventory at all times. The meticulous cataloging and tracking of every asset within the organization, from core infrastructure elements to more minor tools, streamlines the management of current assets but also provides valuable insights for future asset procurement and disposition decisions. By having a comprehensive view, organizations can ensure that their asset inventory reflects the true state of their resources.

Maintaining accurate inventory facilitates preventive maintenance and effective risk mitigation. With a precise and detailed inventory, organizations gain the ability to proactively schedule maintenance activities, effectively planning for necessary inter-ventions before minor issues develop into significant, costly problems. A preemptive maintenance strategy extends the lifespan of assets and ensures their optimal perfor-mance, ultimately contributing to uninterrupted business operations.

Accurate and detailed information about the location and condition of assets is invaluable in identifying potential risks and vulnerabilities. With this knowledge, organizations can develop and implement targeted risk management strategies, sig-nificantly reducing the likelihood of asset-related failures or security breaches.

Software Licensing Tracking

Streamlining license management is integral to an organization's governance, risk management, and compliance efforts. While traditionally seen as separate from asset management, it can also play a role in ASM by ensuring availability and support response. This broader approach includes the efficient tracking of all software licen-ses—from large-scale enterprise applications to individual user licenses—and also extends to maintaining records of maintenance contracts and managed services.

By incorporating software license tracking into a comprehensive asset management strategy, organizations can maintain an accurate inventory of their software assets, ensuring full utilization and compliance with licensing agreements. This becomes particularly crucial for managing complex software portfolios that may include a variety of applications, each with its own set of licensing terms and expiration dates.

Detailed tracking provides a clear overview of all software assets, preventing under-licensing, which could lead to legal issues, and over-licensing, which could result in unnecessary expenditures. Tracking licensing enables organizations to identify and address unused or underutilized software licenses, providing an opportunity to reallocate resources or terminate unnecessary licenses, thereby avoiding wasteful spending. Tracking is also integral to maintaining compliance with software licensing agreements, mitigating the risk of legal issues and financial penalties.

This also addresses the unique challenges posed by different types of open source licenses within software asset management. For instance, licenses such as the GNU General Public License (GPL) can significantly affect how proprietary software inte-grates open source components. The GPL and similar licenses often require that any derivative work based on GPL-licensed software must also be released under the same license, potentially obligating organizations to distribute their proprietary software under GPL, which demands that the software be made available for free. This can inadvertently lead to legal and financial impacts if not managed carefully.

Including maintenance contracts and managed services as part of the asset manage-ment process emphasizes the importance of availability and support readiness as components of the organization's overall security posture. For ASM specifically, this ensures that every critical system has the correct software license and the necessary support structure in place. Knowing the level of support you are entitled to and having immediate access to contact information for escalations can significantly reduce downtime and mitigate risks.

Additionally, by integrating these elements into the ASM framework, organizations will be better prepared to respond to incidents and system failures. The integration ensures that all aspects of software and hardware management are aligned with security and operational standards, which is vital for maintaining the resilience and integrity of IT environments.

With a clear understanding of their software license landscape, organizations are better positioned to manage renewals proactively and negotiate more favorable terms with vendors. By leveraging insights from their comprehensive asset view, they can take advantage of opportunities like volume licensing or other cost-saving licensing arrangements, further optimizing their software asset investments.

Comprehensive license tracking also significantly reduces the risks associated with software audits. In an era where audits are increasingly common, being prepared with accurate documentation of all software licenses is crucial. This level of preparedness decreases the likelihood of facing penalties during audits and minimizes operational disruptions that can arise from last-minute scrambles to compile necessary information. An organization with a well-managed asset view can swiftly provide proof of compliance, showcasing its responsible and proactive approach to software license management.

Compliance Audit Evidence

The compliance benefits of a comprehensive asset inventory go beyond software, as it also facilitates audit preparedness. A detailed view encompasses crucial information about each asset in an organization, including its procurement, operational usage, maintenance history, and security measures.

During compliance audits—be they for financial reporting, data security, or specific industry regulations—having a wealth of organized data at hand is a game-changer. It empowers organizations to confidently adhere to regulatory standards and show that their asset management practices align with legal and industry norms. The depth and accuracy of these records provide tangible evidence during audits, showcasing to auditors and regulatory bodies that the organization maintains clear and thorough oversight of its assets and is managed diligently, following pertinent laws and guidelines.

By maintaining an all-encompassing view of assets, organizations can identify and address compliance gaps before they escalate into issues during an audit. This forward-looking approach is especially critical in data protection, where regulations such as the GDPR, SOX, and HIPAA necessitate stringent data management practices. An accurate and complete asset record ensures that all assets are managed and updated in alignment with the latest regulatory standards, providing a solid defense against potential noncompliance.

Moreover, when the time comes for an audit, a comprehensive asset view significantly streamlines the process. With all necessary information systematically organized and easily accessible, auditors can conduct their reviews more efficiently and thoroughly. This level of preparedness and organization reduces the resource burden and disruption. It also enhances an organization's reputation with auditors and regulatory entities as a compliant and well-managed establishment. It's important to conduct regular internal reviews, leveraging asset data, to prepare for external audits, rendering what can often be a daunting process into one that is predictable and manageable.

Summary

After finishing this chapter, you should have deeper insight into the first steps in ASM: the identification and classification of assets. We've discussed the definition of asset inventory and the relationship between it and asset enrichment. We emphasized the importance of each and discussed that they extend beyond mere listings to include information such as interconnections, dependencies, business context, and potential security vulnerabilities. This step of ASM lays the foundation for the rest of the process and is pivotal for prioritizing security measures and optimizing asset utilization. The data gathered about each asset collectively informs strategic decisions that enhance your organization's cybersecurity posture.

In the next chapter, we'll explore how automating asset discovery can overcome the limitations of manual tracking systems. Automation not only enhances efficiency and accuracy but also adapts to the evolving digital landscape, ensuring a comprehensive view of both physical and virtual assets spread across diverse environments. We'll also discuss advanced asset management techniques for maintaining security and compliance.

CHAPTER 5

Automating Asset Discovery

Any organization starting its ASM journey needs a complete asset inventory. Too often, that involves some unfortunate but well-meaning person grabbing a notepad and exploring which departments own certain assets. Unfortunately, once they've jotted down every laptop, server, and software license they can find, the list is still full of holes. Remote workers' devices are missing, cloud services hide in plain sight, and virtual machines lurk in the shadows.

Reality sinks in as your notepad overflows with scribbled pages: manual asset discovery is a nightmare. It's time-consuming, error-prone, and hopelessly incomplete in the face of modern IT complexity. Spreadsheets can't capture the complete picture when assets live on-premises, in the cloud, and everywhere in between.

Welcome to the wild world of asset management, where "good enough" discovery is never enough, yet often it's the best an organization has. The good news is that there is a smarter approach, and that's important in ASM, where a single overlooked asset can spell disaster with unmanaged risk.

This smarter approach is called *automated asset discovery*. It's the secret weapon for mapping that tangled web of hardware, software, and services that power our businesses. With the right tools, you can illuminate every corner of the IT environment, from physical servers to virtual desktops to SaaS applications.

The hard truth is that in today's hybrid, multicloud world, you can't protect what you can't see. Incomplete asset visibility is a ticking time bomb, waiting to explode into security breaches, compliance violations, and costly inefficiencies. But with automated, comprehensive discovery, you'll have the insight to tackle any challenge thrown your way. So skip the notepad and embrace the power of automated asset discovery—your future self (and possibly your boss) will thank you.

Importance of Automating Asset Discovery

From our discussion in the last chapter, it should be clear that manual asset discovery efforts are time-consuming and ill-equipped to deal with the modern IT landscape. Automated tooling does the heavy lifting, alleviating the burden of already busy staff. It scans across networks, looking for different services, storage, networked devices, or any related IT assets that may belong to your organization.

Basic tools simply do network sweeps of internal resources or rely on agents to relay data back. More advanced versions monitor user behaviors to determine what systems and services are in use and build the inventory from there. Either way, the technology does most of the work, with many even sanitizing and organizing findings into a sensible inventory, so staff only has minor fixes to resolve later.

We'll cover some of the tools that are available later in this chapter, but first, let's look at some of the reasons why you should automate asset discovery and some of the challenges you may face.

Breadth of Enterprises

One of the prime reasons that organizations turn to automated asset discovery is that they are just too large to rely on a manual effort. There are simply too many assets to identify and track, even for small businesses with only a few dozen people.

The vast scale and diversity of assets across modern enterprises require automation for comprehensive visibility. This complexity is compounded by integrating cloud technologies, IoT, mobile devices, and virtualization. Enterprises operate with a mix of legacy and cutting-edge technologies across multiple locations, making manual tracking cumbersome and often inaccurate. Automated tools are adept at scanning and managing across locations and asset types. Cloud services and remote data centers are as easy to investigate for automated tools as on-premises devices. This level of insight is crucial for attack surface management, where complete visibility is required to effectively categorize risk.

On the other hand, manual processes can still discover and inventory external assets, but they are prone to oversight and errors and rapidly become outdated. Failing to fully incorporate remote or cloud assets into the inventory results in flawed risk assessments, leaving attack surfaces undetected and unprotected.

Managing growth and change

Further complicating the asset management process is that companies are no longer relatively static, no matter the size. Previously, aside from changes in staffing, which was fairly predictable, a company's assets were slow to change. Servers and network devices were physical hardware requiring procurement and installation processes, making them fairly easy to track.

Enterprises no longer rely on just physical hardware and assets. Much of it has gone virtual or to the cloud. In these dynamic environments, staff can create and destroy new systems in the blink of an eye. For cloud especially, this can be an automatic process as infrastructures scale rapidly to meet demand and then are eliminated when demand drops.

Tracking these environments with manual processes is impossible with the volume and pace of change. Even if manual efforts were attempted, any inventory would rapidly become inaccurate, leaving visibility gaps and unmanaged attack surfaces.

Addressing global organizations

The problem extends beyond an organization's size and number of assets. It also matters where all the assets reside. They may be physical assets in a data center with a fixed location or cloud assets residing in a general geographic location. Many organizations also have a global presence, with offices and assets located in different countries. Sending staff overseas to inspect data centers and network closets is inefficient and cost-prohibitive.

Automated asset discovery systems are designed to bridge this gap by ensuring that every component of the organization's network is monitored with the same level of rigor, thus eliminating any weak points that might exist due to less stringent management in remote locations. The uniformity is essential for maintaining high security and operational standards and ensuring compliance with international corporate policies and regulatory requirements.

Automated systems also come with the added benefit of providing a centralized overview of all assets, regardless of their physical location. This streamlines the management process and ensures that all regional offices adhere to the same security and operational standards.

Adapting to evolving technology landscapes

As rapidly as cloud, IoT, and mobile devices have become core parts of the enterprise, it would be foolish to assume that it is the end of technology changes. New technologies are constantly emerging, and some will eventually make their way into common usage.

Even when automated tooling is in place, it is not always flexible and scalable enough to adapt to new technologies. When the cloud first emerged, many automated discovery and asset management tools could not properly track and manage these assets. The same holds true for containerization, where images could get reinstantiated thousands of times, rapidly propagating vulnerabilities. Even now, automated tooling that targets a specific environment is often required to track these environments adequately.

Automated discovery is more than just having a tool to do the work and gather data. The right tool will need to meet existing needs yet be flexible and scalable enough to adapt to future changes in technology and business operations.

Cloud Complications

Managing cloud environments is one of the biggest challenges for organizations in maintaining an accurate inventory. Many mistakenly think the cloud works exactly like physical assets in a data center, just somewhere else. This could not be further from the truth. Cloud technologies are more than just servers and network devices; they encompass a broad array of services, including storage solutions, databases, and application platforms that are often highly integrated and scalable. Additionally, container technologies and microservices architectures add further complexity to the landscape, allowing for even more rapid deployment and scaling.

In cloud environments, assets are more numerous and more fluid, with instances spinning up and shutting down in response to real-time demands. Cloud resources such as servers can be instantiated and terminated within moments to accommodate fluctuating demands in these settings. While advantageous for operational flexibility and efficiency, this capability creates a highly variable inventory of assets that can be difficult to track manually, inhibiting investigations for incidents.

However, more than just the dynamic nature complicates the landscape. There is also the DevOps mindset to consider.

As organizations have embraced the cloud, they have needed to shift how they build and deploy infrastructure. Traditional methods of manually configuring systems have completely gone out the window. Newer approaches rely on infrastructure as code (IaC), where configurations are stored in files containing all the information to build, configure, and deploy an asset without human intervention. This technology is at the heart of how assets are built and destroyed on the fly in the cloud.

DevOps relies heavily on IaC to help streamline and optimize IT infrastructure provisioning and management. DevOps teams use IaC to automate the development, testing, and production environment setup. The automation ensures that new environments can be spun up or torn down quickly and reliably, supporting continuous integration and continuous deployment practices.

IaC also enables DevOps teams to self-service provisioning within their environments and independently manage application dependencies, minimizing the need for constant intervention from operational teams. This self-service capability greatly accelerates development and testing cycles by reducing bottlenecks in resource provisioning. In a DevOps environment utilizing IaC, assets such as servers, containers, and services are often ephemeral—they can be created, modified, and destroyed in an automated fashion as part of deployment. The fluidity, while advantageous for speed, makes it extremely challenging to track assets manually since the system's state may change frequently and rapidly.

Unlike traditional vulnerabilities, which are encapsulated in CVEs, many risks in IaC manifest as configurations rather than inherent flaws. A configuration may not be problematic in itself, but the deployment context can turn it into a significant risk. For example, a globally accessible storage bucket might be suitable for serving static website images. Still, it would pose a serious threat if used to store sensitive documents like PDFs of credit card applications. The context-sensitive nature of configurations requires constant awareness and an understanding of the deployment's specific purpose.

From an asset management perspective, IaC-driven environments introduce the potential for rapid, large-scale deployment of misconfigurations. The speed means risky configurations can quickly propagate, making real-time visibility essential to identify what's been deployed as soon as possible.

However, it also leads to a growth in assets that may not be adequately tracked or managed, increasing the organizational attack surface. The automation and speed at which IaC can execute changes mean that the infrastructure landscape can quickly and dramatically alter. Manual tracking methods cannot keep up with the volume and velocity of these changes, leading to outdated or incomplete asset inventories.

Identification of shadow IT and unsanctioned services

Despite all the advantages of the cloud for rapid provisioning and deployment, organizations that poorly track their work build up a collection of untracked and unmanaged assets known as shadow IT. Over time, these applications and services increase risk due to their lack of management and alignment with organizational security policies.

Alternatively, shadow IT can proliferate through DevOps practices, encouraging rapid development and deployment cycles. As noted before, it's easy for teams and individuals to set up and use infrastructure and applications in the cloud without involving IT. The ease of access enables users to implement solutions that meet their immediate needs without waiting for IT approval, leading to an increase in unsanctioned IT activities.

The lack of oversight leads to many risks related to shadow IT. Shadow IT can easily bypass established corporate security controls and compliance processes. These technologies may be left unpatched, with exposed data or a lack of proper authentication mechanisms, making them easy targets for attackers. These are all risks that proper IT oversight should catch and address.

Though it's not just the security holes that make shadow IT a risk, it is also a significant issue for data resilience. Shadow IT complicates data management, resulting in data silos where valuable corporate data is stored outside of secure, backed-up corporate systems. In the event of an attack or system failure, the data can be irreparably damaged or deleted, creating a business continuity risk.

From a legal and compliance perspective, shadow IT exposes the organization to significant risk. Sensitive data may reside in these systems with little oversight regarding what is stored, who has access, and when data was viewed or altered. In the event of a breach, organizations will have no means of determining the extent of data stolen or damaged. For many compliance mandates such as HIPAA, they will have to determine, sometimes forensically, what was stored and assume that it all was inappropriately accessed. The investigatory costs are only part of the overall damage, as these compliance frameworks also come with monetary fines, legal expenses, and significant reputational damage when the public is notified.

Automated inventory and discovery tools are one major way to discover and manage shadow IT. The tools can detect and inventory unauthorized services and applications running in the cloud, giving IT departments visibility into what services are being used and by whom. Similarly, discovery via billing can shed light on what inventory may have been purchased outside of standard IT procurement. By identifying these unsanctioned resources, IT teams can evaluate them for security vulnerabilities, compliance issues, and operational impacts.

Automated tools are essential for identifying and continuously monitoring new assets. Once detected, IT can decide whether to integrate them into the official IT environment, shut them down, or find sanctioned alternatives that meet users' needs without compromising security. For attack surface management, this allows the assets to be appropriately assessed for risk, helping ensure that no hidden attack surfaces exist.

A need for specialized tooling

When looking at discovery in the cloud, it's important to discuss the areas in which the cloud makes discovery tooling for on-premises environments ineffective. It all comes down to the inherent architecture and operations of cloud assets.

The discovery problem starts with the dynamic scalability and elasticity of cloud resources. In traditional data centers, once an asset is deployed, it often remains in a static location and configuration that exists outside the bounds of general maintenance. To expand capacity, new servers must be added and new hardware must be physically purchased, configured, and deployed. Changes in this environment are more deliberate and longer lasting, making them easier to detect which helps teams maintain an inventory.

The cloud completely changes this paradigm, allowing the creation and elimination of new instances of cloud assets on the fly to adapt to load fluctuations. For example, say an organization currently has three identical instances running in the cloud: A, B, and C. Similar instances, D and E, may need to be created automatically when the load scales up, to help manage increased demand.

This change alone would be challenging for many on-premises tools to detect and track. However, it gets more complicated as the scaling logic may eliminate A, C, and D when demand drops, leaving only B and E to manage the base load. Effective automated tooling needs to detect the dramatic change in assets and know that B and E are identical instances of the original, which all the instances map back to.

The ability to scale dynamically like this is based on using IaC, which allows for extremely fast deployment. The change in assets in the last example could happen in a matter of seconds, taking just enough time for new instances to be created or destroyed.

In on-premises environments, discovery tools can run on a periodic schedule—daily, weekly, or monthly—and maintain an inventory that is accurate enough to meet the rate of change in these environments. Being far more dynamic, the cloud does not allow for such latency between reviews. Keeping an up-to-the-moment inventory of assets requires continuous monitoring.

Continuously updating assets is necessary to maintain tight visibility and control over cloud environments. Unlike on-premises environments, where the physical infrastructure of servers, network devices, and storage units is directly accessible to users and administrators, the cloud adds a layer of abstraction. The abstraction simplifies operations but also limits the depth of visibility, which impedes the effective management of attack surfaces. With this limited depth, it's challenging to fully assess cloud-based assets, making continuous updates and monitoring critical to understanding what is deployed and where potential vulnerabilities may lie.

For tools to deliver continuous visibility, they need to directly integrate with cloud service providers' APIs to gather detailed information about all types of resources, including virtual machines, containers, serverless functions, and managed services. This will help them gather advanced information on configurations that can be used to assess the scope of the attack surface and its related security posture. That information is necessary to identify misconfigurations and compliance violations specific to cloud environments.

There are many cloud-native asset detection tools to choose from, and the best-in-class solutions can discover resources from service providers beyond just AWS, Google Cloud, and Microsoft Azure. Many organizations use a combination of cloud providers, including smaller ones such as Alibaba Cloud and Oracle Cloud Infrastructure.

However, when we are talking about the cloud, it is also important to note that there are multiple service models of IaaS (infrastructure as a service), PaaS (platform as a service), and SaaS (software as a service), each with different levels of control. Tracking new services can be incredibly challenging for SaaS products, which can be purchased, turned on, and deployed with little more than a credit card by any team in an organization.

SaaS applications may seem benign on the surface, including tools like Grammarly or Canva, which add services to enhance productivity and quality. However, SaaS also encompasses more advanced software, such as email with Office 365 or Salesforce, that allows the storage and processing of sensitive information in the organization. Without detecting these cloud assets, the organization has an expanded attack surface without any visibility or control in maintaining it. While not every automated tool will be able to identify SaaS across the organization, some purpose-built tools can accomplish this and integrate the data with existing inventory and detection tooling.

Types of Automated Asset Discovery

Now that we understand the various challenges to address in maintaining an accurate inventory of assets, we can better understand the different tools and technologies available, as well as their limitations. Understanding the limitations and challenges makes it easier to determine the best tools for identifying your organization's assets.

Network Scanning

One of the longest-running methods of automated asset discovery is network scanning. Tools run automated sweeps of known network spaces to identify all devices connected to the network at that given time. Unless explicitly configured not to, most assets will respond in some manner, letting the scanner know that something is active at the address. These tools, such as Nmap, shown in Figure 5-1, have been part of the IT tool kit for some time and provide basic visibility into connectivity and exposed ports. With this information, organizations can form a baseline understanding of assets.

Network-scanning tools help expose unauthorized or rogue devices that may pose security threats. This goes beyond shadow IT, which may originate internally, and includes unauthorized devices that may have been plugged into network ports, creating potential entry points for attackers. These devices may even be used for sniffing network traffic and leaking sensitive information or setting up rogue WiFi, allowing unauthorized individuals to "borrow" organizational bandwidth.

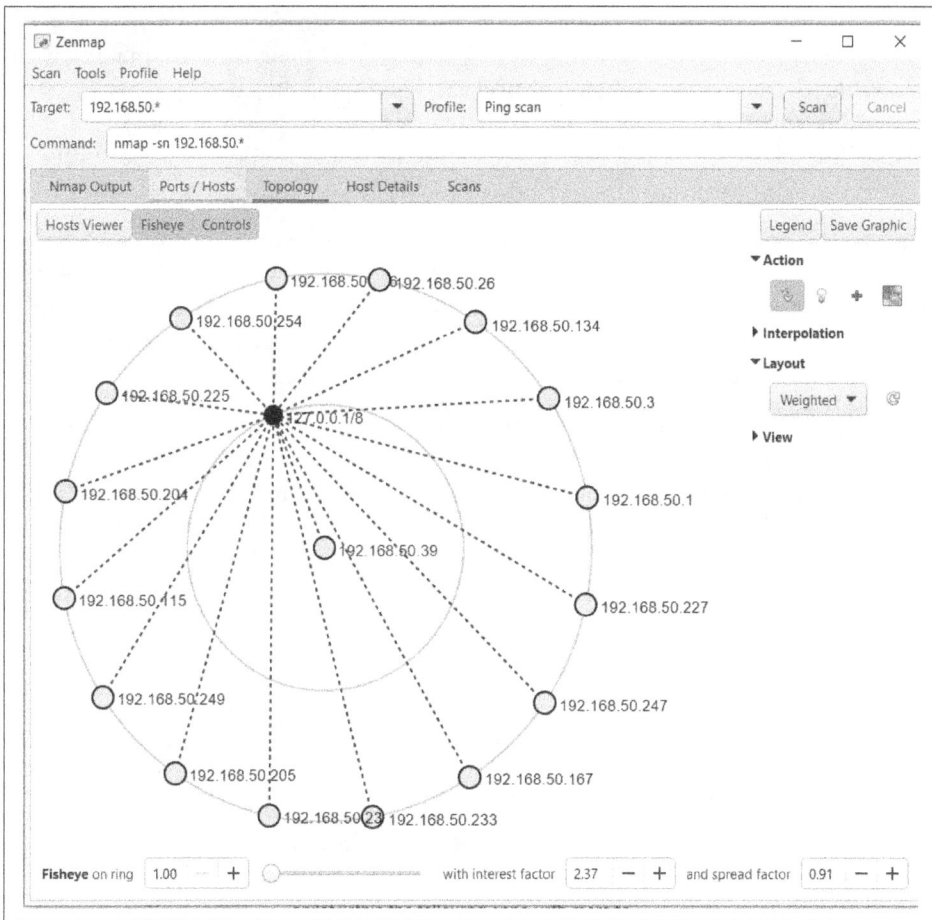

Figure 5-1. Network-scanning tools provide a basic overview of network-connected assets. The visibility is limited by network topography and security rules that may restrict the ability to directly connect by the scanner.

The quality of network scanning will vary, and there are tools that run a scheduled scan as well as those that monitor network devices such as routers and switches to detect changes in real time. Continuous assessment of wireless networks is vital for maintaining an up-to-date listing of all connected devices at any given time. While this information is important for maintaining a safe and secure network, it can also help identify changes in performance, enabling IT teams to respond quickly to changes as they occur, before they lead to massive outages and downtime.

More advanced versions of these tools can also conduct in-depth scans of the devices they see. They can identify different software in use and their versions, making them a valuable tool for vulnerability identification. Identifying outdated systems and software vulnerable to cyberattacks allows IT teams to proactively patch and remediate them before they become targets. This reduces the overall window of opportunity for attackers to exploit known vulnerabilities.

One of the challenges automated network scanners face comes from network segmentation. Most enterprise networks are segmented and subnetted to limit the flow of traffic and isolate more sensitive data to reduce impact in the event of a security incident. While this is valuable for limiting the scope of traffic, it also creates visibility obstacles for network-scanning tools.

To address these challenges, organizations may run scanners on each segment or employ tools more directly connected to their network hardware. That allows them to traverse across the segments on a more elevated level, providing the same level of visibility as if it were all one giant, connected bubble. Doing this is necessary as many of the most critical assets, such as servers hosting sensitive data or systems necessary for business operations, will likely be located on limited access segments restricted by strict access control lists.

Cloud Analysis

Tools for cloud analysis are designed to address many of the cloud challenges outlined previously. These solutions:

- Provide valuable information for managing and optimizing cloud-based assets in the organization
- Help improve resource utilization
- Enforce stringent security measures
- Ensure seamless integration across platforms
- Maintain scalability to keep pace with cloud services

To accomplish these goals, cloud analysis tools create visibility into the cloud infrastructure to identify all technologies. This is tricky as the cloud is not just an extended data center but an amalgamation of different services, some of which, like AWS Lambda, do no more than execute code without provisioning servers. These assets do not map out like a collection of servers but instead appear as a series of lightly interconnected services.

To provide this visibility, cloud tools must seamlessly integrate with existing cloud platforms used by your organization. While less robust tools may only provide visibility, more mature solutions enable coordinated management and control over various cloud services, as seen in Figure 5-2, ensuring that data and resources across different platforms are well synchronized. Such integration helps IT teams simplify management tasks and support more accurate and timely decision making regarding asset deployment and maintenance.

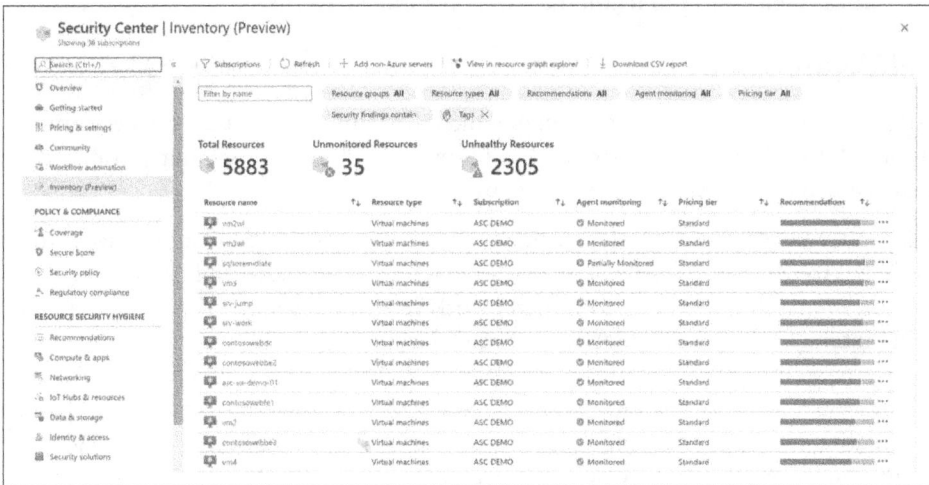

Figure 5-2. *This is an example of a cloud asset inventory from Azure. Most cloud service providers have some basic inventory showing only what is hosted in their environment.*

Part of what makes cloud discovery tools unique is their ability to detect assets dynamically, scaling in response to the organization's needs. They can determine the root asset and tie back all correlating instances to it, helping preserve continuity without bloating the management interface with every instance that was ever made.

More advanced tools go beyond detecting and monitoring these environments to enforce predefined security policies. They help detect and respond to security lapses in real time, such as unauthorized access attempts, noncompliance with data protection regulations, or unexpected changes in configuration settings. Using a proactive approach to security management helps prevent data breaches and maintain the integrity of cloud-based information systems.

Many cloud tools can track resources, as seen in Figure 5-2, and optimize costs as a side benefit. Because cloud technologies are a pay-as-you-use option, the ability to detect opportunities to reduce costs can significantly benefit organizations, especially those with an extensive cloud infrastructure.

These tools track resource consumption in real time, identifying idle or underutilized assets such as unneeded storage, inactive virtual machines, or excessive bandwidth usage. By pinpointing these inefficiencies, organizations can make informed decisions to scale down or turn off resources that are not delivering value, thus optimizing costs and reducing waste.

Despite the wide-reaching growth of the cloud, many asset detection and tracking solutions still focus on and excel either for the cloud or on-premises, necessitating multiple solutions to holistically detect and manage all assets. To overcome this, it is best to look for tools that integrate and export data so teams can select a single interface as their source of truth, reducing operational overhead.

API Identification

APIs serve as critical gateways through which different systems and services communicate. APIs often exist as part of the IT infrastructure that is poorly watched or managed unless it is in software created by the organization.

Like other assets, the first step to managing APIs starts with identification. Tools such as Probely, Salt Security, and Noname automatically scan and catalog all active organizational APIs, similar to how network scanners operate. They map out how APIs interact, identifying connections and dependencies that might not be immediately apparent. This mapping highlights potential security vulnerabilities in API integrations, such as insecure data transmissions or unauthorized access points, facilitating the implementation of targeted security measures. By clarifying these connections, organizations can better anticipate and mitigate risks associated with API interactions.

The comprehensive scanning is crucial for preventing unauthorized access and misuse of APIs, which are often targeted by attackers to gain access to sensitive data and systems. The tools enhance security protocols by identifying all APIs and controlling access points for external and internal software communications. This ensures that only authorized entities can interact with critical systems, significantly reducing the risk of security breaches.

API management tools also track the versioning of different APIs. Over time, some APIs become deprecated or fall out of compliance with security standards. Identification tools ensure that all API versions are up-to-date and compatible, preventing issues related to version mismatches that can lead to system failures or data errors. This prompts timely updates or replacements, thus safeguarding the organization from the security threats of obsolete technologies.

Data Discovery

Data discovery is a core component of automated asset discovery, focusing on identifying and managing the sensitive data used throughout an organization. The process is essential for protecting personal and corporate information and complying with data protection regulations.

Automated data discovery tools scan and identify sensitive data across the entire network, including the cloud and external storage locations. Doing so can be challenging as data may reside in structured formats such as databases and unstructured formats such as emails, texts, or documents. The mix of formats makes it difficult to identify and classify the different varieties of sensitive data, including personal, financial, and health data that may be stored within.

As organizations have experienced rapid growth over the past few years, there are often large volumes of hidden or forgotten data stores to be discovered by these tools. These repositories frequently contain outdated or no-longer-used data that still falls under regulatory protection but is not managed correctly or secured. By bringing these data stores to light, the tools reduce the risk of leaks and help ensure that all data, regardless of its current use, is accounted for and securely managed following relevant protection standards. Automated discovery tools are adept at detecting such data stores, which might otherwise remain unnoticed and vulnerable to breaches.

Once sensitive data is located, automated data discovery tools classify it based on its sensitivity and type. The accuracy of classification for these tools is vital for effectively securing and managing the discovered data. For example, financial information might require encryption and stringent access controls, whereas less sensitive data might not require rigorous protections. Misclassification of a data type might lead to inappropriate controls being implemented or costly failures in compliance that may only come to light after a breach.

Meeting data governance and compliance regulations is one of the core benefits of automated data discovery tools. The information gathered by these tools helps to maintain an accurate inventory of all data assets within the organization, which is essential for effective data governance. By collecting this information, organizations can guarantee that all data is managed and utilized in compliance with organizational policies and legal requirements. This aids compliance and risk management, supporting operational efficiency by eliminating redundancies and ensuring data availability.

Challenges in Automated Discovery

The discovery of assets is challenging, whether automated or not. IT environments, even outside of the cloud, have become more dynamic, with frequent changes to asset configurations. Hybrid environments spread technologies across local and cloud environments, reducing the effectiveness of traditional security perimeters and complicating the automated discovery process.

While important in building a comprehensive inventory, automated discovery does not accomplish everything. Automated tools can't fully accomplish tasks such as identifying asset ownership, mapping dependencies, and clarifying interrelationships for business continuity. These elements require human oversight to ensure accuracy, as automated systems may miss the nuances of how assets connect and support critical business functions. Balancing automated discovery with manual verification is essential to maintaining comprehensive asset management.

Identification challenges

One of the primary challenges in automated discovery is the ability to distinguish between assets that are similar in appearance but differ significantly in function or security requirements. Automated tools must be sophisticated enough to identify subtle differences in assets to avoid mistracking assets, which leads to inefficiencies and confusion in asset management.

Duplications of data can lead to misallocation of resources and security gaps. Alternatively, mistracking assets as duplicates leads to security oversights and improper management due to missing records.

Identification is made even more challenging due to the diversity of assets in modern IT environments, including on-premises hardware, virtual machines, and extensive cloud services. The diversity adds layers of complexity to the identification process, as each type of asset may require different handling. This is especially true for hybrid environments where organizations blend on-premises, cloud-based, and virtual infrastructures.

Integration often brings compatibility challenges, as tools designed for one environment may not function optimally in another. Many organizations have turned to automated identification and management tools to address this. Leveraging multiple tools allows them to navigate and catalog assets across these varied environments using sophisticated discovery algorithms.

However, the additional tools add their own level of complexity and integration challenges. Tools that operate independently may not easily share data with other solutions, leading to data siloing and additional management overhead. More advanced tools designed to interoperate also require more effort to configure and deploy, adding to the initial deployment overhead and forcing organizations to determine what will serve as the single source of truth by amalgamating organizational asset data.

Categorization challenges

With the wide array of different assets in IT environments, it becomes difficult to appropriately categorize them. This is partially due to the evolution of new asset types, including novel software applications, cloud services, IoT devices, and more. Automated tools may be equipped to dynamically recognize and categorize those that have been established for some time, but may end up blocked on newer variations.

A similar problem may arise for multifunctional assets that deliver a selection of capabilities. For example, a network device such as a firewall, web application firewall, or SASE (secure access service edge) provides a selection of services to an organization. Simply classifying it as a firewall is shortsighted, as the SASE component also secures cloud infrastructure. Instances like this may require human intervention to override automated classifications, allowing more accurate risk and threat assessments when determining organizational attack surfaces.

To adapt to this diversity, these tools must be flexible when developing complex categorization schemes. More rigid tooling will require assets to fall into predefined categories, which may not adequately encompass the full scope of what the asset does. The limited categorization has wide-reaching consequences when determining potential attack surfaces. Additionally, these schemes should adapt to the organization rather than vice versa, allowing it to accommodate the unique needs and characteristics of the organization, adapting to its specific operational, regulatory, and security requirements.

Flexibility is valuable for ensuring the accurate categorization of assets. The information is necessary for effectively directing resources and implementing appropriate security measures. It needs to include the sensitivity and significance of an asset to determine how it should be protected. For instance, assets storing sensitive network diagrams require stricter security controls than those storing publicly known data.

Failures in asset categorization can lead to significant risks. Inaccurate categorization by automated systems can result in misapplied security controls, leaving sensitive or critical assets inadequately protected. Misclassification can expose the organization to data breaches and other security threats. To prevent such scenarios, continual updates and checks are necessary.

Features That Deliver High ROI

When considering different automated asset identification and management solutions, it is essential to show organizational value. Some features appear valuable but are difficult to quantify a value for. In the following section, we will cover some features that are easier to directly tie to organizational value, making it easier to secure funding and provide a trackable ROI.

Search Capabilities

When working with any asset management system, leveraging the gathered data is of utmost importance. This capability is essential for managing large data sets, allowing users to quickly and efficiently locate specific assets within a large and complex inventory, and minimizing the time spent searching for information. By enabling rapid access to asset details, organizations can avoid delays and enhance productivity, ensuring that personnel can focus on more critical tasks rather than navigating through cumbersome databases.

Advanced search options include filtering capabilities based on asset type, status, location, and other relevant criteria to further refine the efficiency. These advanced options enhance the ability to pinpoint specific assets based on precise needs or concerns, such as identifying all devices in a particular region due for updates or locating all assets under a particular risk category.

Search capabilities also need to provide accurate, up-to-date information when time is of the essence, such as during security incidents or urgent auditing requests that may require rapid decision making and effective problem resolution. Accessing current information instantly allows security teams to react swiftly to potential threats and compliance teams to perform audits with the most recent data, mitigating risks and ensuring regulatory compliance efficiently.

To help create a holistic view of data, these tools need to seamlessly integrate into existing IT management systems. The integration enables coordinated actions and facilitates data sharing across platforms, improving workflow efficiency. By linking search functionalities directly with other IT management tools, organizations can automate and synchronize updates and management tasks across the system, reducing redundancy and enhancing accuracy in asset handling.

Data Presentation

Equally as important as being able to query the data is the ability to effectively present it in ways teams can quickly access, understand, and act on. Clear and intuitive data presentation significantly facilitates the decision-making process for IT and security teams. By reducing the cognitive load and simplifying the interpretation of complex data sets, teams can make accurate assessments swiftly, enhancing their ability to respond to issues as they arise.

Customizable dashboards, such as the example in Figure 5-3, amplify efficiency further by allowing data visualization to be tailored to meet the specific needs of various user roles within an organization. The customization ensures that each team member is presented with the most relevant and actionable information, enhancing user engagement and operational effectiveness.

Many of these dashboards allow for the visualization of asset relationships and networks, which plays a critical role in security and network management. By employing visual aids such as graphs and network diagrams, IT teams can better understand the interconnectedness of assets and pinpoint potential vulnerabilities within the asset network. Many solutions allow you to build customer dashboards, which enables organizations to identify specific scenarios that are important to them. This capability makes it easier to assess possible impacts of security threats and strategize appropriate countermeasures.

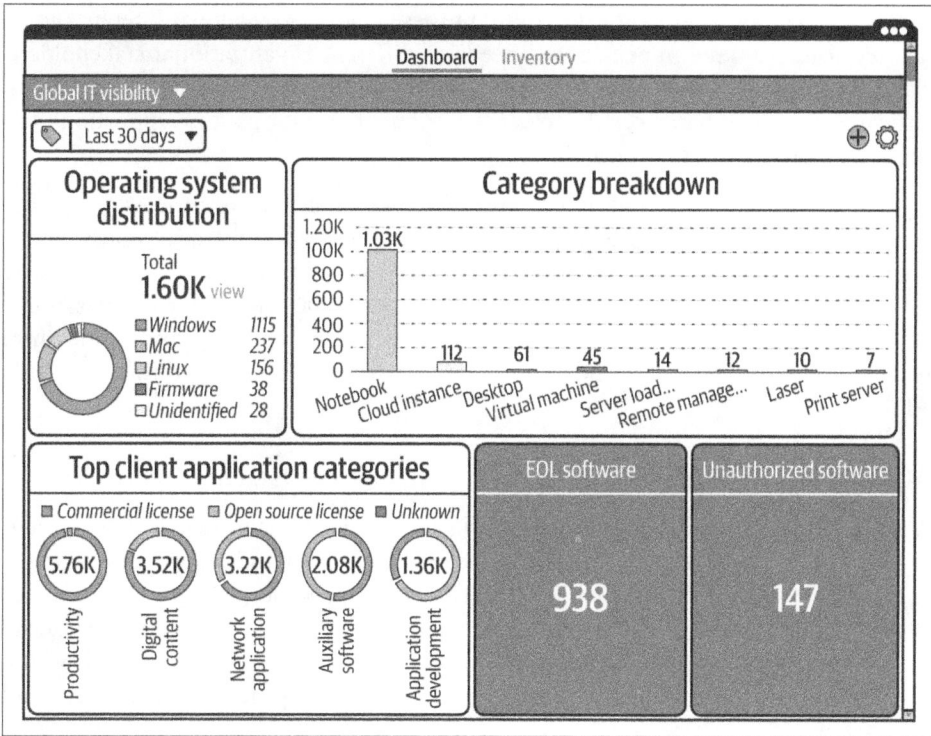

Figure 5-3. An example of an asset management dashboard that shows a combination of categorized assets. The most advanced dashboards allow users to customize the interface to show the most relevant information.

Analytics and Reporting

Part of the value of asset identification and management systems is the ability to derive comprehensive analytics and reporting. Extensive analytics provide insights into asset utilization, security posture, and compliance status, enabling stakeholders to make well-informed decisions and strategic adjustments.

Trend analysis functionality within these systems helps in long-term planning and resource management. By analyzing data over time, trend analysis tools can identify patterns, forecast future resource needs, and aid in budget planning. This functionality helps organizations anticipate changes and prepare strategically for future demands, ensuring they remain agile and responsive to evolving market conditions or operational needs.

Customizable reports enhance the utility of these analytics by allowing reports to be tailored to the unique informational needs of different organizational stakeholders. The customization improves communication and understanding across departments, ensuring each team has access to relevant and targeted information supporting their specific functions and responsibilities.

It is important to note that information becomes dated over time, so regularly generating reports supports ongoing oversight and aids administrative and strategic planning processes. It also ensures that all levels of management have up-to-date information, assisting in effectively tracking performance metrics and operational efficiency. This capability is also essential for meeting reporting and compliance requirements, placing easily understandable data in the hands of auditors with little effort.

Advanced Features

Advanced features such as machine learning and artificial intelligence in asset discovery significantly add to these systems' capability to predict and respond to potential security issues. By utilizing predictive analytics, it's possible to forecast trends and detect unusual behaviors among assets, allowing organizations to take proactive measures before problems escalate. The ability to learn from ongoing data refines security protocols over time, making the asset discovery process both reactive and anticipatory.

Additionally, the seamless integration with security tools, such as security information and event management (SIEM) systems, strengthens the organization's overall security posture. Comprehensive integration ensures that security responses are well coordinated, leveraging the strengths of both asset discovery tools and SIEM systems to create a robust defense strategy against potential threats.

Automated asset discovery tools may also incorporate security enhancements and mechanisms. Automated alerting mechanisms play a pivotal role in this setup, as they promptly notify relevant stakeholders of critical changes or emerging vulnerabilities within the system. This prompt notification facilitates taking swift action to mitigate risks, significantly improving the organization's security responsiveness. The systems may also integrate essential security measures such as multifactor authentication and encrypted communications, which are crucial for protecting the integrity and confidentiality of data throughout the asset management life cycle.

Summary

This chapter provided an overview of automating asset discovery in modern IT environments. When we say modern, we're referring to those characterized by large or dynamic asset pools, some of which span across local, cloud, and global infrastructures. We emphasized how automation not only streamlines the discovery and inventory process but also significantly mitigates the risks associated with manual tracking errors, such as incomplete inventories or outdated information. Automation is particularly valuable for handling cloud environments and virtual assets, where changes are rapid and continuous, making manual tracking impractical and accuracy difficult at best.

As organizations face the increasing complexity of managing hybrid IT environments, the benefit of automated tools that integrate seamlessly with existing systems, providing real-time updates and comprehensive visibility, becomes undeniable. These tools do more than simplify management; they help quickly identify shadow IT and unsanctioned services that expand the organizational attack surface. As we move into Chapter 6, we will build on this foundation of effective asset management to explore strategies for prioritizing assets.

PART III

Prioritization and Remediation

Now that you've got a solid grip on identifying and cataloging your assets, it's time to take the next steps: prioritization and remediation. These chapters will cover how to determine what matters most when measuring risks across your attack surfaces.

While this may initially appear challenging, it doesn't have to be overwhelming. We'll discuss how to prioritize your assets—because not all of them need the same level of attention—and how to assess your internal and external vulnerabilities.

Here's the key: not every organizational asset carries equal organizational value. Some are your "crown jewels"—those critical systems that keep the lights on and drive your business forward—while others, though important, won't bring everything to a halt if compromised. We'll walk through how to rank assets so that you can allocate your security resources smartly. With attack surface analysis, you'll learn how to monitor for risks and stay ahead of potential threats continuously.

Once you understand what assets are prioritized, you can determine how best to remediate the identified risks. With this information, organizations can make better, more targeted investments, gaining more value for every dollar of the security budget spent.

By the end of Part III, you'll understand how proper prioritization makes remediation possible. You'll know exactly where to focus your efforts, how to measure your attack surface, and where to apply remediation first for maximum security posture impact. Let's jump in!

CHAPTER 6

Prioritization and Crown Jewel Analysis

Prioritization in attack surface management builds on the inventory a company has already taken to determine an order to how assets will be secured. This involves looking holistically at how various aspects fit into the overall business ecosystem and assessing the value they provide. As part of the holistic look, many stakeholders across the organization will need to be engaged to help provide the context to critically evaluate different prioritization levels.

This chapter will investigate the wide range of criteria for making these prioritization determinations.

Understanding Prioritization

Prioritization is how ASM determines what resources require the most protection. It does this by systematically determining the relative importance of various assets so that resources can be allocated effectively. The process encompasses a wide range of assets, including the physical (e.g., machinery, buildings), the digital (e.g., data, software), and intellectual properties (e.g., patents, trademarks). It takes into account the full scope of these assets to ensure that all facets of an organization's infrastructure are considered.

The primary goals of asset prioritization are to enhance security, improve resource allocation, and ensure operational continuity. By identifying and focusing on the most critical assets, organizations can strengthen their security posture against potential threats.

Effective prioritization also aids in better resource management, directing limited budgets, personnel, and time toward the most valuable assets. Additionally, prioritization supports operational continuity by ensuring that the most essential functions of the organization remain protected and functional, helping achieve strategic business objectives.

Prioritizing assets is also closely tied to risk management. Organizations can develop a more effective risk response strategy by evaluating each asset's potential threats. Doing so helps ensure that the most critical and vulnerable assets receive the highest level of protection. This approach safeguards key systems and enhances the organization's overall risk management framework.

Effective prioritization relies on robust decision-making frameworks or models, such as the risk-value matrix or business impact analysis. These frameworks help comprehensively assess the value and vulnerability of assets, enabling informed decision making. Organizations can systematically evaluate which assets are most important and should be prioritized by employing such models, ensuring a logical and transparent prioritization process.

ASM uses prioritization to optimize resources. As budget, personnel, and time are finite, allocating them where they are needed most is essential and ensures they are used efficiently. The approach provides the highest level of protection and attention to the most critical assets, maximizing the return on investment, and minimizing efforts on less important assets.

Part of how ASM effectively prioritizes assets is by involving key stakeholders in the process, which creates a more holistic understanding of the business context and asset value. Stakeholders, as experts in their slice of the organization, provide valuable insights and perspectives that might otherwise be overlooked. Their input ensures that the prioritization process is aligned with strategic goals and operational needs. Engaging stakeholders also fosters a sense of ownership and accountability across the organization, enhancing the effectiveness of the prioritization process.

Prioritization does not happen in a bubble and should integrate with other organizational processes such as enterprise risk management, compliance, and IT governance. The integration creates synergy, as prioritization efforts can enhance these processes and vice versa. For instance, prioritizing assets can support business continuity planning by identifying essential operations that organizations must maintain during disruptions. Similarly, aligning prioritization with compliance requirements ensures efficient alignment with regulatory obligations.

While it's easy to consider asset prioritization a one-time activity, it isn't, and treating ASM like a one-off chore will lead to ineffective long-term results. Instead, the process is dynamic and requires ongoing assessment and adjustment. It must be regularly reviewed and updated to accommodate changing business needs, asset values, and threat landscapes. The dynamic approach ensures that the prioritization remains relevant and effective in addressing current and emerging challenges.

Comparisons to Other Strategic Processes

Asset prioritization enhances an organization's security posture and aligns it with strategic objectives by integrating asset management with strategic planning. Doing so ensures that every aspect, from daily operations to long-term projects, contributes directly to achieving the strategic vision. The alignment makes resource utilization more efficient and keeps the organization focused on its strategic objectives.

Additionally, IT governance directly benefits from this integration by providing tactical support that improves resource management and ensures compliance with regulatory requirements. IT governance leverages the outcomes of asset prioritization to manage resources more effectively and efficiently, ensuring that core systems and data are protected and aligned with compliance standards.

Organizations can develop targeted risk management strategies by evaluating assets based on their value and vulnerability. Such an approach takes into account regulatory requirements that mandate the protection of specific types of assets. Using this data, in combination with risk assessments and impact analyses, helps risk management efforts concentrate on the most valuable and vulnerable assets while simultaneously meeting compliance requirements to help organizations avoid penalties.

Prioritization efforts also help improve operational continuity and crisis management. Identifying critical operations and assets that must be maintained during disruptions is one of the first steps in the prioritization process, and when done right, guarantees that the organization can continue functioning. The proactive approach complements business continuity planning, which focuses on restoring operations after disruptions. While business continuity planning is concerned with reactive recovery, asset prioritization ensures that the most necessary operations and assets are protected from the outset.

Asset prioritization is distinct from project management, which is typically finite and outcome-oriented. As an ongoing, cyclical process, asset prioritization continually reassesses and adjusts the importance of assets based on changing conditions. Project management can benefit from the insights gained through prioritization by focusing efforts on projects that impact the most valuable assets, thereby achieving project goals more effectively.

Similarly, asset prioritization differs from performance management, which aims to improve organizational efficiency and effectiveness. While performance management seeks to enhance productivity and operational efficiency, asset prioritization focuses on security and optimal asset utilization. Both processes support organizational performance through different mechanisms, with performance management improving efficiency, and asset prioritization ensuring that essential assets are protected and utilized to their fullest potential.

Importance of Prioritization

While earlier sections establish why asset prioritization matters, it's equally important to consider what's at stake without it. Without a clear prioritization strategy, organizations often spread resources too thin, treating all assets with equal urgency and, in doing so, diluting the effectiveness of their security measures. This increases exposure to avoidable threats and leads to inefficient use of time, budget, and personnel.

Effective prioritization acts as a strategic filter, enabling security teams to differentiate between routine safeguards and mission-critical protection. When resources are channeled toward assets with the greatest business and regulatory impact, organizations gain stronger defenses and a clearer alignment between security actions and business outcomes. It's not just about reducing risk. It's about amplifying the value of every security investment.

Moreover, prioritization supports informed decision making and strategic planning. Organizations can develop targeted security measures that address their most significant vulnerabilities by understanding which assets are essential for revenue generation, operational efficiency, and regulatory compliance. That strategic focus helps optimize investment in security technologies and personnel, ensuring that efforts are not wasted on less impactful areas.

Effective prioritization facilitates better stakeholder communication, providing a clear rationale for security investments and initiatives. Ultimately, prioritization strengthens the organization's overall security posture, ensuring that high-priority assets are protected, risks are managed proactively, and resources are used efficiently.

Benefits to security posture

Prioritizing assets is fundamental to enhancing an organization's security posture. It involves identifying and securing key resources, thereby reducing the attack surface. It also focuses efforts on the most valuable targets for attackers. By focusing on these prioritized assets and implementing stronger access controls and monitoring measures, organizations can significantly minimize threat exposure and prevent major data breaches. This targeted approach protects sensitive data classified as crown jewels or high-value assets.

Resource optimization is another valuable benefit of asset prioritization. Organizations ensure maximum security impact with minimal expenditure by directing limited security resources—such as budget, personnel, and time—toward the most important assets. This strategy deploys the most skilled security staff to handle the highest-priority assets, maximizing their expertise and effectiveness. It optimizes investment in security tools and technologies for these assets, ensuring a higher ROI and avoiding unnecessary spending on lower-risk, less valuable assets.

One of the most significant benefits of asset prioritization in ASM is the strategic alignment it achieves, aligning security efforts with business objectives. Focusing on assets crucial for business operations ensures that security measures support business continuity and strategic goals. The alignment helps security teams communicate more effectively with executives, linking asset protection directly to business outcomes. It also shows direct business value, making security less of a "thing we have to do" and more of a "thing which supports the business."

Part of this alignment is the improvement in an organization's ability to respond to incidents, resulting in a direct value to the organization. Organizations can reduce downtime and recovery costs for incident response preparedness by developing detailed and targeted response plans focused on prioritized assets. Incident response teams can quickly identify the most critical systems and tailor their actions accordingly. Enhanced monitoring and detection of prioritized assets also lead to faster detection of breaches and more accurate alerts, improving metrics such as mean time to detect and mean time to respond.

The prioritization process must be continuously reviewed and refined to maintain these benefits. Doing so requires creating a feedback loop for adjusting security policies and controls. It allows adaptive security measures to evolve with emerging threats.

However, like all ASM steps, asset prioritization should not happen in isolation, but should involve different business units in the process; it cultivates a risk-aware culture where employees understand and value the importance of protecting key assets. The cultural shift that understanding can bring means the prioritization process is not only top-down but also is integrated into the daily practices of the entire organization, improving overall security and resilience.

Enhancing resource allocation

Asset prioritization significantly enhances resource allocation by ensuring that organizational resources—such as people, processes, and technology—are directed toward protecting and managing the assets most essential to the organization's goals and supporting its risk management strategy. This approach optimizes financial resources by enabling targeted investment in security technologies suited to the most valuable assets, thereby avoiding unnecessary expenditure on less impactful assets. As a result, organizations can ensure that the most effective and suitable security solutions are implemented where they are needed most. By focusing spending on areas with the highest return on investment, companies avoid the financial drain of over-protecting lower-priority assets, thus allowing for more efficient budget allocation.

Strategic deployment of human resources is another key benefit of asset prioritization. This is especially important considering the shortage of security personnel that has existed for over a decade and is likely to continue. By directing skilled personnel to areas where their expertise will have the greatest impact, organizations can more efficiently leverage their talent.

Asset prioritization also helps grow and maintain staff by informing the development of tailored training programs for the skills necessary for protecting high-value assets. This results in a more knowledgeable workforce that is well-prepared to manage sophisticated threats against essential assets.

Parallel to the human efficiency improvement is the operational efficiency improvement through asset prioritization. By ensuring that physical and digital assets are utilized to their fullest potential, organizations can focus maintenance and upgrade efforts on assets that drive the most value, preventing resource wastage. It helps to streamline operations by identifying which assets require immediate attention and which can be scheduled for routine checks. The approach allows for more focused monitoring and proactive maintenance of core systems, leading to increased operational uptime and reduced downtime.

Asset prioritization helps the efficient utilization of resources in disaster recovery planning by identifying which assets must be restored first to minimize business disruption. This approach allows organizations to allocate recovery resources effectively, supporting the swift restoration of business-critical functions. Focusing on the most essential assets makes recovery efforts more streamlined and targeted, reducing unnecessary expenditures on less vital areas. Additionally, the prioritization strengthens the resilience of core operations, ensuring that resources are available and optimally used for their protection and maintenance. The efficiency enables organizations to plan and execute contingency measures more effectively, safeguarding core operations against potential failures or disruptions. As a result, asset prioritization enhances overall operational resilience and ensures that all resources are deployed in the most impactful and cost-effective manner.

Prioritization Criteria

Determining prioritization criteria in ASM is no small task, as it involves multiple elements that are all important to the organization and may require business stakeholder buy-in. It needs to take into account the value to the organization, operational impact, and data sensitivity. Each of these plays a role in determining the prioritization of an asset.

The value to the organization considers how crucial an asset is to generating revenue and achieving strategic objectives. Operational impact evaluates how the failure or compromise of an asset would affect the organization's ability to carry out its core functions. Lastly, data sensitivity assesses the level of protection required for assets that handle sensitive information.

When developing an ASM strategy, the prioritization needs to weigh and balance each of these factors to ensure that the most critical assets receive the appropriate level of protection. The holistic approach fortifies the organization against potential threats and supports its long-term operational and strategic goals.

Value to the Organization

Understanding the financial value of assets is one of the first steps in determining which ones to prioritize. By assessing the economic impact of various assets, organizations can make informed decisions that align with their strategic objectives and optimize resource allocation.

Revenue generation is a straightforward starting point for this investigation, as assets that directly contribute to it are often prioritized higher. These include primary production equipment, key software platforms, and other systems necessary for delivering products or services. Ensuring their continuous operation minimizes downtime and disruptions, thereby protecting revenue streams.

However, value extends beyond directly generating revenue. An asset's financial value sometimes comes from its ability to reduce potential costs. When properly maintained and secured, assets can help prevent significant financial losses because the frequency and impact of downtime is reduced, thereby avoiding the costs associated with halted production, service disruptions, or data breaches. That's why regular maintenance and robust security measures should also be a factor you consider when prioritizing assets and considering value.

Similarly, cost reduction can be emphasized by avoiding financial risks associated with asset failure or compromise, which are also primary factors in asset prioritization. If assets are compromised, this could lead to substantial financial liabilities, such as fines, lawsuits, or regulatory penalties. Establishing stronger controls around high-risk assets reduces exposure to financial liabilities and supports a comprehensive risk management strategy.

Organizations may also prioritize assets based on long-term financial outcomes. While upgrading a mainframe system and its applications to a modern database and application stack may cost more initially, the long-term impact is significant. Prioritizing upgrades reduces future spending on legacy hardware and niche skill sets. Over time, focusing on assets that offer the highest ROI improves organizational financial health. Determining this type of prioritization is more strategic and requires decisions to be data-driven and aligned with organizational goals.

Considering the long-term financial implications of asset management is vital for sustainable growth. Prioritizing assets that support long-term financial strategies ensures that resources are allocated to maintain and enhance critical assets over time. It also aligns asset management and ASM with broader financial planning, contributing to strategic goals such as sustainable growth and shareholder value enhancement. By focusing on effective asset prioritization, you can demonstrate prudent financial management, potentially increasing investor confidence and stock value.

Operational Impact

Operational impact plays a valuable role in determining asset prioritization. Prioritization directly influences operational efficiency and effectiveness by ensuring essential assets receive the necessary focus and resources, supporting overall productivity and stability within the organization.

When determining how to prioritize assets based on their operational impact, several key criteria should be considered so that resources are allocated efficiently and core operational functions are maintained.

One primary criterion is the contribution of assets to core operations. Organizations should prioritize assets that are fundamental to the business's daily functioning and essential for achieving primary business objectives. For example, machinery that keeps the production line moving in a manufacturing firm is indispensable. Similarly, a call center that handles an organization's sales and supporting technology is important. Disruption of these assets can halt entire operations, leading to significant financial losses and inefficiencies.

 There is often a substantial overlap between essential assets and revenue generation. However, assets don't always generate direct revenue but rather provide the services that lead to revenue. Take, for example, a company like Amazon, where video streaming is a benefit of its Prime membership. Assets that support the video service are core to the company's operations and add value to Prime membership, but the actual money made is through sales and purchases of merchandise. The "free" videos get people coming back to Amazon, where they make purchases that drive revenue.

Downtime sensitivity plays a role in this prioritization process. Assets that, if down, would significantly disrupt operations must be prioritized. Examples include network servers, manufacturing equipment, and essential utility systems. Assets where continuous operation is crucial to prevent operational halts and maintain business continuity have more weight than those that do not.

Assets' value may also be determined by their impact on productivity. Those that streamline workflows and eliminate bottlenecks should have a higher prioritization, such as automated assembly lines, supply chain management systems, and advanced software tools that support employee productivity and operations. For example, enterprise resource planning systems that link various departments and streamline business processes are not directly valuable but improve efficiency and productivity. These assets provide increased output and better service quality, making them valuable to the organization.

Sometimes, the operational value is more challenging to determine, especially regarding assets that align with strategic business objectives and goals. For example, innovative technologies that support the company's growth strategy or new market expansion efforts help operational efforts align with broader organizational targets. These assets may not currently show value, but damage or loss to them could impact future organizational growth. This is part of why integrating multiple business units and leadership into the ASM process is vital. Looking at assets purely through an IT or security lens will overlook these more complex initiatives, leading to missed opportunities and potential gaps in strategic planning and execution. By involving diverse perspectives and expertise, organizations can comprehensively evaluate and prioritize assets, ultimately supporting current operations and long-term goals.

The last and most valuable operational factor to consider is those assets that further safety and compliance efforts. Assets that maintain safety standards and regulatory compliance reduce risks associated with noncompliance and safety incidents. In health care, prioritizing medical devices and patient data systems ensures compliance with health regulations and patient safety standards. For general operations, these assets may include the systems that monitor environmental conditions, manage hazardous materials, or ensure workplace safety protocols are followed. Prioritizing them is essential for minimizing legal and operational risks, protecting employees, and maintaining a safe and compliant operational environment.

Data Sensitivity and Classification

When determining how to prioritize assets, a major area to consider is the sensitivity of the data they store or process. Sensitive information encompasses various types of data that require protection due to their confidentiality, potential impact on privacy, or the consequences if disclosed, altered, or destroyed without authorization. Understanding the different categories of sensitive information and their specific protection needs is essential for effective asset prioritization.

One primary category of sensitive data is personally identifiable information (PII), which includes any data that can be used independently or with other information to identify, contact, or locate a single person. Examples include names, addresses, Social Security numbers, dates of birth, and biometric records. Due to the direct risk to individual privacy, PII is highly regulated under laws like GDPR in Europe, among other global privacy regulations. These regulations require organizations to implement strict access controls, encryption, and data minimization practices to protect PII, prioritizing assets that store or process it due to regulatory and privacy implications.

Another important type of sensitive information is protected health information (PHI), which encompasses any information about health status, provision of health care, or payment for health care that can be linked to an individual. This includes medical records, lab results, and insurance information. In the US, PHI is primarily regulated by HIPAA, while in Europe it falls under GDPR. These regulations impose stringent requirements on health data confidentiality, integrity, and availability. Compliance with HIPAA involves ensuring the secure transmission, storage, and disposal of PHI, making assets handling this type of data essential for prioritization due to the high stakes involved in regulatory compliance and patient privacy.

Financial information is another category that demands careful prioritization. It includes data related to personal or corporate finances, such as bank account details, credit card numbers, and investment records, much of which is also regulated. Unauthorized access to financial information can lead to fraud, identity theft, and substantial financial loss. Assets storing or processing financial information must be prioritized to prevent financial crimes and protect the organization's and its clients' financial integrity.

Intellectual property (IP) is sensitive information that is often overlooked when prioritizing assets. IP includes patents, trade secrets, copyrights, and trademarks, while trade secrets can encompass manufacturing processes, recipes, and other proprietary knowledge that provides a competitive edge. Assets associated with IP are prioritized because their compromise could result in significant competitive and financial losses.

Corporate data may include IP, but it goes further, including strategic plans, financial forecasts, and internal communications for maintaining competitive advantage and operational integrity. Prioritizing assets that store or process corporate data helps secure the organization's strategic initiatives and internal operations.

The final and perhaps most critical factor to consider is the role of assets in supporting compliance and safety efforts. Those that help maintain regulatory standards and uphold safety measures reduce noncompliance risks and potential safety incidents. In health care, prioritizing medical devices and patient data systems is essential to meet regulations and safeguard patient safety. More broadly, this may involve systems that monitor environmental conditions, manage hazardous materials, or enforce workplace safety protocols.

Methods of data classification

Despite knowing we must protect our sensitive data, discovering and classifying it is challenging. Data exists all over the organization, in structured formats such as databases and unstructured formats such as documents, emails, and messages. Not everything is neatly categorized and classified by type. Data classification helps us organize data based on sensitivity, regulatory requirements, and business value so that the company can ensure that it handles each type of data appropriately. A structured approach to data management facilitates better protection, compliance, and operational efficiency.

One of the methods involved in data categorization is criteria-based classification. This approach evaluates data based on its sensitivity to unauthorized disclosure, which can impact privacy, security, or operational continuity. Sensitivity levels typically range from public and internal to confidential and highly confidential. By considering the potential impact on the business if data is lost, corrupted, or accessed by unauthorized parties, organizations can assess factors such as financial loss, reputational damage, and legal consequences. The method helps prioritize data protection efforts based on the severity of these potential impacts.

Another approach is content-based classification, which leverages automated tools and manual intervention to organize data. Automated classification tools scan data contents to categorize them based on predefined rules or criteria, such as keywords or patterns. They are particularly effective for managing large volumes of data efficiently. However, manual tagging and categorization are also essential, especially for sensitive or ambiguous data that automated tools might misclassify. Relying on the expertise and judgment of trained personnel ensures that these data types are accurately managed.

A slightly different approach is context-based classification, which focuses on how data is accessed and used within the organization. This method considers the roles and responsibilities of users interacting with the data and adapting to dynamic data environments. It also considers the applications processing the data and the locations where it is stored or transmitted. By ensuring that data receives an appropriate level of protection according to its exposure and usage context, context-based classification provides a tailored approach to data security.

Specific requirements guide regulatory-driven classification. For example, the EU's GDPR mandates stringent controls for personal data. At the same time, HIPAA in the US focuses on protecting health information. Similarly, PCI DSS sets standards for securing payment card information, requiring that data is managed in compliance with relevant legal standards, facilitating compliance audits, and reducing the risk of penalties. Organizing data according to regulatory requirements also streamlines reporting and audit processes, making it easier for organizations to demonstrate compliance with regulatory bodies.

It's important to incorporate various data classification methods into an asset management strategy to prioritize data assets. By doing so, organizations can implement appropriate security measures, allocate resources well, and comply with legal standards by understanding their data's sensitivity, context, and regulatory requirements.

Regulatory compliance implications

With all the regulations governing data privacy and protection, it is valuable to understand the ones that are most relevant to a business. Each has its own scope, applicability, and compliance requirements that must be understood to categorize data properly. Additionally, many of these regulations overlap, so a single piece of data may fall under multiple regulations simultaneously, requiring compliance with each.

The GDPR is a cornerstone of data protection within the European Union, but its reach extends globally. Any organization operating within the EU or offering goods or services to individuals there must comply with GDPR. The regulation sets a high data protection standard, emphasizing individuals' control over their personal data. Key provisions include rights for data subjects, such as access, the right to be forgotten, and data portability. Organizations must ensure they have a lawful basis for processing personal data, implement data protection by design, and report breaches within 72 hours.

Like GDPR, the California Consumer Privacy Act (CCPA) and the subsequent California Privacy Rights Act (CPRA) enhance consumer protection for residents of California. These laws apply to businesses that collect consumers' personal data, do business in California, and meet certain thresholds. Key obligations include:

- Informing consumers about the purpose of the personal information being collected
- Allowing consumers to access their personal data
- Providing a way to request personal data deletion
- Opting out of the sale of individuals' personal information

To comply with these regulations, businesses must prioritize assets that handle consumer data, ensuring transparency and protecting consumer rights.

In the United States, HIPAA governs the protection and privacy of identifiable health information. HIPAA applies to health care providers, health plans, clearinghouses, and business associates. Compliance involves implementing administrative, physical, and technical safeguards to protect the privacy and security of PHI. Regular risk assessments and breach notification procedures are also mandatory. Prioritizing assets that manage PHI is critical to ensure these safeguards are robust and effective, thereby protecting sensitive health data and maintaining compliance.

PCI DSS focuses on securing credit card transactions to reduce fraud. It applies to all entities storing, processing, or transmitting cardholder data. PCI DSS requires maintaining a secure network, protecting cardholder data, implementing strong access control measures, regularly monitoring and testing networks, and maintaining an information security policy. Organizations must prioritize assets involved in credit card transactions to adhere to these standards, safeguarding financial information and minimizing the risk of data breaches.

The Federal Information Security Modernization Act (FISMA) addresses the security of information systems and data used by US federal agencies. It emphasizes the importance of developing, documenting, and implementing an agency-wide program to secure information systems and data. FISMA requires agencies to conduct annual reviews of their information security programs, categorize information based on the level of risk, and implement appropriate security controls. Prioritizing assets under FISMA's scope ensures that federal data is protected, compliance is maintained, and the integrity of federal information systems is upheld.

Compliance vs. risk-based prioritization

When considering asset prioritization, organizations must navigate compliance-based and risk-based approaches, each offering distinct advantages and challenges. Both are valuable in the prioritization process and must be considered together to create a balanced and effective security strategy.

Compliance-based prioritization primarily focuses on aligning security efforts with statutory and regulatory requirements. This approach is driven by the need to adhere to laws and guidelines to avoid legal penalties and reputational damage. Regulatory requirements often set specific criteria that organizations must meet to ensure legal compliance. These standards are usually mandatory and nonnegotiable, meaning organizations must allocate resources to fulfill these obligations regardless of their risk assessment outcomes. Compliance-based prioritization necessitates stringent documentation and audit trails to demonstrate adherence to external auditors, emphasizing actions like data protection impact assessments and regular security audits.

In contrast, risk-based prioritization centers on identifying and mitigating risks based on their potential impact and likelihood. This method is more flexible and tailored to the organization's unique threat landscape and business context. It involves evaluating potential threats to determine which pose the most significant impact and the likelihood of occurring, adjusting dynamically as the threat landscape evolves. Tools such as risk assessments and threat modeling are utilized to prioritize security initiatives, so the organization's most valuable assets receive the highest level of protection. This approach optimizes limited resources by allocating them based on the severity and potential impact of identified risks.

The integration of compliance-based and risk-based prioritization are integral in developing a robust security posture. Organizations must often balance compliance requirements with risk management priorities to allocate resources effectively and ensure comprehensive protection. Strategic decision making involves assessing whether compliance-driven actions also mitigate significant risks, thereby achieving dual benefits from specific initiatives. For instance, measures implemented to comply with data protection regulations may simultaneously address critical vulnerabilities identified through risk assessments.

Creating a unified security posture involves integrating compliance and risk management efforts. Developing policies and practices that satisfy compliance needs while addressing the most significant risks can improve security. By leveraging the strengths of both approaches, organizations can ensure they meet legal obligations and protect against the most pressing threats. This balanced approach safeguards against legal and financial penalties and fortifies the organization's resilience against evolving cyberthreats.

Obtaining Business Context

Understanding the business context is fundamental to attack surface management because it helps align security measures with the organization's operational and strategic priorities. Mapping business functions is the first step, as it identifies which activities are core to the organization's mission and which are supportive but not central. By distinguishing between them, organizations can prioritize resources and focus their security efforts on protecting the most valuable assets. That prioritization is essential because the assets that are vital to delivering essential services or products will be safeguarded against potential threats, thereby maintaining the organization's competitive edge and operational integrity.

Various tools and techniques are employed to effectively map business functions and assess their impact on the organization. These might include process flowcharts, business impact analysis, and stakeholder interviews, which provide a comprehensive view of how different functions interact and contribute to the overall business objectives. Once these functions are mapped, an impact assessment is conducted to evaluate the potential consequences of disruptions or security breaches. The assessment helps quantify the operational, financial, and reputational impacts, guiding the allocation of resources toward the most impactful areas.

Mapping Business Functions

Mapping business functions helps identify core and noncore functions within an organization for asset prioritization. The distinction helps allocate resources effectively and helps core operations receive the necessary focus and investment.

Understanding core functions is fundamental to this process. Core functions are activities directly related to the organization's primary purpose and value proposition. They are critical for delivering the services or products that define the business. For example, in a health care organization, core functions might include patient

---

record management, medical diagnostics, and billing systems, as these are essential for delivering health care services, whereas noncore functions like employee payroll or office supply procurement, while important, do not directly impact patient care.

The performance of core functions directly impacts the organization's success and competitive positioning. As such, they often receive the highest level of investment and strategic focus, driving the primary revenue streams and ensuring long-term sustainability. Prioritizing resources, including financial and human capital, toward these functions is essential for maintaining optimal performance and fostering innovation.

Conversely, assessing noncore functions involves identifying activities that, while necessary for daily operations, do not directly contribute to primary business objectives. Examples might include facility management, payroll, or certain IT services. These functions support the core activities but do not directly influence the business strategy. As they do not drive the primary value proposition, noncore functions are prime candidates for outsourcing or automating. Outsourcing them can streamline operations and reduce costs, freeing up resources to allow the organization to focus more intensely on areas that contribute directly to competitive advantage and value creation.

However, organizations should not underestimate the integration and support provided by noncore functions. Although not central to the organization's primary mission, noncore functions may be vital in enabling core functions to operate smoothly. Effective management of these supporting activities is crucial because inefficiencies can indirectly impact the performance of core functions. Careful analysis is required to ensure that noncore functions are adequately resourced without draining resources from central business areas. Efficiency measures, such as process improvements and technology integration, are often applied to manage costs and performance in these areas.

Organizations can better allocate resources and enhance operational efficiency by distinguishing between core and noncore functions. Core functions are prioritized for investment and strategic focus, ensuring they receive the support needed to drive the organization's success. Noncore functions, while essential, are managed to support the core functions efficiently, often through outsourcing or automation. This balanced approach ensures that all aspects of the business contribute effectively to the overall strategy, supporting operational excellence and long-term growth.

Tools and Techniques for Mapping

To make the mapping of business processes more manageable, there are multiple tools and techniques that provide visual and analytical representations of business processes, aiding in identifying inefficiencies and areas for improvement. One practical approach is business process modeling notation (BPMN). BPMN provides:

- A graphical representation of business processes
- Workflows in a standard format
- Easy-to-understand methods

This method is widely used to map out a process's steps, making it easier to pinpoint inefficiencies and potential areas for enhancement.

Similarly, flowcharts serve as a simple yet powerful tool to diagram a process. They show various steps and decision points, clarifying how tasks are completed and who is responsible. Both BPMN and flowcharts help break down procedures into understandable and manageable parts, facilitating process improvement initiatives.

Data collection techniques such as surveys and questionnaires play a vital role in mapping business functions by gathering information from employees and stakeholders about the processes they are involved in. These tools help capture the current state of processes and identify gaps or inefficiencies. Engaging team members through these techniques involves them in the process improvement journey and allows for the efficient collection of large amounts of data.

Additionally, conducting interviews and focus groups with process participants and managers provides deeper insights into nuances. These methods capture knowledge that might not be visible through other techniques, offering a detailed understanding that enriches the mapping process.

Visualization software also significantly enhances the mapping of business functions. For example, enterprise resource planning systems integrate various functions into one complete system, streamlining processes and information across the organization. These systems help map out resource use and workflows, connecting different business functions from production to sales. They can also be used to simulate changes and improvements, providing a dynamic view of how adjustments can impact overall operations. Mind-mapping tools like XMind or MindMeister offer another visual approach, creating diagrams of linked and organized thoughts and tasks. These tools are beneficial in brainstorming sessions and organizing complex processes into clear, communicable visual structures.

Analytical techniques further support the mapping of business functions. Value stream mapping, a lean management tool, analyzes the current state and designs a future state for the series of events that take a product or service from its inception to the customer. It focuses on identifying waste and inefficiencies, emphasizing the value added at each process step.

SWOT (strengths, weaknesses, opportunities, threats) analysis can also be adapted to process mapping, providing a strategic view of the operational environment. This analysis helps identify internal and external factors that could impact a process, aiding in planning improvements based on comprehensive insights.

Impact Assessment

Impact assessments help drive prioritization in ASM. They use qualitative and quantitative methods to evaluate the potential consequences of security threats and vulnerabilities. These methods provide a comprehensive understanding of how different risks can affect an organization, helping prioritize assets and allocate resources effectively.

Qualitative methods focus on contextual insights, exploring processes, behaviors, and organizational attitudes. Techniques such as interviews, focus groups, and observational research help uncover vulnerabilities that may not be captured through numerical data. For example, interviews with stakeholders can reveal the operational significance of specific assets, while observations may highlight security gaps in everyday workflows.

Quantitative methods rely on numerical analysis to measure and predict security risks. Surveys, statistical modeling, and data analysis tools like SPSS, R, or Python help assess trends, quantify financial impacts, and evaluate threat likelihood. For instance, statistical analysis of past security incidents can identify high-risk areas and inform data-driven security decisions.

Integrating both approaches creates a balanced strategy. Quantitative methods highlight the most pressing threats through measurable trends, while qualitative insights explain their underlying causes and offer context-specific solutions. This combination enables organizations to design targeted security interventions, from policy updates to employee training, ensuring a well-rounded and effective cybersecurity approach.

Determining Actual Prioritization

Determining actual prioritization within ASM is a nuanced process involving more than just listing assets by their apparent importance. It requires a comprehensive evaluation of each asset's value to the organization, its operational impact, and its data sensitivity. Decision-making frameworks, such as risk-value matrices and business impact analyses, often support this evaluation, which helps quantify and compare the relative importance of different assets.

The process is iterative and dynamic, integrating inputs from various organizational stakeholders to ensure a holistic view. Prioritization must also adapt to changing business needs, technological advancements, and evolving threat landscapes. By continuously reassessing and adjusting priorities, organizations can ensure that their most essential assets receive the appropriate protection and resources, ultimately enhancing their overall security posture and operational resilience.

Determining Crown Jewels

One of the first things to determine in prioritization is the crown jewels. These assets are essential for the organization's operations, strategic objectives, and overall survival. Identifying them involves assessing several key criteria to ensure they receive the highest level of protection and resource allocation.

Determining crown jewels starts with looking at business criticality, as shown in Figure 6-1. Assets directly tied to revenue generation are considered crown jewels, for example. They include those involved in production, service delivery, or any processes that generate significant income, making them crucial for sustaining the organization's financial health.

Legal and regulatory requirements further delineate the importance of certain assets. Assets that comply with specific laws and regulations, such as GDPR or HIPAA, are prioritized to prevent legal actions and fines resulting from noncompliance. Similarly, assets governed by contractual obligations with clients or partners are important, as their compromise could lead to breaches of contract and significant legal liabilities. Factoring in these requirements ensures that the organization maintains its legal standing and contractual integrity.

The sensitivity and confidentiality of the data contained within crown jewels also play a significant role. Assets holding sensitive, confidential, or proprietary information are prioritized because unauthorized access or loss could threaten the company's competitive position and privacy obligations, potentially leading to intellectual property theft. Strict access controls are necessary for these assets, ensuring that physical and digital information are tightly managed and protected from unauthorized access.

Risk exposure is another valuable criterion for identifying crown jewels. This involves evaluating assets' vulnerability to cyberattacks, theft, or natural disasters. It goes beyond the likelihood of a threat and focuses more on the potential impact to determine the organizational risk. Factors such as the irreplaceability of certain assets—like bespoke software, specialized machinery, or personnel with key expertise—elevate their priority status, as their loss would be difficult and costly to mitigate.

Strategic importance is also a valuable factor. For instance, research and development assets or investments in emerging technologies are vital for the organization's growth and innovation. Moreover, assets that influence stakeholder confidence, such as those required for maintaining trust and confidence among investors, customers, and regulators, should be prioritized. Maintaining the integrity of these assets is essential for sustaining the organization's reputation and stakeholder relationships.

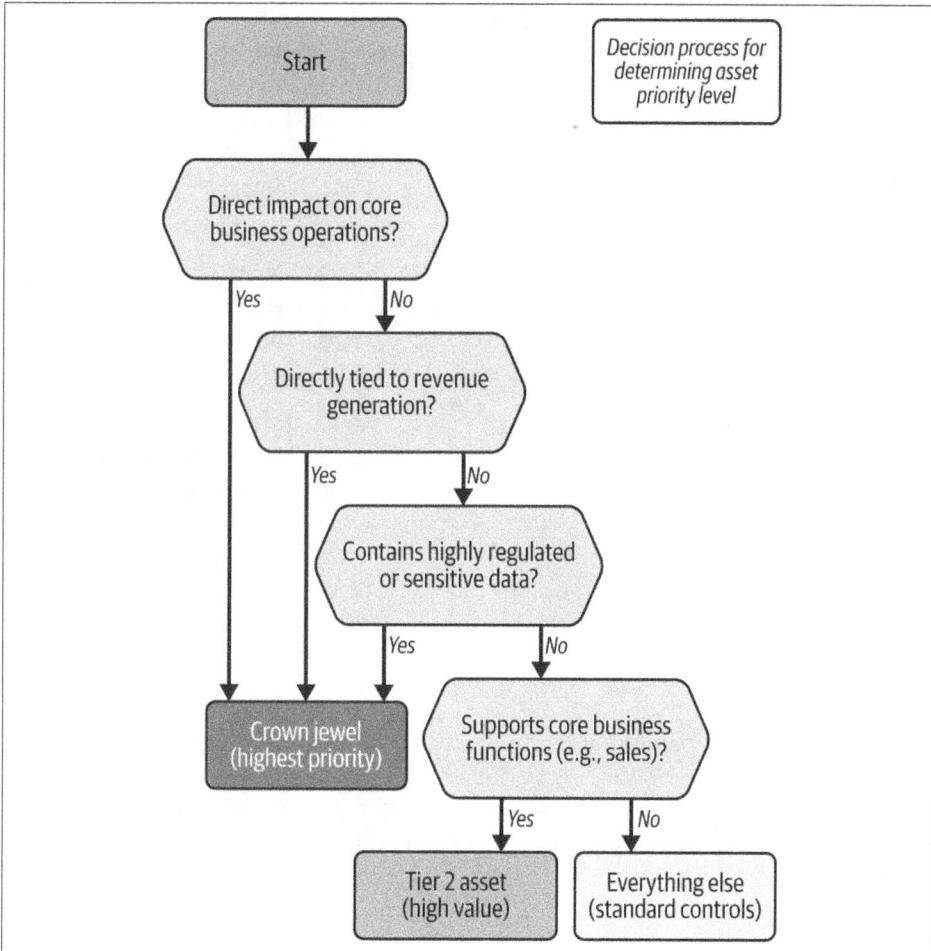

Figure 6-1. A structured approach to identifying crown jewels, high-priority assets, and standard-control assets based on business criticality, revenue impact, regulatory requirements, and operational support factors.

Periodic Review and Update of Crown Jewels

Like many aspects of ASM, asset prioritization is not static, so the periodic review and updating of crown jewels is essential to maintaining an organization's security posture. This process involves regularly evaluating and reassessing critical assets to ensure their importance and the security measures protecting them remain aligned with the evolving business environment, threat landscape, and organizational changes.

As companies evolve, their strategic priorities shift. Regular reviews ensure that their assets align with current objectives and operations, maintaining relevance and importance. Similarly, responding to market and technological changes helps the organization remain agile. As markets and technology develop, new assets might become critical while old ones might decrease in importance. Periodic reviews help identify these changes and adjust protection efforts accordingly, ensuring that security measures always focus on the most relevant assets.

Technological and operational upgrades also necessitate regular reassessment. Upgrading systems and technologies that support crown jewels requires a revaluation of protection measures to ensure they remain effective; changes in how assets are used or the processes they support may alter their criticality. Reviews can help update asset protection strategies to reflect these operational changes.

Similarly, the security landscape is constantly changing. New vulnerabilities, attack vectors, and threat actors continually emerge, making it essential to review security measures and threat assessments often. A proactive approach helps keep the crown jewels secure against evolving threats. On the defensive side, advancements in security technologies provide new tools and methods to protect assets more effectively. Periodic reviews facilitate the integration of these advancements into the protection strategy for crown jewels, ensuring that the organization leverages the latest security innovations.

Legal and regulatory requirements also change over time. New laws and regulations are passed, requiring organizations to ensure that the protection of crown jewels meets these evolving standards to avoid fines and penalties. Regular reviews ensure readiness for audits and compliance checks, maintaining compliance and demonstrating due diligence.

Organizational changes, such as mergers, acquisitions, or restructuring, can alter the importance or nature of assets. Periodic reviews accommodate these changes by reassessing which assets remain critical. These changes can affect asset ownership or custodianship transitions, in turn affecting asset management. Regular reviews ensure that new custodians understand their responsibilities and the importance of the assets they manage, maintaining continuity and security.

Identifying Other High-Value Assets

If an organization has crown jewels—its most critical and valuable assets—it stands to reason that there are also lesser assets that, while not as crucial, still hold significant value. These lower-tier assets play essential roles in supporting day-to-day operations, maintaining financial stability, and contributing to long-term strategic goals.

As part of ASM, delineating tiers helps organizations focus their efforts more heavily on the most valuable assets. This does not mean lower-tier assets will be denied proper management and protection. Instead, they will come after those of a higher tier. A tiered breakdown is most important when determining the value of security investments, helping organizations target their limited resources most effectively.

Tier 2 assets

While not essential to an organization's immediate survival, Tier 2 assets play significant roles in supporting core business functions and maintaining financial stability. Proper identification and categorization of these assets involves assessing their importance in the broader operational landscape. Tier 2 assets may include secondary operational systems, backup data repositories, or noncritical intellectual property. Though their compromise might not lead to catastrophic failure, their loss could still result in notable operational disruptions or financial setbacks.

The risk and impact assessment of Tier 2 assets are integral to their prioritization. While these assets might not have the same dire consequences as crown jewels if compromised, their failure could still lead to substantial disruptions. Evaluating the risk and potential impact helps determine the appropriate level of protection and resource allocation.

Management strategies for Tier 2 assets are less robust than those of crown jewels, focusing on more scaled security measures. These measures include standard encryption, access controls, and regular security audits. The goal is to safeguard these assets while balancing security investments with cost efficiency. Efficient resource allocation is more important for this tier, ensuring expenditures are proportional to the risk and impact associated with these assets.

Monitoring and maintaining Tier 2 assets is essential to operational readiness and security. Regular reviews are necessary to reassess their importance and the adequacy of current protection measures, especially as business needs and technologies evolve. Preventive maintenance averts disruptions that could indirectly affect core operations. A proactive approach ensures that Tier 2 assets remain functional and secure, supporting overall business continuity.

Tier 2 assets are also integral to business continuity and disaster recovery plans. They may not be the first things restored, but they still provide essential functions and are necessary to attend to after a primary system failure. Effective disaster recovery planning will take this into account, making sure that adequate and available backups are in place and that these assets are factored into the restoration strategy.

Feedback from business units

Incorporating feedback from business units is essential for asset prioritization and management, ensuring that security strategies align with each department's practical needs and objectives. Each business unit has unique insights into the risks that affect its operations, and by integrating this feedback, organizations can prioritize assets more accurately and tailor protection strategies to address specific vulnerabilities. This collaborative approach improves risk awareness across the organization and fosters a cohesive security culture in which each unit feels responsible for asset protection.

Engaging business units in the asset management process builds a sense of ownership, strengthening security efforts through improved communication and coordination. By understanding how assets are used daily, security teams can make informed decisions about their criticality, prioritize resource allocation effectively, and even identify underutilized assets that could better support business goals. Alignment between asset management and business objectives helps security measures be technically sound and strategically relevant, directly contributing to the organization's overall success.

Ultimately, continuous feedback from business units supports the evolution and adaptability of asset management strategies, allowing organizations to respond to technological changes, market shifts, and new business challenges. This dynamic feedback loop helps asset management to continuously improve, maintaining robust protection for high-value assets while adapting to a changing environment.

Ranking Everything Else

Ranking assets in the "everything else" category involves a strategic approach to make sure that, while these assets might not be the crown jewels, they still receive the necessary protection and management. The process begins by recognizing that even secondary assets play a crucial role in supporting the overall functionality and efficiency of the organization. Though not as important as the primary assets, the assets are indispensable for the smooth operation of daily business activities.

Identifying and categorizing these assets accurately is essential to avoid potential operational disruptions that could stem from neglecting their importance. Prioritizing lesser assets involves a comprehensive evaluation of their operational impact, financial implications, and the risks associated with their compromise. The process includes assessing how the failure of the assets might affect productivity, cause financial setbacks, or create vulnerabilities within the organization's security framework. By systematically ranking these assets, organizations can create a balanced allocation of resources that addresses both critical and secondary needs.

Developing a prioritization matrix

A prioritization matrix is a decision-making tool that ranks tasks, projects, or assets based on specific factors, such as importance, urgency, and resource availability. The matrix provides a structured way for organizations to evaluate and prioritize multiple items by scoring them against chosen criteria, helping allocate resources more efficiently. For example, a prioritization matrix for asset management might rank assets based on criteria like operational impact, security vulnerability, regulatory compliance requirements, and replacement costs. Assigning a score to each factor helps organizations quickly identify high-priority items that need immediate attention and those that can be addressed later.

By carefully designing the matrix framework, implementing and using it, integrating it with decision-making processes, engaging key stakeholders, and committing to regular reviews and continuous improvement, organizations can be assured that their prioritization efforts are adaptable to changing needs.

The first step in developing a prioritization matrix is designing its framework, which involves selecting the criteria that will be used to assess and rank items, as shown in Figure 6-2. Typical criteria might include the impact on business operations, associated costs, risks involved, and the time required for implementation. These criteria should reflect the organization's strategic goals and risk management priorities. Once the criteria are identified, the next step is to assign weights to each one based on its relative importance to the organization. This weighting influences how much each criterion affects the overall prioritization of an item, so more important factors have a greater impact on decision making.

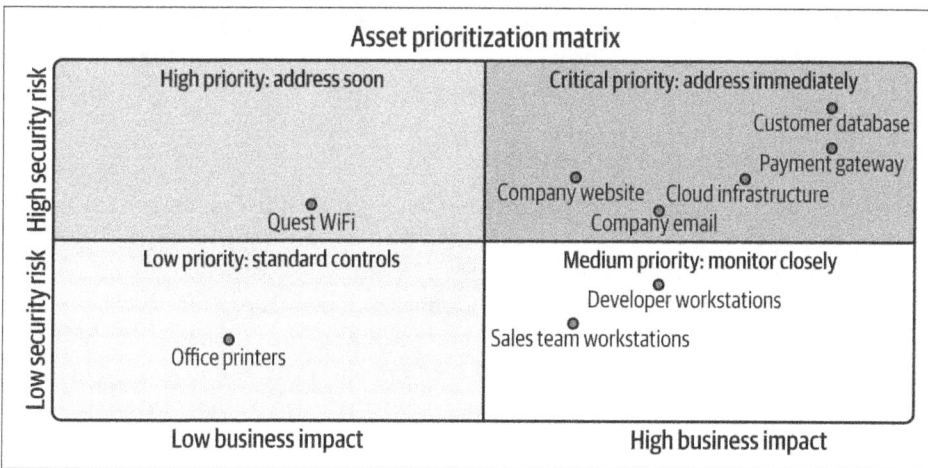

Asset prioritization matrix

	Low business impact	High business impact
High security risk	High priority: address soon Quest WiFi	Critical priority: address immediately Customer database Payment gateway Company website Cloud infrastructure Company email
Low security risk	Low priority: standard controls Office printers	Medium priority: monitor closely Developer workstations Sales team workstations

Figure 6-2. A visual framework for evaluating organizational assets based on business impact and security risk dimensions, helping security teams efficiently allocate resources to the most critical assets while establishing appropriate controls for lower priority assets.

The matrix layout can be created after establishing the criteria and their respective weights. This involves setting up a grid with criteria listed on one axis and the items or assets to prioritize on the other. The layout facilitates a clear visual comparison across multiple dimensions, making it easier to see how different items stack up against each other. A consistent scoring system, such as a scale from 1 to 5 or 1 to 10, should be developed for each criterion, where higher scores represent higher importance or greater risk. This scoring system ensures fair comparisons across all items, promoting objective and balanced decision making.

Integrating the prioritization matrix with decision-making processes is necessary for its proper use. Establishing clear guidelines for interpreting the matrix's results, such as defining thresholds or cutoff scores, helps determine which projects or assets should be prioritized for action. Additionally, allowing for dynamic adjustments in the matrix as new information becomes available or as business priorities shift keeps the prioritization relevant and aligned with current needs.

Engaging key stakeholders from various departments in developing and reviewing the prioritization matrix is vital. Their insights can help all relevant perspectives and expertise be considered, leading to a more comprehensive and accurate prioritization. Maintaining transparency in how criteria are weighted and how scores are assigned builds trust in the process. It secures buy-in from all parts of the organization, fostering a collaborative approach to resource allocation.

Regular reviews and continuous improvement are necessary to keep the prioritization matrix effective. Scheduling regular reviews ensures that the matrix meets the organization's needs and adapts to any internal or external environment changes. Implementing a feedback mechanism to gather input on the effectiveness of the matrix and suggestions for improvement helps refine the tool over time, making it more responsive to the organization's evolving priorities.

Implementing a dynamic prioritization model

Implementing a dynamic prioritization model is an adaptive approach that continuously evaluates and adjusts the priority of tasks, projects, or assets based on changing conditions and new information. The model is particularly beneficial in environments where flexibility and responsiveness are mandatory for success, since it improves an organization's ability to respond swiftly to shifts in the business environment, such as changes in market demands, technological advancements, or emerging risks. By regularly updating and reassessing priorities, companies can ensure their efforts align with current strategic goals and operational needs.

One of the core strengths of a dynamic prioritization model is its reliance on data-driven decision making. Real-time data integration allows the model to react dynamically to immediate statuses of various metrics like market trends, performance indicators, or risk assessments. Advanced analytics and forecasting techniques are employed to predict changes and potential impacts, which guide the prioritization process. That approach makes sure decisions are informed by the most current and relevant information, supporting the organization's ability to anticipate and respond to future challenges.

Implementing technology and tools is necessary for the dynamic prioritization model. Automated tools and specialized software manage and update priorities without manual intervention, increasing efficiency and reducing the likelihood of errors. Ensuring seamless integration with existing IT systems and management tools maintains consistency and data accessibility across platforms, allowing for a unified and coherent approach to prioritization.

The success of a dynamic prioritization model comes from stakeholder engagement and transparent communication. Regularly engaging stakeholders from different levels of the organization fosters a collaborative approach, gathering valuable input and communicating changes in prioritization. Transparency in the decision-making process clarifies how priorities are determined and adjusted, building trust and supporting organizational compliance. This openness encourages stakeholder buy-in and reinforces the importance of the prioritization efforts.

Like all the other aspects of ASM, evaluation and continuous improvement are integral to the success of a dynamic prioritization model. Conducting periodic performance reviews helps assess the model's effectiveness and identifies areas for improvement. Establishing feedback loops from users and stakeholders helps refine and optimize the model over time. The iterative process keeps the prioritization model relevant in addressing the organization's evolving needs, leading to a more agile and resilient operational framework.

Summary

Asset prioritization in attack surface management is fundamental to safeguarding an organization's most important resources. Organizations can optimize their security measures by systematically identifying and categorizing assets based on their value, operational impact, and data sensitivity. This thorough approach improves resource allocation and fortifies the organization's overall security posture. However, prioritization is just one piece of the broader ASM puzzle. The prioritized list of assets must seamlessly integrate into a comprehensive risk management strategy to protect an organization from its myriad threats.

In risk management, the focus shifts from identifying and ranking assets to understanding and mitigating the various risks these assets face. Risk management in ASM involves a continuous process of risk assessment, threat analysis, and the implementation of mitigation strategies to protect prioritized assets from potential threats. The next chapter will explore the methodologies and tools used to assess risk, evaluate threat landscapes, and develop proactive measures to minimize vulnerabilities.

By linking asset prioritization to a structured risk management framework, organizations can create a dynamic and responsive ASM strategy that identifies the most valuable assets and protects them in an ever-evolving threat environment.

CHAPTER 7

Measuring Attack Surface

In this chapter, we explore the process of measuring an organization's attack surface, focusing on both internal and external aspects. We will explore how identity and access management are pivotal in securing these surfaces and introduce essential techniques like threat modeling and attack surface mapping. These methods are crucial for assessing and enhancing the security framework, providing a comprehensive overview and actionable insights into protecting an organization's digital and physical assets against potential threats.

Attack Surface Analysis

Attack surface analysis (ASA) is an essential practice in ASM that identifies, classifies, and prioritizes vulnerabilities across an organization's digital and physical assets. By defining and understanding the scope of potential risks within networks, applications, and systems, ASA serves as a crucial tool for ensuring robust security measures are in place. This comprehensive visibility is pivotal for organizations to safeguard their infrastructure against various threats.

The significance of ASA extends beyond mere identification; it is foundational in shaping an organization's security strategies. By providing a clear map of vulnerabilities, ASA enables security teams to effectively develop targeted measures and policies that address specific weaknesses. That approach improves the security of sensitive assets and supports the broader objectives of risk management.

ASA also helps organizations adapt to the rapidly evolving risk landscape. The dynamic nature of cyberthreats requires a proactive approach to security management, where continuous updates to the understanding of the attack surface are necessary. ASA facilitates this by offering ongoing assessments that reflect current vulnerabilities, ensuring that security measures are always aligned with the latest threat intelligence.

Its integration with other security technologies, such as SIEM systems and endpoint protection, further amplifies ASA's effectiveness. The integration creates a layered security approach that maximizes an organization's detection and mitigation capabilities. By coupling ASA with these advanced technologies, organizations can strengthen their defensive posture significantly, making it more difficult for threats to penetrate their systems.

How Does ASA Work?

The ASA process begins with the comprehensive identification of all assets within an organization, as shown in Figure 7-1. This crucial first step involves cataloging every piece of software, hardware, and network environment to ensure that no component is overlooked. By understanding what assets exist, security teams can better prepare to protect them.

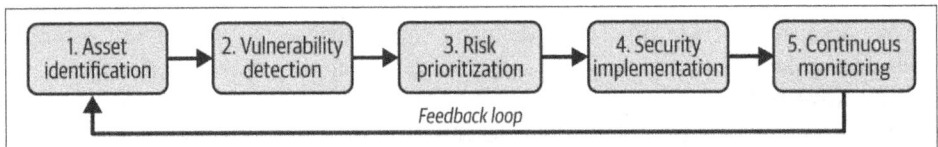

Figure 7-1. *The continuous attack surface assessment cycle used for maintaining an effective security posture against evolving threats.*

Once assets are identified, the next phase is vulnerability detection. Security teams utilize a combination of automated tools and manual assessments to uncover weaknesses within the system. These methods allow for thorough scrutiny of the identified assets to spot vulnerabilities that attackers could exploit.

After detecting vulnerabilities, the task of prioritizing risks commences. It involves assessing each vulnerability's potential impact and exploitability to determine which issues should be addressed first. Prioritization ensures that resources are allocated effectively, focusing efforts on the most significant threats to reduce risk efficiently.

Underlying this process is automation, which is necessary for streamlining each step, especially in large or complex environments. While manual processes would work, they can quickly become unwieldy and create an excessive workload for teams as organizations expand. Automated systems help offload some of the burden by rapidly processing vast amounts of data and identifying methods faster than manual methods ever could. Automation is especially important considering how rapidly threats evolve and must be handled; manual processes just can't keep up.

Continuous monitoring augments all of this to ensure that any changes in the asset base or emerging threats are detected in real time, allowing for immediate response. Without such monitoring, changes could be made dramatically, changing the organizational risk posture without teams being aware of and able to implement the appropriate controls to address it. Continuous tracking helps organizations stay one step ahead of potential attackers by adapting their security measures as new information becomes available.

How ASA Enhances Security Posture

ASA fundamentally transforms how organizations approach security protocols by providing a holistic view of all vulnerabilities. A comprehensive perspective is crucial for a more effective and targeted response to potential threats. ASA also fosters proactive security measures, allowing organizations to anticipate and mitigate risks before they escalate into actual attacks. Furthermore, ASA feeds into strategic security planning by delivering actionable intelligence that informs decisions on where to allocate resources and how to tailor security investments, ensuring that efforts are focused where they are most needed.

Organizations can better align their security practices with industry compliance standards and best practices by conducting ASA. This alignment helps maintain the trust of partners and customers while avoiding penalties associated with noncompliance. ASA ensures that security measures not only meet but often exceed regulatory requirements, positioning the organization as a leader in security within its industry. A thorough understanding of compliance through ASA helps in structuring a robust security framework that is adaptable to changes in compliance landscapes.

Another significant advantage of implementing ASA is improving incident response times and effectiveness. By having a clear and updated picture of where critical assets and vulnerabilities lie, organizations can swiftly respond to security incidents. That readiness minimizes potential damage from attacks and reduces downtime, enhancing overall operational efficiency. ASA's role in continuously monitoring the attack surface also ensures that the organization can quickly adapt to new threats, keeping its defense measures current and effective.

Internal and External Attack Surfaces

The internal attack surface of an organization includes all components within its network that could potentially be vulnerable to security breaches. The list encompasses hardware, software, and network configurations accessible internally, such as user devices, internal servers, databases, and essential network infrastructure like routers and switches. Managing the internal surface involves strict control over employee access, credential management, and the handling of privileges to mitigate risks associated with insider threats and accidental data exposures.

External attack surfaces, in contrast, consist of elements accessible from outside the organization's internal network. These include public-facing web applications, APIs, email systems, external network connections, and interactions with third-party vendors or cloud services. The security of these external points must defend against external threats from hackers and cybercriminals who might exploit vulnerabilities to gain unauthorized access or disrupt organizational services.

Both internal and external attack surfaces are intrinsically linked, requiring comprehensive and integrated security strategies for robust protection. Vulnerabilities in one area can lead to security breaches in the other, illustrating the need for cohesive management.

An example of how vulnerabilities in external attack surfaces can lead to broader security breaches is when a compromised web server is used as a pivot point into a connected database. If the database is poorly secured, the attacker could pivot to internal databases, potentially escalating access to more sensitive data.

Internal Attack Surface Analysis

Internal ASA is a thorough review and assessment of an organization's internal IT infrastructure vulnerabilities. This analysis scrutinizes all components accessible internally, such as hardware, software, network configurations, and access controls. The goal is to uncover potential security weaknesses that could be exploited by insiders or via compromised internal accounts. Such assessments are vital for strengthening defenses against insider threats, unauthorized access, and accidental data leaks, ensuring that robust internal security measures are effectively implemented.

While the upcoming sections delve into critical areas, it's important to note that they are not exhaustive; they represent essential components that must be considered as part of a comprehensive attack surface analysis strategy.

Network security

Network security is one of the first attack surfaces most people consider when looking at internal attack surfaces. The challenge here is that networking covers a lot of ground, addressing every way technologies communicate internally. It's helpful to break the different review areas into manageable bites so as not to become overloaded.

One place to start is assessing preventive measures such as network segmentation and isolation, because they support the compartmentalization of sensitive areas within the internal network. This limits the damage potential of security breaches and reduces the attack surface. Additionally, verifying robust access controls helps to check that only authorized personnel and devices can access critical network segments. These measures are fundamental to preventing unauthorized access and establishing a secure network environment.

Reviewing detection strategies is another vital component of ASA for networks. It involves checking the effectiveness and responsiveness of an intrusion detection system (IDS) to be confident it is correctly monitoring network activity for suspicious behavior. Similarly, assessing the thoroughness of traffic monitoring systems is important for identifying any anomalies that may indicate security breaches or malicious activities. These assessments help organizations spot potential threats early, enabling timely interventions to mitigate risks.

Maintaining data integrity and confidentiality is expected for everything traversing the network, requiring protective technologies such as network encryption. It's no longer sufficient to assume that data cannot be intercepted or modified just because it traverses an internal network. Given that implementing secure network connections is easy, there is no reason it should be avoided. As part of the ASA, an evaluation should verify that all data transmitted across the network is adequately encrypted, safeguarding it from interception and tampering by unauthorized entities.

User account management

In ASA, verifying access establishment and control mechanisms helps assess the strength and effectiveness of authentication protocols, such as multifactor authentication. This ensures that only authorized users can access the system, mitigating unauthorized access risks. Equally important is evaluating the implementation of role-based access control (RBAC) systems. Doing so helps check that access permissions are appropriately aligned with users' roles, reducing the potential for excessive access that could lead to security breaches.

Regular audits and account life cycle management are key assessments within ASA. By auditing user accounts and permissions, organizations can detect and rectify improper access configurations or outdated privileges, maintaining a secure access environment. Assessing account life cycle management practices ensures that user accounts are appropriately managed throughout their lifespan—from creation to deactivation or deletion—preventing orphaned accounts from posing a security risk.

Assessing the effectiveness of user education and training programs is essential in ASA. It involves evaluating how well the organization educates its workforce on security best practices and the importance of secure account management. Ensuring that all users are well-informed and compliant with security policies improves the overall security posture by reducing the likelihood of accidental breaches or misuse of access privileges. This assessment helps cultivate a security-aware culture that supports broader ASA objectives.

Automated process identities

For ASA, assessing identity and access management for automated processes ensures that entities like scripts and bots are managed with the same rigor as human identities, securing them and providing them with appropriate privileges. Additionally, evaluating the access restrictions placed on these processes prevents them from having more access than necessary for their functions, thereby minimizing potential misuse and enhancing overall security.

Assessing the monitoring and auditing mechanisms for automated processes is integral to ASA. The review helps verify that continuous monitoring systems and regular audits are in place and functioning effectively to detect and respond to abnormal or unauthorized actions. These practices maintain control over automated processes and keep them operating within their defined parameters.

The assessment of security configurations and integration with centralized security management systems is also essential. Evaluating how automated processes are integrated into the organization's broader security framework improves visibility and control. The review includes verifying the security of configuration management systems that handle automated deployments, so that they are impervious to unauthorized changes that could lead to security breaches.

Physical security

Most organizations have a physical presence of some variety, whether for their offices or wherever their IT assets exist. Assessing access and entry controls for these environments ensures physical security measures effectively let the right people in and keep the wrong people out. This involves verifying the mechanisms that control physical access to critical infrastructures, such as data centers and server rooms, to prevent unauthorized access. Rigorous visitor management is also crucial; assessing how visitors are logged, badged, and supervised protects sensitive areas from potential security breaches. These assessments help maintain a secure perimeter and safeguard critical organizational assets.

Surveillance systems are a key part of physical security. They must be evaluated to check that cameras and monitoring systems are optimally placed and functional to deter and detect unauthorized intrusions. The goal is to establish a reliable system that can provide real-time alerts and evidence in the event of security incidents. Continuous monitoring is essential for responding promptly to physical threats and maintaining the integrity of secure areas.

The assessment of environmental controls is an important aspect of protecting infrastructure against damage from environmental risks like fire, flooding, or extreme weather. The controls include systems like fire suppression, water leak detection, and climate control that safeguard critical assets from hazards. Having these systems in place and functioning as intended can prevent significant physical damage and potential operational disruptions. Regularly evaluating and maintaining these systems helps them operate effectively and continue to provide the necessary protection.

Security training equips personnel to recognize and respond effectively to physical security threats and should be part of this assessment. It should cover everything from preventing common attacks, such as tailgating, where someone slips through a door without proper access, to being prepared for and acting in emergencies.

External Attack Surface Analysis

External attack surface analysis identifies and assesses vulnerabilities and risks linked to an organization's publicly accessible IT assets. This type of analysis is essential for understanding and mitigating potential threats that exploit external vectors, such as public-facing web applications, APIs, and server endpoints. By conducting a thorough external attack surface analysis, organizations can proactively prevent cyberattacks by addressing vulnerabilities before they can be exploited by external actors.

Cloud services

Assessing data protection and access control within cloud services helps safeguard sensitive information. Organizations can validate that their cloud-stored data is protected from unauthorized access by verifying the implementation of data security measures such as encryption, secure APIs, and robust access controls. That evaluation is essential for protecting data integrity and privacy and complying with regulatory requirements that govern data security. Properly implementing these controls can prevent data breaches and maintain trust in cloud-based systems, making it a core component of cloud security governance.

To safeguard against unauthorized access, the effectiveness of authentication and authorization mechanisms must be assessed. With robust mechanisms, organizations can effectively control who accesses their cloud resources, significantly reducing the potential entry points for attackers. These assessments help prevent breaches that could expose sensitive organizational data. They involve checking that the security measures are configured correctly and function as intended, providing a reliable barrier against external threats and internal misuse of data access.

Many breaches in the cloud are due to improper configuration, making them entirely avoidable. Assessing proper configuration and ongoing management of cloud services is pivotal to ensuring that cloud environments remain secure and compliant. This verification process involves checking for correct settings and configurations to guard against common misconfigurations that could introduce vulnerabilities within the cloud infrastructure. By aligning the configurations with security best practices and compliance standards, organizations can significantly reduce the risk of security incidents, maintaining a robust security posture in their cloud operations.

Vendor management, particularly for SaaS services, requires evaluating whether providers meet security and industry standards. This includes verifying regulatory compliance, assessing security protocols, and confirming that their infrastructure aligns with organizational security requirements. The process is a key part of maintaining data integrity and protecting against potential security breaches facilitated by vendor shortcomings.

The assessment of monitoring and incident response strategies in cloud environments involves checking that mechanisms for continuous monitoring are in place and that robust incident response plans are ready to be executed when security breaches occur. Assessing these areas allows the organization to quickly detect and respond to security threats, minimizing potential damage and maintaining the integrity of cloud-based systems.

The cloud assessment should also include monitoring and incident response strategies to prepare for possible incidents. These controls maintain the security and integrity of cloud-based systems, since continuous monitoring systems must be operational and capable of swiftly detecting any unusual or unauthorized activity. Moreover, having robust and well-defined incident response plans is essential. These plans must be ready to activate immediately upon detection of a security breach to mitigate potential damage.

APIs

APIs form the communications gateway to applications, opening up the potential for unauthorized access and potential misuse. Assessing them includes verifying the implementation of secure authentication methods such as OAuth, which helps make sure that only authorized users can access the API. Additionally, it involves evaluating access controls that limit user and system interactions with the API, preventing unauthorized operations. Proactive verification maintains the security and integrity of the APIs, supporting the overall security framework of the organization.

For ASA, we also want to assess preventative measures for APIs, which is vital to prevent exploits and attacks. Doing so includes verifying the implementation of rate limiting to mitigate abuse and DDoS attacks, which helps the APIs handle unexpected traffic surges without compromising service. Additionally, assessing input validation practices is crucial to block malicious data entries and prevent common attacks such as SQL injection. These preventative measures are fundamental in maintaining the robustness of API interactions and protecting against potential vulnerabilities.

Keeping a healthy API environment requires API monitoring and maintenance strategies through regular audits. Monitoring this process allows organizations to proactively identify and address emerging security vulnerabilities or gaps within their API infrastructure. By conducting these assessments consistently, organizations can keep their APIs secure against evolving threats, maintain the integrity of their systems, and protect sensitive data from unauthorized access or breaches.

When evaluating APIs, remember that the endpoints are connected to attack surfaces and can be exposed through them. A thorough evaluation of these endpoints helps identify and seal off unnecessary access points, significantly improving the security of the API infrastructure. Organizations can effectively reduce the overall attack surface by managing which APIs are exposed and how they are secured.

Web application security

Due to their accessibility and potential vulnerabilities, web applications are frequent targets for cyberattacks. This means companies should rigorously assess vulnerability management practices within these applications. Such an assessment should include regular security testing routines like penetration testing, designed to proactively identify and remediate vulnerabilities. By regularly scanning for and fixing vulnerabilities, organizations can fortify their web applications against potential exploits, enhancing their overall cybersecurity posture and reducing the risk of successful attacks.

As part of vulnerability management, there should be a process for applying patches to address vulnerabilities. Assessing the patch management process helps to confirm that updates and fixes are applied promptly, which helps protect against known vulnerabilities and threats. Timely patching strengthens the defenses of web applications by closing security gaps that attackers could exploit, thereby significantly reducing the risk of breaches and maintaining the continuous integrity and availability of web services.

Web applications also host valuable data that cybercriminals can target, making their protection important. Check that data encryption is effectively employed both in transit and at rest to secure sensitive information from potential interception. In addition, assess the strength of input validation practices, as these help defend against injection attacks such as SQL injection and XSS, preserving the integrity of the web applications to prevent data loss.

Part of securing web applications is ensuring that attackers cannot easily access them. The access control mechanisms we use for this protection must be rigorously evaluated to verify that strong authentication and authorization practices, including multifactor authentication (MFA) and RBAC, are in place. Restrict access to sensitive functionalities appropriately, minimizing the risk of unauthorized data manipulation or exposure.

Alternatively, as with any exposed service, we also want to be sure that attackers cannot prevent legitimate users from accessing them. DDoS attacks can flood resources, grinding performance to a standstill. However, these attacks are not always malicious—unexpected interest in your company or product can drive a flood of extra traffic, which may overwhelm systems.

Because web applications are continuously exposed, they require monitoring and the ability to respond to threats. Web application assessments should include evaluating the operations of different systems, such as IDS, that monitor suspicious activities. They should also check the effectiveness of the incident response plan to validate that it is ready to be executed effectively. This readiness is vital to address security breaches swiftly and minimize their impact.

Third-party risk assessment

Third parties handle specialized functions like IT services, payroll, and logistics for organizations, allowing them to focus on core business areas. They also provide expertise in cybersecurity and legal services, enhancing operational efficiency without needing internal development of these capabilities. These services increase the organizational attack surface as they access data and systems, creating potential security vulnerabilities that must be managed through stringent security measures and continuous monitoring.

Assessing the risk associated with third parties starts with reviewing the vendor selection and management process. Conduct thorough security assessments before onboarding new vendors to ensure they meet the organization's security standards. The contracts with these vendors should have clear security requirements and compliance standards to be met. The contractual requirements should align with organizational standards so that vendors are legally obligated to maintain the agreed-upon security practices, which protect the organization's data and systems from potential third-party risks.

Monitoring third-party vendors helps to maintain ongoing compliance with security standards and contractual obligations. That includes regularly reviewing their performance to confirm adherence to contractual security obligations and conducting periodic security audits. Audits help validate the security practices of third parties and enforce compliance, providing an additional layer of security by continuously assessing the risk they pose.

Like most things in IT, third-party risk management includes having robust incident response plans for vendors. This assessment ensures that third parties have clear protocols for responding to security breaches, which helps minimize potential damage. Their contracts should be assessed to verify they contain terms related to liability and compensation in the event of data breaches. This helps delineate the financial and operational impact on the organization should an incident occur. It establishes who is responsible and to what degree, allowing the organization to select appropriate ways to mitigate its residual risk, such as buying cybersecurity insurance.

Perimeter defense

Perimeter security serves as the first line of defense against external threats. By verifying the effectiveness of defenses like firewalls, intrusion detection systems, and anti-DDoS measures, organizations can keep their network perimeter robust enough to block unauthorized access and filter malicious traffic. A proactive approach helps prevent potential breaches that could compromise sensitive data and disrupt business operations, maintaining the integrity and availability of an organization's network infrastructure.

When looking at the perimeter, an assessment should start with verifying the implementation and maintenance of robust firewalls that manage and control incoming and outgoing network traffic based on established security rules. Next, evaluate the effectiveness of intrusion prevention systems, which actively monitor network traffic to detect and prevent vulnerability exploits before they impact the network. Properly configuring and maintaining these technologies helps defend the network against external threats and unauthorized access.

Border routers also rely on rules to manage and filter traffic at network borders. These controls need to be assessed to help maintain the integrity and security of the network by preventing unauthorized access and ensuring that only legitimate traffic enters the network.

While these devices help to control access through the network perimeter, tunnels still make their way in by design. As such, assessing the security of VPNs, particularly their encryption standards, is vital in any perimeter security review. Doing so ensures that data transmissions remain protected against interception or breaches from external sources. Thoroughly reviewing and verifying the robustness of VPN and encryption protocols helps to maintain a secure connection, safeguarding the network against vulnerabilities and unauthorized access.

Monitoring and detection also form a key part of perimeter defense, involving continuous analysis of network traffic to identify unusual patterns that may indicate potential security threats. Assessing the implementation of SIEM systems is essential. These systems aggregate and analyze log data from various network sources, enabling real-time security monitoring and rapid incident response. This ensures that potential threats are quickly identified and addressed, maintaining the network's overall security.

Public infrastructure exposure

External attack surfaces cover a wide range of public infrastructure providing foundational services and technologies exposed to the public internet, such as domain name systems (DNSs), email servers, and hosted services. These components are crucial because they ensure the availability and accessibility of an organization's digital resources and pose potential security risks if not properly secured. Exposure to these services can become vectors for cyberattacks, impacting an organization's operations, reputation, and security.

When assessing domain and DNS security, it's important to focus on several key areas to ensure the robustness of protections against DNS spoofing and other DNS-related security threats:

- DNS security extensions should be evaluated to confirm they are properly implemented and functioning, since they ensure the authenticity of DNS responses.
- To prevent domain hijacking, the security of domain registration should be verified, including checking the WHOIS privacy features and registration lock.
- Regular DNS audits should be conducted to identify misconfigurations or vulnerabilities that could be exploited.

Checking for DNS resilience measures, such as geo-redundancy and DDoS protection, also helps to ensure that DNS services remain available and reliable under attack conditions.

Evaluating email security involves verifying the implementation of authentication protocols such as SPF, DKIM, and DMARC (*https://oreil.ly/EYqvl*). These protocols are essential for defending against email spoofing, ensuring that emails purportedly coming from the organization are authentic, and maintaining their integrity. That assessment helps protect against phishing attacks and other malicious activities that could compromise sensitive information, maintaining the trustworthiness and security of organizational communication channels.

Managing public data exposure prevents unintentional information leaks that attackers could exploit. Assessing data exposure control includes monitoring and managing what organizational data is made publicly accessible. Verifying SSL/TLS certificates for securing communications involving public infrastructure ensures that data in transit is encrypted, protecting it from eavesdropping and tampering. The assessment helps secure public-facing services and protect the organization's data against external threats.

Areas of Overlap

When analyzing attack surfaces, remember that not all risks are strictly internal or external due to the presence of shared technologies and common issues that straddle both realms. This overlap, where technologies serve dual roles within and outside the organizational boundaries, necessitates a unified security strategy that can effectively address vulnerabilities across interconnected areas. A comprehensive approach means that security measures are not siloed but work cohesively to protect the organization's digital landscape from potential threats.

Identity and access management

Identity and access management (IAM) is a framework of business processes, policies, and technologies that facilitates the management of electronic or digital identities. By controlling user access within a network through rights and restrictions, IAM lets the right individuals access the right resources at the right times for the right reasons. IAM is a significant attack surface because it directly influences security by protecting against unauthorized access to systems and data, thus reducing the risk of data breaches and other security incidents.

IAM systems must be assessed for the proper implementation of robust authentication controls such as MFA and single sign-on (SSO). MFA strengthens security by requiring multiple verification forms, reducing the risk of unauthorized access, while SSO minimizes password fatigue and the likelihood of password-related breaches. These mechanisms ensure secure and user-friendly access, improving overall security posture without sacrificing efficiency.

IAM involves assessing whether access controls like RBAC are appropriately implemented and aligned with the principle of least privilege. RBAC lets individuals access only those resources that are necessary for their roles, minimizing potential internal and external threats. The least privilege principle further tightens security by restricting user permissions to the bare minimum required for their job functions, reducing the risk of accidental or malicious breaches.

Assessing IAM processes also requires evaluating the identity life cycle management processes such as provisioning, deprovisioning, and regular audits of access rights. Timely provisioning and deprovisioning of accounts prevent unauthorized access by only allowing current, authorized users to access resources.

Regular audits and reviews help maintain appropriate access levels over time, adapting to any role or employment status changes. A thorough examination of IAM practices confirms that the organization's approach to identity management aligns with best practices and security standards, safeguarding sensitive information and systems from potential threats.

Vulnerability management

Vulnerability management is a cybersecurity process in which security vulnerabilities within an organization's technology environment are identified, prioritized, and addressed. The process helps protect systems and networks from attacks by ensuring that vulnerabilities are discovered and remediated before they can be exploited by malicious actors. Vulnerability management reduces the risk of data breaches and other security incidents, thereby enhancing an organization's overall security posture.

The first step in vulnerability management is systematically identifying vulnerabilities across all assets through regular scanning and assessments. Using automated tools ensures comprehensive coverage while integrating real-time threat intelligence, which helps recognize emerging vulnerabilities swiftly. A proactive approach is crucial for maintaining a robust defense against potential security breaches.

Vulnerabilities should be prioritized based on the risk they pose to the organization, combined with a contextual analysis that considers the specific business environment. Prioritization helps allocate resources more efficiently and addresses the most critical vulnerabilities first, thereby reducing the potential impact on the organization.

The remediation and mitigation phase involves timely patch management to correct vulnerabilities as soon as they are detected. Implementing compensating controls can provide temporary protection when immediate remediation is not possible. This ensures that vulnerabilities are managed effectively, minimizing the window of opportunity for attackers.

Tools for Assessing Attack Surfaces

Having a strong cybersecurity strategy depends on having effective tools to manage and assess attack surfaces. These tools, ranging from automated scanners to sophisticated threat intelligence platforms, provide the necessary capabilities to detect vulnerabilities, monitor security configurations, and respond to emerging threats. By leveraging these technologies, organizations can systematically identify and address security gaps, enhancing their ability to protect against cyberattacks and maintain robust security across their digital infrastructure. Taking a comprehensive approach ensures that all aspects of the attack surface are continuously monitored and managed to mitigate risks.

Automated scanning tools enable organizations to proactively monitor and identify vulnerabilities across their digital infrastructure. Systematically scanning networks, systems, and web applications means these tools provide a continuous overview of security weaknesses, allowing for swift detection and response. The automation not only streamlines the vulnerability identification process but also ensures that the organization can address security gaps promptly, thereby enhancing its ability to prevent potential cyberthreats and maintain robust defense mechanisms.

Configuration management tools maintain an organization's cybersecurity by actively monitoring and managing the settings of its technology infrastructure. They enforce security configurations, ensuring that all systems adhere strictly to established security protocols. Proactive management helps prevent vulnerabilities that could arise from misconfigured systems and guarantees compliance with security best practices. By maintaining rigorous control over system configurations, these tools significantly reduce the risk of security breaches linked to configuration errors.

Threat intelligence platforms bolster an organization's ability to defend against cyberthreats by providing real-time data about emerging risks. These platforms gather and analyze global security information to deliver relevant and actionable insights. The information enables security teams to understand the landscape of potential threats, anticipate attackers' tactics and strategies, and proactively adjust their defenses accordingly. Organizations can swiftly respond to incidents and strategically prevent breaches by staying informed about the latest threats.

Penetration testing tools help assess the robustness of an organization's security framework. These tools mimic real-world threats, simulating cyberattacks and allowing security teams to uncover and address vulnerabilities before they can be exploited by malicious actors. This process tests the effectiveness of existing security measures and highlights areas where improvements are necessary. The insights gained from these tests enable organizations to strengthen their defenses, making them less susceptible to actual attacks and better prepared to respond to security breaches.

Visualization tools provide detailed maps representing all the organization's assets and security statuses. Offering a comprehensive view, these tools help security teams identify critical vulnerabilities and prioritize their remediation efforts based on their risk level. The ability to visually understand and manage the extent of exposed surfaces improves the strategic planning and implementation of necessary defenses.

Threat Modeling

Threat modeling is a process designed to identify, prioritize, and assess potential threats to a system. It begins with thoroughly understanding a system's architecture to pinpoint and evaluate potential security vulnerabilities. That proactive approach not only aids in planning but also enhances an organization's security posture by anticipating and mitigating vulnerabilities before they are exploited.

As an integral component of developing robust security strategies, threat modeling is routinely applied across various software development and system management stages, ensuring comprehensive protection and preparedness against potential security challenges.

Threat Modeling Informs Risk Management

Threat modeling enables organizations to anticipate potential threats early in system design. Through incorporating security considerations directly into the design phase of projects, vulnerabilities can be addressed from the outset, embedding robust security practices into the system's foundation. This approach enhances overall security and integrates seamlessly into development workflows, ensuring security measures are not an afterthought but a fundamental aspect of system architecture.

In risk management, threat modeling proves invaluable by allowing organizations to prioritize their security resources effectively. It identifies the areas of highest risk, enabling targeted allocation of resources where they are most needed, optimizing security investments, and ensuring cost-effective mitigations. Prioritization is critical for maintaining security standards while managing financial overhead, making threat modeling an essential tool for cost-efficient and impactful security planning.

The iterative nature of threat modeling supports continuous improvement in security strategies. As an ongoing process, it facilitates regular reassessment of threats and adaptation to evolving security landscapes. The iterative process creates a feedback loop, where each cycle of threat modeling informs and enhances subsequent security measures and risk management strategies. By continually refining these practices, organizations can stay ahead of potential threats and adapt to new challenges.

Threat Modeling Methodologies

Threat modeling methodologies integrate into attack surface analysis, providing a systematic approach to identifying, prioritizing, and mitigating potential security threats in various systems. These methodologies simulate attacker behaviors and scrutinize system vulnerabilities to pinpoint security weaknesses, comprehensively evaluating potential threats. By structuring the evaluation process, these methodologies enable organizations to map out their entire attack surface, prioritize risks based on severity, and proactively address security issues before they are exploited, significantly reducing overall risk.

Integrating these methodologies into regular ASA empowers organizations with a deeper understanding of their security vulnerabilities, facilitating a more informed allocation of resources toward the most critical risks. This proactive defense strategy fortifies the security posture and enhances the effectiveness of organizational defenses.

STRIDE

STRIDE (*https://oreil.ly/KJqxQ*) is a comprehensive threat modeling methodology developed by Microsoft, designed to improve the security of software applications and systems, shown in Figure 7-2. By categorizing potential security threats into six distinct types—Spoofing, Tampering, Repudiation, Information Disclosure, Denial of Service, and Elevation of Privilege—STRIDE provides a systematic framework for identifying vulnerabilities. This methodical categorization helps in the detailed assessment of threats and aids in crafting security measures to mitigate them.

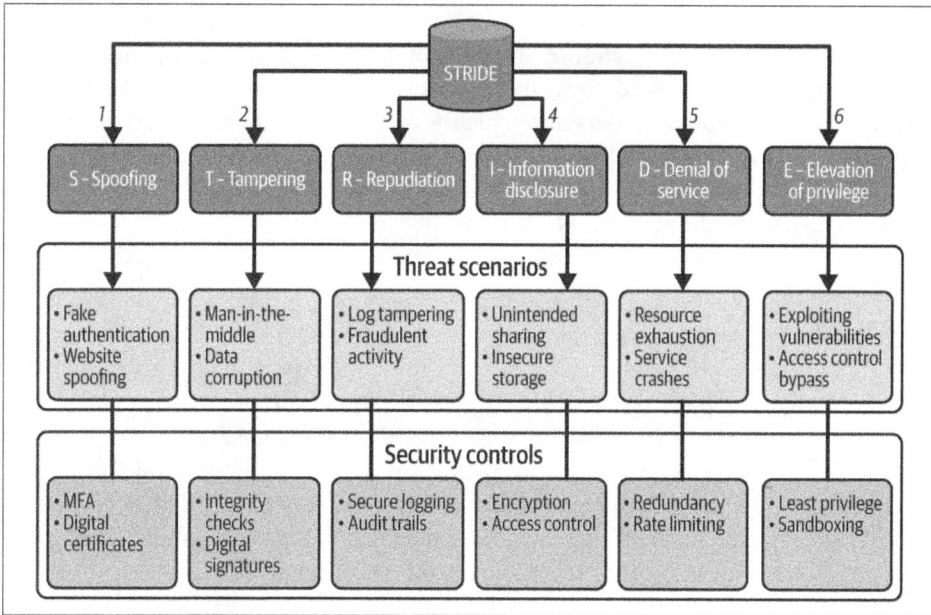

Figure 7-2. *The STRIDE Threat Modeling Framework with corresponding threat scenarios and security controls for each category.*

Utilizing STRIDE allows for systematically evaluating potential security issues, ensuring that each threat category is addressed thoroughly. The methodology is especially beneficial during the early stages of system design, where it can pinpoint vulnerabilities and proactively integrate security solutions. The early integration of security considerations helps to prevent potential exploits. It strengthens the overall security posture of the application or system being developed, making STRIDE an essential tool in the arsenal of developers aiming to fortify their systems against diverse security threats.

DREAD

DREAD (*https://oreil.ly/TemCO*) is a threat modeling methodology, also originally from Microsoft, used to quantify and prioritize the risks associated with potential threats in information systems. The acronym DREAD stands for Damage, Reproducibility, Exploitability, Affected Users, and Discoverability—each component is crucial in assessing how a threat impacts an organization. DREAD helps organizations assign numerical values to threats, making it easier to prioritize which vulnerabilities need immediate attention and resources, and ensuring that efforts are focused effectively to mitigate the most significant risks.

The prioritization process within DREAD is instrumental in helping organizations target their security measures more precisely. By rating each aspect of a threat—from the potential damage it could cause, to how easily it can be replicated or discovered—DREAD guides teams to understand which issues pose the greatest risk and should therefore be addressed first. This structured approach to prioritization ensures that resources are allocated where they are needed most, enhancing the organization's ability to manage and mitigate risks proactively and efficiently.

PASTA

The Process for Attack Simulation and Threat Analysis, or PASTA (*https://oreil.ly/ GZs76*), is a comprehensive threat modeling methodology that systematically identifies and analyzes potential security threats. It employs a seven-step process that meticulously integrates business objectives with technical analysis, from defining business objectives to identifying critical assets and culminating in modeling potential attacks against the security architecture. This method is particularly effective as it considers technical vulnerabilities and aligns the security strategy with business goals, ensuring that the most significant risks to the organization are addressed.

PASTA facilitates a detailed, context-driven security analysis that goes beyond typical threat assessments by focusing on the attacker's perspective and potential attack vectors. Each stage of the PASTA process aims to bridge the gap between business operations and technical security measures, making it invaluable for organizations looking to tailor their security measures to their business needs. The business-centric approach helps prioritize risks more effectively, allowing organizations to allocate resources strategically and enhance their overall security posture.

MITRE ATT&CK

MITRE ATT&CK (*https://oreil.ly/PTuGh*) is a globally accessible knowledge base that captures and organizes observations of real-world adversary tactics and techniques. It provides a comprehensive matrix that details the specific tactics and techniques that cyberthreat actors employ during their operations. This framework helps organizations understand not just the "how" but also the "why" behind cyberattacks, enhancing their ability to develop defense strategies that are finely tuned to counteract specific adversarial behaviors.

With its empirical basis, MITRE utilizes real-world data to model the behavior of cyber adversaries, offering an extensive database that supports defensive planning. This resource is pivotal for security teams aiming to craft effective and informed defense mechanisms. By providing a detailed understanding of potential threat patterns, MITRE helps organizations enhance their detection, prevention, and mitigation strategies, making it an essential tool in the fight against cyberthreats.

While all of this information may appear overwhelming, the next section will help you determine a good fit for your organization.

Which to Use?

Choosing the right threat modeling methodology can be challenging for companies due to each method's diversity and specific focus. STRIDE, DREAD, PASTA, and MITRE ATT&CK all cater to different aspects of cybersecurity, ranging from early design stage threat identification to detailed analysis of adversary tactics. This variety can cause confusion, as organizations must consider their specific security needs, the nature of their digital assets, and their strategic security goals to select the most effective approach. The decision involves balancing thoroughness, resource availability, and the relevance of each methodology to the organization's unique threat landscape. Here's a brief explanation of each with example use cases:

STRIDE

Best utilized in the early stages of software development, STRIDE helps identify potential security threats systematically. This methodology is particularly beneficial for developers intent on embedding security within the architectural design of applications, offering a structured way to foresee and mitigate risks from the outset.

DREAD

This methodology excels in environments where threats must be prioritized and managed based on their potential impact. DREAD evaluates threats based on damage potential and reproducibility, making it ideal for organizations that require a clear prioritization framework to manage and mitigate risks.

PASTA

Tailored for organizations aiming to integrate their security protocols with overarching business objectives, PASTA employs a detailed seven-step process. This approach considers technical threats and aligns them with business impacts, making it particularly effective in complex environments where business continuity is paramount.

MITRE ATT&CK

A comprehensive choice for those looking to enhance their defense against specific adversarial behaviors, the MITRE ATT&CK framework is invaluable for SOCs (Security Operation Centers) and incident response teams. It provides detailed insights into the tactics and techniques used by threat actors, aiding in developing targeted defense strategies tailored to real-world attack patterns.

For a more in-depth breakdown by functionality, take a look at Table 7-1. This table explores each feature of the different threat models for a quick side-by-side comparison and easy reference.

Table 7-1. Brief threat modeling reference

	STRIDE	DREAD	PASTA	MITRE ATT&CK
Purpose	Identify and categorize security threats systematically	Quantify and prioritize risks associated with threats	Analyze and simulate attacks by aligning technical and business objectives	Provide a detailed knowledge base of real-world adversary tactics and techniques
Focus	Threat categorization into six types: Spoofing, Tampering, Repudiation, Information Disclosure, Denial of Service, Elevation of Privilege	Risk prioritization using Damage, Reproducibility, Exploitability, Affected Users, Discoverability	Context-driven analysis considering both business objectives and technical vulnerabilities	Adversary behavior, tactics, techniques, and operations based on empirical data
Methodology	Framework-based, useful in early system design stages for proactive security integration	Numerical scoring system for each aspect of a threat to prioritize mitigation efforts	Seven-step process that bridges business goals with technical security analysis	Knowledge matrix offering actionable insights into adversary behaviors for detection and defense
Advantages	Ensures comprehensive evaluation during system design; mitigates vulnerabilities early	Helps allocate resources effectively to address the most significant risks	Aligns technical security with business needs, prioritizing risks strategically	Empirical, real-world data enhances understanding and preparedness against sophisticated threats
Application	Software applications and systems development	Information systems risk management	Enterprise-level threat modeling with a focus on aligning security with business goals	Defense strategy development, detection improvement, and proactive threat mitigation
Unique feature	Categorization into six distinct threat types for thorough assessment	Risk quantification and prioritization through scoring	Attack simulation integrated with business objectives	Real-world adversary tactics and techniques database with detailed threat patterns and insights

With this quick reference, it should be easy to find a methodology that best aligns with your organization. Take note, though, that there is never a perfect fit, so look for reasonable alignment and don't spend too much time chasing perfection.

Integrating Threat Modeling with Attack Surface Mapping

Attack surface mapping (*https://oreil.ly/wCxIx*) is the process of identifying and cataloging all potential entry points and vulnerabilities across an organization's systems and networks. By creating a detailed "map" of an organization's external-facing assets—such as applications, servers, APIs, and other IT resources—attack surface mapping provides a complete view of where attackers might attempt to gain access. This map includes known assets and potentially hidden or forgotten components, offering a comprehensive snapshot of exposure points.

Attack surface management, on the other hand, is the broader practice that encompasses identifying these assets and vulnerabilities and continuously monitoring and mitigating associated risks. ASM builds on the foundation provided by attack surface mapping by prioritizing vulnerabilities based on risk, assessing changes in the attack surface over time, and enabling timely, strategic responses to new threats. While attack surface mapping gives a static view of exposure, ASM turns this insight into a dynamic, proactive security process that evolves alongside an organization's infrastructure and the threat landscape.

When integrated with threat modeling, which involves analyzing potential attack scenarios and identifying likely targets, attack surface management becomes even more powerful. Together, these processes enable organizations to understand which vulnerabilities are most critical, allowing security resources to be efficiently prioritized. This strategic alignment ensures that defenses are thorough and focused on the highest-risk areas.

Ultimately, combining attack surface mapping with attack surface management and threat modeling creates a proactive security approach. Organizations continuously assess, prioritize, and mitigate risks as their environments and potential threats evolve. This integrated approach maximizes resource efficiency and strengthens the organization's security posture, ensuring that the most impactful defenses are always in place.

How Threat Modeling Improves Attack Surface Management

Threat modeling significantly enhances ASM by providing detailed insights into specific vulnerabilities. This process identifies targeted weaknesses within the attack surface and contextualizes these risks. Threat modeling allows organizations to develop more focused and effective ASM strategies by understanding potential attack paths and their impacts. An in-depth analysis helps to refine and prioritize security efforts, ensuring that resources are allocated to the most critical areas, thus bolstering the organization's overall defense mechanism.

It also boosts the strategic aspects of ASM by facilitating informed security decisions. By identifying and understanding the most critical threats through threat modeling, decision-makers can engage in more strategic planning and prioritization within ASM. Such an approach allows ASM processes to adapt dynamically as new threats emerge and are modeled, ensuring that security measures remain current and effective.

Threat modeling improves ASM's efficiency by streamlining the response to potential threats. Identifying specific threats through detailed analysis, organizations can quickly deploy targeted response strategies, shifting from a reactive to a proactive security posture. Precise identification allows for better resource allocation, focusing efforts on areas of the attack surface that pose the greatest risk.

How ASM Complements Threat Modeling

ASM enhances the threat modeling process by providing a detailed and up-to-date inventory of all organization assets, including internal and external components. The comprehensive coverage allows for a thorough evaluation of vulnerabilities and potential attack vectors.

ASM's capability to offer real-time updates ensures that the data used in threat modeling reflects the most current state of the attack surface, enabling security teams to identify and respond to emerging threats swiftly and accurately.

It also bolsters threat modeling by providing granular and specific details about the attack surface, allowing for targeted threat analysis. The detailed information enables threat modeling to focus precisely on areas most susceptible to attacks.

ASM's detailed mapping of system architecture and connections enriches the context in which threats are assessed, aiding in understanding each threat's potential impact. The integration between ASM and threat modeling facilitates a more nuanced, context-aware risk assessment process.

The synergy between ASM and threat modeling extends into strategic defense alignment. The integration facilitates proactive security planning, allowing for designing and implementing tailored security measures that directly address identified vulnerabilities and threats. Moreover, this alignment optimizes resource allocation, ensuring that security resources are directed toward the areas of highest risk, thereby maximizing the effectiveness of the organization's security efforts.

Summary

As we conclude this chapter on integrating threat modeling with attack surface mapping, it's clear that combining these methodologies not only fortifies an organization's understanding of its security landscape but also sharpens its defensive strategies. That holistic view is crucial for identifying vulnerabilities and planning effective responses ahead of time.

Next, we'll walk through remediation strategies. We will explore how the insights gained from thorough threat modeling and ASM guide the development of remediation efforts to address and mitigate identified risks.

CHAPTER 8

Remediation

In this chapter, we'll discuss remediation. We'll work through the nuanced process of evaluating the security needs of digital assets. Then, we'll look at when to monitor, patch, decommission, or eliminate these assets based on the risks they face, which factors in the severity and potential impact on business operations.

This chapter will cover the importance of validating the effectiveness of remediation actions, maintaining thorough documentation throughout the process, and consistently reporting outcomes. These actions ensure compliance with regulatory requirements and bolster your organization's security posture. Having a clear remediation plan in place also enables informed decision making and strategic adjustments in response to evolving threats.

Assessing the Remediation Need

Before diving into specific remediation actions, it's imperative to first assess the overall need for intervention. Not every vulnerability or security issue requires the same level of response, and determining the right approach hinges on understanding the full scope of potential risks. This process involves evaluating each vulnerability's severity, its potential impact on business operations, and the broader context within the organization's security posture. By carefully assessing the risk, organizations can allocate resources efficiently, avoid unnecessary disruptions, and ensure their security efforts align with their most pressing risks.

Identifying the Severity of Vulnerabilities

Identifying the severity of vulnerabilities within a digital ecosystem is a meticulous process that hinges on a structured vulnerability assessment framework. The process begins with applying the common vulnerability scoring system (CVSS), which provides a standardized severity rating by assessing the vulnerability's fundamental nature and contextual factors such as exploitation complexity and impact. This rating system is further refined through an exploitability analysis, which scrutinizes the technical details of the vulnerability alongside the availability of related exploit codes or kits.

The severity assessment should be adapted to each organization's unique environment. Actual severity is influenced by the specific environmental context of the infrastructure, where existing security controls and compensating measures play into the rating. This ensures the evaluation reflects the organization's unique defenses and vulnerabilities because security is rarely a one-size-fits-all process. Your impact evaluation needs to consider potential business repercussions, ranging from data exposure and service disruption to indirect effects like reputational damage and regulatory consequences.

Historical data also plays a valuable role, providing insights from past incidents to predict possible outcomes and refine the assessments. This historical perspective is complemented by threat intelligence feeds, in which real-time information updates predictions and severity ratings to better reflect the reality of the current threat landscapes. Additionally, input from IT, network security, and application teams further enhances the assessment's accuracy and comprehensiveness.

When determining the appropriate course of action, the availability of patches and other workarounds factor heavily into the decision-making process. For more urgent situations where no patch is available, organizations may have to leverage what is known as compensating controls, which are security controls that help mitigate a specific risk but may not properly eliminate it. They are there to reduce risk until a proper fix can be implemented.

An example would be cutting off network access to a port hosting a vulnerable service. Sometimes, these controls are temporary and can be removed when a patch becomes available. However, in some cases, a proper patch from the manufacturer may never be released, forcing organizations to rely on long-term workarounds. This is common with niche or proprietary systems, such as industrial control systems, which are frequently used to monitor and automate processes across various sectors.

Assessing Potential Impact

Assessing a vulnerability's impact is more than just looking at the CVSS score. While this score is a great starting point for quick-and-dirty evaluation, there is far more at play that needs to be considered.

One of the first areas of consideration is business continuity, which requires a detailed evaluation of the vulnerability's potential to disrupt vital operations. The analysis must understand the direct effects on core services and extend to dependent systems, which may also be impacted, potentially leading to broader operational challenges. The duration and extent of these disruptions are important information for preparing mitigation strategies.

Financial consequences are a significant area of impact in vulnerability assessments. Estimates should include potential losses from operational downtime, incident response costs, and possible regulatory fines. Financial assessment aids in prioritizing vulnerabilities based on their economic impact, guiding resource allocation to areas posing the highest risk to revenue.

However, the scope of vulnerability impact extends beyond financial costs. Remediation efforts require the allocation of personnel, time, and technology, and companies should consider how diverting these resources might affect other projects or operational capabilities. Effective resource management ensures these allocations do not jeopardize other vital business functions, sustaining operations while addressing cybersecurity risks.

Data security and privacy concerns add another wrinkle to assessing a vulnerability's impact. Analyzing the types of data at risk can affect the overall impact, especially when sensitive information, including personal, financial, or confidential data, could be exposed. Each comes with unique consequences due to unauthorized access or loss. These impacts may be as simple as undermining the reliability of data analytics and decision-making processes or as complex as impacting regulatory compliance. While the former may damage decision making, the latter can rapidly escalate to legal penalties and fines.

No matter the data, any vulnerability leading to a breach may require disclosure, which will inevitably damage customer trust and market positioning. While those impacts are less easily quantified than potential fines, they are no less damaging. The loss of consumer confidence is often long-lasting, affecting business sustainability and growth.

The technical and infrastructural impacts of vulnerabilities also require thorough evaluation. Assessing how a vulnerability might serve as a gateway for further compromises is valuable for understanding the full scope of the potential impact. Doing so involves analyzing the potential for vulnerabilities to allow unauthorized access or escalate in severity, which could compromise broader network aspects.

As part of the evaluation, organizations must consider the vulnerability risk leading to attacks that could propagate across the network. Some vulnerabilities may impact a single system, while others allow a level of access that attackers can use to pivot to other interconnected devices. This is where understanding how a given vulnerability is used and how different devices are interconnected comes into play. Highly connected systems or vulnerabilities that can rapidly escalate—such as remote code execution (RCE) (*https://oreil.ly/KB-Ad*), which allows attackers to run arbitrary code on remote systems—may require prioritization, even on less critical assets.

The impact on stakeholders, including customers and business partners, must be considered by evaluating how security issues and their remediation affect user experiences. This includes potential service disruptions that could affect customer interaction and loyalty.

Only by holistically examining all these factors can a true impact be determined. While simpler methods may be reasonable for an estimate, failing to consider the deeper impact may leave organizations remediating issues that appear to be more impactful but, in reality, do little to reduce the attack surface or overall risk.

Cost-Benefit Analysis of Remediation

Conducting a cost-benefit analysis of remediation begins with calculating the direct costs involved, such as the expenses for labor, necessary technology solutions, and any third-party services required to address the vulnerabilities.

Assessing the costs for essential tools and resources needed for patching, software updates, and system modifications is integral for an accurate cost-benefit analysis. Beyond the immediate financial outlay, evaluating the opportunity costs, such as the potential loss of productivity or the diversion of resources from other important projects, is also important. These opportunity costs must be weighed against the overall business objectives to ensure that remediation efforts align with long-term strategic goals.

The primary benefit of remediation is risk reduction, which directly translates into financial and operational stability. By addressing vulnerabilities effectively, organizations minimize the risk of data breaches, system downtime, and compliance violations, which can lead to costly penalties and disruptions.

Beyond immediate risk mitigation, remediation efforts yield long-term savings by reducing incident response costs and preventing operational setbacks. A proactive approach safeguards resources and strengthens an organization's overall security posture. Maintaining a strong remediation strategy also enhances customer trust, protects reputational integrity, and ensures compliance with industry regulations.

Decision-making criteria are pivotal for determining financial viability and understanding the broader impacts of remediation efforts. Conducting a break-even analysis (*https://oreil.ly/XF_8g*) allows organizations to pinpoint when the ensuing benefits will balance remediation costs. The analysis offers stakeholders a clear financial perspective, aiding in strategic planning and resource allocation.

Calculating the ROI further refines this approach by comparing the costs of remediation against the financial losses potentially avoided by preventing future security incidents and breaches. This metric is an integral factor in justifying investments in cybersecurity and showcasing how proactive measures can lead to significant financial savings over time.

Beyond quantitative measures, qualitative factors play a pivotal role in shaping cybersecurity strategies. Enhancements in employee morale stemming from a secure working environment and the potential for innovation through adopting advanced security technologies contribute to a robust security posture. Although less tangible, these factors significantly influence organizational culture and innovation capacity.

How remediation actions are prioritized should be strategically based on a detailed cost-benefit analysis to ensure that resources are directed first toward vulnerabilities that, once mitigated, yield the most significant reduction in risk relative to their remediation costs. Such prioritization improves the efficiency of security efforts and the robustness of defense against the most potentially damaging threats.

Aligning these remediation efforts with the organization's strategic business objectives ensures that every security investment directly contributes to the broader company goals. Strategic alignment helps create a resilient cybersecurity framework that supports and protects core business activities, ensuring that security measures are reactive and proactive components of the organization's overall strategy. Alignment helps maintain operational continuity and achieve long-term security objectives.

Prioritization of Findings

Prioritizing findings in cybersecurity is where we start moving from an overwhelming pile of problems to determining which ones matter, as not every vulnerability poses the same threat level. With ASM, we continuously reevaluate the risk to optimize security outcomes, including everything from maximizing resource allocation to closing the vulnerabilities attackers are most likely to exploit first.

Ease of Exploitation

When examining cybersecurity vulnerabilities, it helps to start by considering the CVEs framework. CVEs serve as standardized identifiers for security vulnerabilities, which are helpful for identifying, tracking, and resolving threats across platforms. The direct correlation between the severity of CVEs and their exploitability informs the potential impact on an organization, necessitating rigorous assessment and management to mitigate risks effectively.

Assessing a CVE's exploitability often involves metrics from the CVSS, which quantifies how easily a vulnerability can be exploited based on several factors, including its potential impact and the ease of exploitation.

However, the actual ease of exploitation is not just a high, medium, or low; it has a variety of considerations, looking at what level of access is necessary, such as whether an attack can be done remotely or requires physical access. It also includes conditions like the attack complexity, whether it requires existing privileges, or whether it requires user interaction to be successful. Take a look at the chart in Figure 8-1 for a sample of the factors used in generating a CVSS score.

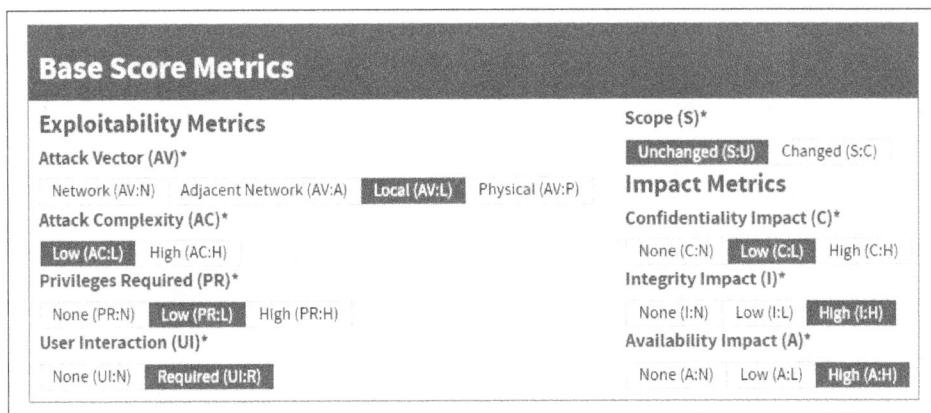

Base Score Metrics

Exploitability Metrics

Attack Vector (AV)*

Network (AV:N) Adjacent Network (AV:A) Local (AV:L) Physical (AV:P)

Attack Complexity (AC)*

Low (AC:L) High (AC:H)

Privileges Required (PR)*

None (PR:N) Low (PR:L) High (PR:H)

User Interaction (UI)*

None (UI:N) Required (UI:R)

Scope (S)*

Unchanged (S:U) Changed (S:C)

Impact Metrics

Confidentiality Impact (C)*

None (C:N) Low (C:L) High (C:H)

Integrity Impact (I)*

None (I:N) Low (I:L) High (I:H)

Availability Impact (A)*

None (A:N) Low (A:L) High (A:H)

Figure 8-1. A sample of factors for a CVSS score.

Considering all of these factors cumulatively generates a score, creating a relatively quick way to evaluate vulnerabilities in relation to one another.

While it's easy to prioritize vulnerabilities that are hard to execute with low impact and those that are easy to execute remotely and have high impact, the middle starts to get more challenging. In this middle range, CVSS scores can be similar but differ strongly on either ease of attack or final impact, making it hard to decide on score alone what should be prioritized.

The impact of a CVE can also vary significantly based on an organization's specific environment and the critical systems affected. The CVSS score generated and listed in a CVE is generic. Updating it for a given environment makes it more accurate but also adds to the workload.

Publicly known exploits also play into this equation. These are vulnerabilities exposed to the general public, often through exploit kits that are widely disseminated on the dark web. The availability of such exploit kits significantly raises the likelihood of cybercriminals actively targeting affected vulnerabilities. Public awareness and kit availability alter the cyberthreat landscape and drive the prevalence of attack types, such as ransomware, which is often a payload of such attacks. When exploits are known publicly, and there is proof of concept code—often termed as "in the wild"—organizations must dramatically increase the prioritization and remediation of these vulnerabilities. If remediation isn't possible for some reason, at the very least, monitoring should be increased until remediation can be accomplished.

When planning prioritization, the availability of a patch greatly influences the urgency of remediation efforts. A vulnerability with a readily available patch may be addressed more swiftly to prevent exploitation, whereas those without may require more strategic and resource-intensive approaches to mitigate risks.

For ASM, managing and tracking vulnerabilities is not a one-time effort but a continuous life cycle. It is necessary to ensure they are identified and assessed, and that remediation efforts are implemented, updated, and adjusted in line with evolving threats and organizational priorities. By constantly assessing, prioritizing, and remediating based on organizational-specific factors and not just the CVSS score, the actual attack surface can be effectively reduced without spending all existing resources chasing down every discovered vulnerability.

Discoverability

Another factor to consider in remediation is discoverability, which is how easily potential attackers can detect or identify valuable assets within a network. High discoverability increases the attack surface, especially in cloud environments where assets like servers, applications, and databases may be publicly accessible. Exposure is exacerbated by common cloud-specific issues, such as misconfigured storage buckets or exposed APIs, which attackers can easily exploit.

Strategies such as using data security posture management (DSPM) tools to detect misconfigurations or implementing data detection and response to identify data exposure help mitigate these misconfiguration risks. Regular security audits, API scanning, and penetration tests are recommended to assess and reduce the visibility of exposed attack surfaces such as APIs. These measures help identify exposed services and entry points, enabling organizations to implement corrective actions promptly to reduce their attack surface.

Internal accessibility is another factor to consider when determining vulnerability exposure. To accomplish their jobs, users need access to network resources and data, but the number of hurdles between them and accessing all data in an organization helps to determine the risk of vulnerabilities exposing data in an incident. Access controls, such as RBAC and advanced authentication technologies, help limit the scope of what users can access, but they also add friction to doing their jobs.

When we look at a vulnerability's discoverability factor, this information helps determine its real impact. For organizations with more access control mechanisms and better segmentation, the true impact of a vulnerability may be far more limited than that of an organization where every user can access every resource. While access controls might seem like common sense, small and medium enterprises generally have very few access controls outside of basic authentication, leaving them in situations like those we just described.

Regular audits help determine the level of accessibility, ensure access rights are appropriate, and detect any security lapses or misuse of access privileges. Moreover, employing strategies like network segmentation, such as virtual private clouds and isolation, helps limit access to sensitive areas of the network, significantly reducing the potential for internal threats.

Attacker Priority

The attractiveness of a target in cybersecurity depends on several factors. One is the value of data, such as financial or personal information, which has a direct value for resale and is used by attackers for extortion. They may threaten to release the information publicly if a fee is not paid, harming the organization's reputation or causing regulatory issues when the exposure becomes public.

Attackers know this and will often consider whether an entity is regulated as a factor for attack. For highly regulated organizations, attackers know there is more value in the data, but there are also likely to be stronger controls, making it harder to access. They often assume that less regulated sectors may have lower defenses, making it easier to pull off a successful attack. The reward may not be as lucrative, but almost every organization has some data worth targeting.

Geopolitical influences also significantly shape the cybersecurity landscape, affecting how and where attacks are most likely. International and political contexts can drive attackers to focus on specific regions or industries, underscoring the importance of understanding broader influences to implement proactive and informed cybersecurity strategies.

Attackers consider existing vulnerabilities and the ease of access to a network or physical locations. Much of this information can be ascertained remotely via vulnerability scans or online research using tools like Shodan or even simple Google searching. These discoverable security gaps make specific targets more appealing to cybercriminals, giving them exploitable paths to create a plan to use well before an attack starts.

A company's visibility and reputation can also attract unwanted attention from cybercriminals, making high-profile organizations more likely targets. These elements encompass everything from how the organization treats its employees to its operations and rankings relative to its peers. For larger cybercriminal groups, a high-profile attack against a well-known company like Microsoft can help them make a name for themselves in the community.

Reputation goes well beyond this and includes historical security incidents, especially well-publicized ones. Previous breaches at a company highlight existing weaknesses that may still be exploitable, increasing the target's risk profile. Even if the published weakness is eliminated, a previous breach indicates earlier lapses in security posture, which may still occur in other areas, increasing the likelihood of a successful attack.

Attackers are not the only ones who can benefit from this data. Historical trends provide valuable insights into the evolution of threat vectors and attackers' preferences, highlighting the significance of trend awareness and analysis. Past security incidents reveal preferred attack methods and frequently targeted systems that can inform future security needs.

Threat Intelligence

While the past is useful for guiding future efforts, knowing what attackers are actively up to is valuable too. Threat intelligence offers strategic insights that guide the development of defense strategies and preparations using intelligence on cybercriminals. By understanding the tactics, techniques, and procedures employed by attackers, organizations can tailor their security measures to counter potential threats. The relevance of intelligence is maximized when it is specifically adapted to meet the unique needs and profiles of individual organizations.

Integrating threat intelligence into operational security workflows is imperative for maintaining a proactive defense posture. Real-time updates from intelligence feeds enable organizations to react swiftly to emerging threats, enhancing their ability to preempt attacks. The seamless incorporation of intelligence into daily security operations helps improve the detection and prioritization of threats, making security responses more timely and effective.

By participating in intelligence-sharing networks, such as ISACs (*https://oreil.ly/iRoaP*) and ISAOs (*https://oreil.ly/N4CLP*), organizations contribute to and benefit from a collective community defense strategy. This collaboration allows for a broader understanding of the threat landscape, as shared intelligence amplifies each participant's ability to detect and respond to threats.

Remediation Complexity

Addressing the complexity of remediation involves a thorough evaluation and management of the required resources, factoring in the complexity of the vulnerabilities and the scope of remediation efforts. Organizations must assess the resources needed, such as labor, technology, and time, while also considering their direct and indirect costs, like potential downtime and productivity impacts.

Another aspect that needs careful consideration is the operational impact of remediation. Downtime or degraded performance during remediation can significantly affect business operations. Therefore, it is crucial to prioritize remediation efforts based on resource availability and the critical nature of the vulnerabilities, minimizing the operational impact and enhancing the resilience of business functions.

Strategic planning for remediation extends beyond immediate needs to include long-term resource planning and budgeting. This forward-looking approach is essential for sustainable cybersecurity management, allowing organizations to anticipate future remediation challenges and allocate resources accordingly. Effective long-term planning ensures that organizations are prepared to address vulnerabilities proactively and maintain defenses as part of their overall business strategy.

Distinguishing between temporary and long-term fixes is imperative for effective vulnerability management. Temporary fixes are often quickly implemented to mitigate immediate risks and maintain operational continuity. They are key when an immediate threat presents itself and there isn't enough time to develop a more permanent solution. However, these fixes might not address the underlying issues, making long-term solutions essential. Long-term fixes, though, typically involve more comprehensive system changes and are aimed at permanently eliminating vulnerabilities.

Strategically implementing these fixes takes planning to ensure temporary solutions transition smoothly into permanent improvements without compromising system security. This transition strategy maintains the integrity of cybersecurity defenses and ensures that the fixes are sustainable over time. The process requires a thorough understanding of the system architecture and the specific vulnerabilities to ensure the final solutions are robust and effective.

The decision-making process for implementing these fixes involves a detailed cost-benefit analysis, where the costs of quick fixes are weighed against the benefits of more durable solutions. Such analysis considers the resources available, the potential risks associated with delayed action, and the overall impact on the organization's cybersecurity posture. Making informed decisions based on this analysis ensures that resources are well utilized, aligning short-term responses with long-term security goals and overall business objectives.

Compensating controls are an alternative solution in risk management, especially when standard remediation approaches are not feasible. These controls are security measures implemented to manage organizational risk levels effectively. By offering practical examples, such as additional monitoring or enhanced access restrictions, compensating controls allow organizations to maintain security standards even when direct fixes are not immediately achievable.

Operational considerations for compensating controls should help thoroughly evaluate their adequacy and the specific criteria for their implementation. These controls must also be installed, monitored, and adjusted as necessary. Ongoing vigilance helps maintain their effectiveness over time and can be adapted to new threats and changes within the organization's IT environment.

The resource implications of compensating controls can be significant, especially in cost and long-term resource allocation. Organizations must consider the financial impact of these controls, which often require investment in new technologies or processes and may even necessitate increased operational spending. Balancing these costs with the benefits they bring must be considered when justifying their use and ensuring they contribute positively to the organization's overall security posture.

Remediation Strategies

Now that we've explored how to assess vulnerabilities, prioritize risks, and consider the complexity of remediation, it's time to dive into the actual strategies for addressing these issues. Remediation strategies might be proactive or reactive, tailored to an organization's specific needs and security posture. Oftentimes, a balanced combination of both offers the best coverage.

In this section, we'll outline proactive measures, like patch management and asset decommissioning, and reactive strategies for containing threats once they've emerged. Balancing these two approaches ensures a comprehensive defense, providing the flexibility to prevent incidents and respond effectively when they occur.

Proactive remediation

Proactive remediation, specifically through patching, is crucial in cybersecurity management (see Figure 8-2). Identifying the correct patches is essential for addressing specific vulnerabilities that affect systems. Utilizing automated patch management tools can improve the efficiency of tracking and applying these patches. Testing the patches in isolated or staging environments should happen before deployment, since this step helps prevent unexpected disruptions in production systems and allows for identifying any issues with patch compatibility or functionality.

Once patches are deemed safe for production, the next step is rollout and ongoing monitoring. Employing phased deployment schedules can help manage risks associated with the patching process. After deployment, continuous monitoring ensures no unanticipated adverse effects occur from the patches and confirms that they mitigate the identified vulnerabilities. An incremental approach keeps the system secure and functional, maintaining operational integrity, while continuous monitoring validates that the solution minimizes potential risks associated with vulnerability exploitation.

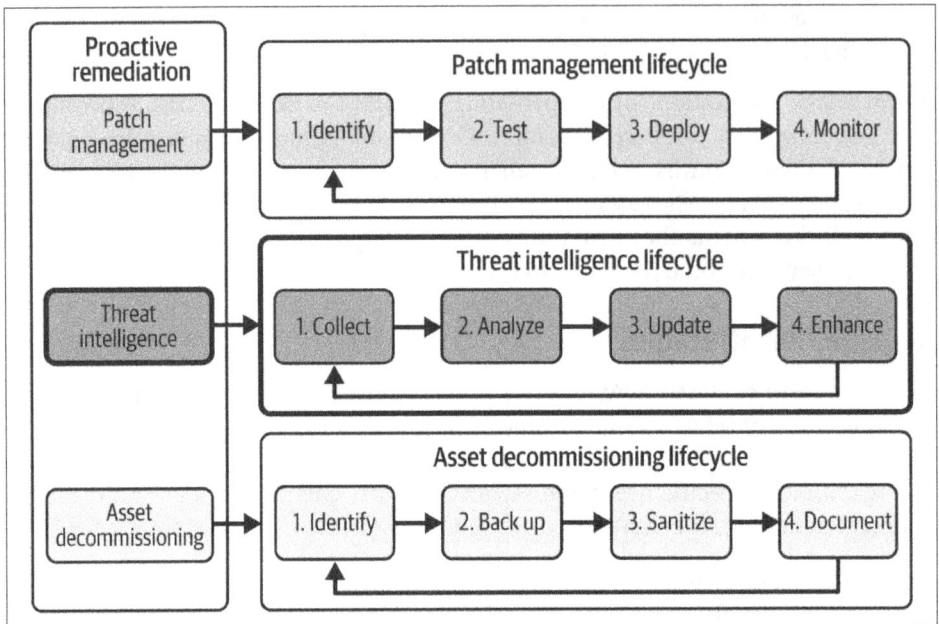

Figure 8-2. *The three pillars of proactive remediation: patch management, threat intelligence, and asset decommissioning. Each operates as continuous cycles rather than one-time actions, ensuring sustained security improvement.*

Threat intelligence is one of the most important proactive measures. It provides data on real-world attacks, both past and current, on other organizations. Some advanced solutions even offer predictive threat intelligence. Integrating threat intelligence into your cybersecurity strategies helps anticipate and mitigate attacks. Security teams can identify threat vectors by better understanding the threat landscape specific to their organization's industry and technology.

Utilizing this data allows for predicting future attacks and facilitates proactive security planning. This informed approach not only shapes the development of better security policies and stronger architectures but also enhances incident response capabilities.

Proactively tackling asset decommissioning reduces attack surfaces by eliminating legacy assets, many of which go unmonitored or unmaintained. These assets include everything from the physical hardware used to digital assets such as user accounts and data. The process should start during the initial identifying and classifying phases of ASM, which involves assessing, identifying, and determining which assets should be decommissioned, prioritizing them based on security risks and redundancy. It's important to ensure that decommissioning is conducted securely, preserving data integrity and adhering to compliance requirements.

The process of asset decommissioning should also address both environmental and legal considerations, which include understanding and complying with legal requirements related to asset disposal and data protection laws. Doing so may consist of retaining certain data for a specified time period, scrubbing and rewriting storage with random data to eliminate the possibility of it being recovered, or physically destroying assets that no longer function properly because they cannot be sanitized.

Failing to properly decommission assets may create an unexpected attack surface from dumpster divers who scavenge old hardware for reuse and may stumble upon sensitive data that is left behind.

Reactive remediation

Reactive remediation addresses containing and isolating threats once they're identified, which may be post-incident. An in-depth incident response plan really shines when the rubber hits the road for an incident. It makes the difference between being able to shut off selective parts of the network and isolate the problem, and having an organization-wide breakdown where the threat is ubiquitous and everything needs to be turned off.

Incident response plans outline the processes that an organization will leverage to recover from or mitigate an attack. An in-depth plan includes clear roles and responsibilities, predefined communication protocols, and detailed procedures for containment, eradication, and recovery. It also incorporates threat intelligence, forensic analysis, and lessons learned to continuously improve security posture. Regular testing and simulations ensure that the response team is well-prepared to act swiftly and effectively, minimizing the impact of security breaches while maintaining business continuity.

The processes in an incident response plan often involve segmenting vulnerable assets within the network—such areas are isolated to prevent the spread of attacks and limit the exposure of critical assets. Implementing virtual local area networks and other network tools helps physically and logically separate sensitive information from general network traffic.

Access controls and firewalls are also used to restrict unauthorized access to networked resources while allowing for dynamic responses to emerging threats. Firewalls serve not only to block unauthorized access but also to monitor and log traffic, which is crucial for forensic analysis in the aftermath of a security breach. This ensures that any malicious activity is contained and analyzed for further security enhancement.

Networks are no longer restricted to on-premises, where firewalls are effective, but extend to SaaS and other cloud services. Much of the reactive security in this area relies on the alerts and analytics collected to drive the incident response. Security alerts help notify administrators of potential attacks, often feeding into security information and event management for amalgamating data for real-time monitoring or intrusion detection systems to actively prevent attacks.

Moreover, the effectiveness of reactive remediation depends on the periodic review of isolated assets. Regular audits are necessary to ensure the isolated segments are secure and the security measures are not compromised. Continuous monitoring technologies are key to the integrity of these defenses, swiftly detecting and addressing any attempts to breach the segregated systems.

Balancing proactive and reactive

Proactive and reactive control provide comprehensive protection across different stages of security management. Proactive controls aim to prevent security incidents before they occur by identifying and mitigating potential vulnerabilities. Examples include regular updates, threat intelligence, predictive analytics, tools like DSPM, and preventive measures like firewalls and encryption. Reactive controls, on the other hand, are designed to respond effectively after an incident has occurred. They include incident response plans, detection and response tools, forensic tools, and systems that help restore operations quickly.

Combining both types of controls ensures an organization is well-prepared to prevent and respond to threats. Monitoring and logging are two areas that work in both the proactive and reactive contexts. Continuous monitoring and logging help detect anomalies early, preventing incidents and refining security measures. By analyzing unusual behavior and trends in network activities, security teams can swiftly react to potential threats, enhancing the overall security posture by updating defense mechanisms accordingly.

Once a breach occurs, logs provide a detailed account of the events, helping to understand the sequence of events, scope of impact, and source of the attack. This detailed documentation supports thorough forensic analysis and serves as critical evidence for compliance with regulations and legal proceedings, ensuring that the organization can adequately respond to and recover from security incidents.

With integrated monitoring and logging strategies, organizations can detect and respond to threats promptly and maintain and improve their security infrastructure based on insights gained from logged data. This dual approach helps continuously safeguard sensitive information and system integrity.

Validation of Remediation Efforts

After implementing remediation actions, the next step is checking that those efforts have been successful and that no new vulnerabilities were introduced during the process. Validation confirms that the remediation strategies were effective, and helps maintain the integrity of the system going forward. Validation includes key practices like retesting for vulnerabilities, continuous monitoring, and creating feedback loops so that remediation efforts align with both security goals and strategic business objectives. Proper validation reinforces security improvements and provides valuable insights for future remediation planning.

Ongoing evaluation involves using sophisticated tools and techniques, such as automated vulnerability scanning, dynamic and static analysis, and penetration testing, all of which should be seamlessly integrated into the software development life cycle. These methods help confirm that identified vulnerabilities have been addressed while proactively detecting new security risks.

The integration into development cycles ensures that modifications or updates are consistently tested, maintaining system integrity and security post-remediation. Such practices help identify residual risks or emerging vulnerabilities, allowing for timely adjustments.

Communication and documentation form the backbone of retesting processes. Transparent communication with stakeholders about retesting outcomes is essential for maintaining trust and ensuring all parties are informed of the ongoing security needs. The documentation records the security posture over time, supports compliance, and aids in refining future remediation efforts, enhancing the overall security framework. We'll cover this in more detail next.

Feedback Loop with Stakeholders

Establishing a feedback loop with stakeholders helps align remediation efforts with security and business objectives. This process calls for continuous engagement with diverse stakeholders, including technical teams, management, and possibly affected customers, to gather comprehensive insights on the impact of remediation efforts. Such feedback is crucial for understanding security measures' efficacy and alignment with business goals.

Operational mechanisms for gathering feedback include structured surveys, direct communications, and regular meetings, which allow stakeholders to provide detailed input on their observations and concerns. The feedback is then analyzed to inform continuous improvements in security practices, so that remediation efforts are responsive to the dynamic nature of cybersecurity threats and business needs.

Moreover, thorough documentation and transparent communication are fundamental to the success of these feedback loops. Maintaining detailed records of feedback and the responses to it helps all involved parties stay well informed about the ongoing remediation processes and outcomes. Ongoing documentation supports accountability and aids in refining future strategies, keeping all stakeholders engaged and aware of the evolving security landscape.

Monitoring for Unexpected Issues or Collateral Damage

Continued monitoring post-remediation is critical to ensure that the remediation actions haven't introduced new vulnerabilities or caused unintended side effects, such as operational disruptions or negative impacts on user experience. By leveraging advanced monitoring tools and techniques—such as real-time log analysis, anomaly detection, behavioral analytics, and automated threat intelligence—organizations can continuously track system performance and security changes. These capabilities enable the early detection of suspicious activity, misconfigurations, or potential breaches, allowing for swift responses such as automated alerts, incident containment, or system rollbacks to mitigate risks before they escalate.

Such ongoing monitoring is not just about problem detection; it is fundamental in improving security practices. Regular reviews of the effectiveness of remediation actions contribute to a cycle of continuous enhancement, ensuring that security measures evolve in line with emerging threats and the changing landscape of the organization's infrastructure. This approach reinforces the overall resilience of the security system, minimizing future risks and optimizing remediation strategies over time.

Documentation and Reporting

Effective remediation extends beyond fixing vulnerabilities; it also requires thorough documentation and reporting. These practices ensure accountability, provide evidence for compliance, and facilitate continuous improvement. Proper documentation helps track progress, measure the effectiveness of security efforts, and align them with broader organizational goals. Let's explore how to create comprehensive remediation reports, document changes and updates, and communicate the outcomes to key stakeholders.

Creating a remediation report

A comprehensive remediation report documents the process of addressing vulnerabilities within an organization. It should provide a clear and detailed record of identified vulnerabilities, the remediation actions taken, and the outcomes of these efforts. It's crucial to tailor the report to the needs of its intended audience, which could range from internal stakeholders like management and IT teams to external entities like auditors and regulatory agencies. Doing so means the information will be relevant and actionable, facilitating better decision making and compliance with organizational and regulatory standards.

The key components of a remediation report should be:

- Summary of the issue
- Detailed description of the remediation process

- Evidence of the remediation's effectiveness
- Any unresolved issues

To create a comprehensive report, timelines, affected assets, and resources utilized throughout the process must be included. This documentation offers a transparent view of efforts and resource allocation, enabling strategic insight for managing future risks.

The report should also outline follow-up actions and recommendations to mitigate ongoing vulnerabilities and prevent future issues. Strategic insights from these outcomes can guide future security policies and enhance the organization's security posture.

Using best practices—like clear language, data accuracy, and standardized templates—supports consistent, streamlined reporting that maintains document integrity and improves efficiency across reporting efforts.

Documenting changes and updates

Maintaining accountability and creating a transparent audit trail requires clear and detailed documentation of changes and updates to the remediation process. This documentation not only aids internal oversight but also supports compliance with regulatory requirements, simplifying both internal and external audits. Organizations provide clear evidence of their compliance and decision-making process by recording each modification—what was changed, why it was necessary, who approved and executed it, and the timing.

Including updates to policies, procedures, or configurations resulting from these changes further helps all adjustments be traceable and consistently aligned with organizational standards. Documenting these updates enables good security protocol management and reinforces that each modification is integrated into operational practices.

Documentation should be continuously updated to capture new changes and findings from ongoing security assessments, helping to improve the organization's security posture over time. To support this, organizations can leverage change management tools and integrated IT management platforms.

Standardized templates and best practices keep consistency across all documentation while safeguarding against unauthorized access. These strategies improve the reliability and accessibility of documentation, making the process more effective and aligned with evolving security requirements.

Reporting to leadership and relevant teams

Organizations should assess their specific reporting requirements—whether executives need concise summaries with key takeaways and visual aids or technical leaders require in-depth analysis with detailed findings and appendices. Understanding these preferences helps reports provide the right level of insight to the right stakeholders. These reports should not be a "one and done" scenario but should be updated regularly with ad hoc reports prepared after major incidents or significant changes in the security landscape.

Visual aids like charts and graphs enhance accessibility, especially for nontechnical stakeholders, helping illustrate complex data clearly. Automating the reporting process or creating dashboards can streamline distribution and improve consistency while soliciting feedback, which ensures the reports evolve to meet organizational needs and support an ongoing security dialogue.

Summary

As we've explored in this chapter, effective remediation is not a single action but a comprehensive process involving careful assessment, targeted strategies, continuous validation, and thorough documentation. Each step, from identifying vulnerabilities to validating remediation efforts, builds a resilient security posture by ensuring that responses are precise, efficient, and aligned with business priorities. By integrating proactive and reactive approaches, organizations can reduce their attack surface while strengthening defenses against evolving threats.

With a solid understanding of remediation strategies, the next step is to minimize attack surfaces through strategic and tactical techniques. The next chapter will guide you through the specific methods—such as network segmentation, vulnerability management, and endpoint controls—that further refine and protect an organization's infrastructure. Combining these tactical actions with overarching security strategies will help organizations achieve a balanced, layered defense that is robust, adaptable, and prepared for the challenges of the modern cyber landscape.

PART IV

Adapting and Monitoring

Now that we've explored identification, classification, prioritization, and remediation, it's time to focus on the continuous process of adapting and monitoring. Security isn't static. Attackers evolve, new technologies introduce fresh vulnerabilities, and organizational changes shift risk landscapes. That's why ongoing monitoring and adaptation are essential to maintaining a strong security posture.

This section will explore how organizations can stay ahead of threats through continuous monitoring, automated detection, and adaptive security strategies. We'll examine how technological shifts—like cloud expansion, IoT adoption, and AI-driven threats—affect attack surfaces and demand new approaches to visibility and defense. You'll learn how to fine-tune alert thresholds, reduce false positives, and integrate monitoring with incident response for faster, more effective remediation.

But monitoring alone isn't enough. True security resilience requires adaptability. We'll discuss how feedback loops, periodic audits, and real-world incident analysis help refine security strategies over time. You'll see how automation and AI enhance threat detection while balancing the need for human oversight to prevent blind spots and biases.

By the end of Part IV, you'll understand how proactive adaptation and real-time monitoring transform ASM from a reactive process into a dynamic security advantage. Whether your focus is on streamlining operations, improving detection accuracy, or integrating AI into security workflows, this section will help you build a monitoring strategy that evolves alongside your organization's needs. Let's dive in!

CHAPTER 9

Minimizing Attack Surfaces

Minimizing attack surfaces takes a combination of strategic and tactical approaches. Strategic methods are broad and long term, setting the foundational security policies and frameworks. Tactical approaches are not as broad; they rely on smaller, more tangible steps that can be accomplished in a shorter duration. By tailoring them to the organization's available resources and requirements, tactics allow strategies to be implemented over time in manageable chunks. Both approaches offer unique benefits: strategic methods provide a comprehensive, future-forward security vision, while tactical approaches allow quick responses to immediate issues.

Each approach plays an important role in creating a holistic, resilient security posture. Which approach is used for a given situation depends. Rather than existing in isolation, strategic and tactical approaches often intersect in meaningful ways. For example, a live cyberattack may demand an immediate tactical response, such as isolating compromised systems. Still, the effectiveness of that response often depends on whether strategic foundations like incident response protocols, access controls, and network segmentation are already in place. This way, strategy sets the stage, while tactics bring it to life under pressure.

As always, the unique business needs, organizational security goals, and details of the situation will determine which is best. Generally, integrating strategic and tactical approaches is the best way to build a well-rounded and resilient security strategy.

How to Minimize Attack Surfaces

When defining your attack surface management strategy, it's important to consider both long-term and short-term goals. Tackling everything at once may not be possible, but each approach informs the other, and both are necessary.

Strategic cybersecurity methods set the vision and direction for security initiatives, including policies, compliance standards, and risk management strategies. These provide the foundational guidelines and objectives that shape the organizational security landscape, ensuring that all security efforts are aligned with the broader business objectives.

Tactical techniques, on the other hand, operate within the framework established by the overarching strategy, focusing on deploying specific tools and courses of action such as firewalls, encryption, a cloud access security broker (CASB), antivirus software, patch management, and incident response. Tactical measures are critical in the day-to-day maintenance of an organization's security posture, swiftly addressing emerging threats and vulnerabilities to prevent potential accidental data exposures and security breaches.

Strategic Methods

Strategic methods focus on reducing the organization's overall attack surface by implementing security improvements across multiple assets and infrastructure areas. This organization-wide focus allows these methods to address the interconnectivity of various assets, ensuring that security enhancements are consistently applied where vulnerabilities may overlap.

Strategic methods often involve high-level security policies, continuous monitoring, and access management systems that enforce a unified standard across different departments and infrastructure segments. By addressing multiple areas simultaneously, they reduce exposure points and create layered defenses that increase resilience against diverse threats.

Defense-in-depth

Defense-in-depth strategies utilize a layered security approach to provide comprehensive protection across various levels of an IT environment, effectively guarding against external and internal threats. This method ensures that even if one layer is compromised, additional layers of security will protect the organization. Tailoring these security layers to address specific vulnerabilities within different network segments enhances protection by focusing on areas with distinct security needs. Customization allows organizations to fortify their defenses against targeted attacks and adapt to the unique challenges of each segment of their network infrastructure.

Implementing multilayered defenses augments organizational security in many ways. By establishing multiple safeguards at various levels of the IT infrastructure, you not only strengthen the security barrier but also ensure that no single point of failure can compromise the entire system. The comprehensive coverage spans from perimeter defenses like firewalls to application-level measures such as antimalware systems and data encryption, ensuring that all aspects of the network are secured against a wide array of threats.

The resilience offered by a multilayered strategy is particularly valuable. With multiple defensive layers in place, the failure of one security measure does not leave the entire system vulnerable. Instead, other layers of security continue to operate, maintaining protection against breaches and reducing the impact of any single compromised element. The redundancy helps maintain continuous security operations and safeguard sensitive data and systems from advanced persistent threats that exploit single-point weaknesses.

The redundancy inherent in a multilayered approach ensures that security measures are overlapping and interconnected, providing a safety net that enhances the organization's ability to respond to and recover from security incidents. Such a setup allows for more flexible and responsive security strategies that adapt to emerging threats and changing organizational needs.

Multilayered defenses are generally made from numerous straightforward security processes rather than one complex and monolithic architecture. While organizational security may appear complex, taken as a whole; with layers, each can be managed and understood separately.

Adopting a simplified approach to security processes can significantly enhance an organization's cybersecurity measures. Streamlining security protocols makes them more transparent and manageable, facilitating easier maintenance and updates. This enables organizations to focus on truly critical security measures, avoiding the complications and potential vulnerabilities associated with overly complex systems.

By reducing unnecessary complexity, organizations can achieve cost-effectiveness and improve system performance. Minimizing redundant or overlapping security layers cuts down on excessive spending and optimizes resource allocation, ensuring that security systems are agile and robust. This approach allows for a leaner, more focused security operation that can adapt more quickly to the changing threat landscape.

A simplified security architecture enhances an organization's responsiveness to emerging threats. Security teams can more easily understand and manage a less complex system, which speeds up the process of making necessary adjustments in response to security incidents. Improved agility ensures that organizations can react swiftly and effectively in the face of evolving challenges.

Identity and access management

Identity and access management systems, particularly through tools like RBAC, single sign-on, and OAuth, greatly simplify the management of user identities and permissions. By implementing SSO, organizations improve user experience by reducing the need for multiple credentials, thereby minimizing password fatigue and related security risks. This streamlines access across various systems and applications, eliminating the need for repeated logins and boosting productivity and user satisfaction.

The integration of RBAC ensures that access permissions are aligned with the user's role within the organization, further tightening security while maintaining ease of access where needed. OAuth complements this by allowing third-party services to authenticate users without exposing their credential details, thereby maintaining a balance between accessibility and security. These systems work in concert to simplify the administrative burden of managing access.

The combination of these technologies also significantly strengthens security frameworks. By reducing the complexity and enhancing the management of user credentials and access rights, organizations can effectively lower their vulnerability to cyberattacks and ensure compliance with regulatory standards. A streamlined approach to IAM empowers organizations to focus more on core business functions and less on the intricacies of identity and access management.

By closely aligning access rights with job roles, RBAC provides a clear framework that supports management and compliance efforts. This makes it easier for organizations to conduct audits and adhere to stringent security regulations.

However, it's important to note that RBAC can rapidly become complex as organizations grow. A simple organizational hierarchy may increase in complexity as users join different teams for projects or even change roles over time. As the roles become more granular to accommodate these needs, RBAC becomes more difficult to manage, though it remains far simpler than manually assigning access to everything.

Integrating OAuth protocols improves the security and simplicity of user authentication processes within an organization. By allowing applications to authenticate users without exposing their password details, OAuth minimizes the risk of credential theft, thereby reducing the attack surface. This secure approach streamlines the authentication process and bolsters overall system security by limiting direct access to user credentials.

Having RBAC complements these benefits by ensuring that access rights are meticulously aligned with job roles, enhancing operational efficiency and ensuring that employees have access only to the information necessary for their tasks. Accuracy in permission assignment is crucial for maintaining organizational productivity and security compliance. RBAC's structured approach simplifies permissions management, making it easier to meet regulatory compliance requirements and conduct thorough security audits and reviews.

Another way to enhance protection is by implementing the principle of least privilege. This security measure limits user access to only what is necessary for their specific roles, minimizing the risk of internal threats. Limiting privileges strengthens security and decreases the number of potential entry points for attackers.

From a compliance and auditing perspective, the least privilege strategy simplifies the process of monitoring and auditing user actions. With fewer permissions granted, the audit trail becomes less complex and easier to review, enhancing the ability to detect unauthorized or inappropriate activities quickly. This streamlined auditing process supports compliance with stringent regulatory requirements, which often mandate tight controls over access to sensitive data to prevent unauthorized disclosure and ensure data integrity.

IAM Systems

While there are many benefits, implementing IAM systems such as RBAC and SSO presents significant challenges, particularly in large organizations with a mix of modern and legacy systems. Integrating these systems often requires substantial IT resources and can initially cause disruptions in daily operations. The complexity is heightened by the diverse requirements and preexisting infrastructures that must be carefully managed to ensure seamless transition and implementation.

While IAM systems are designed to streamline access management, they inherently increase administrative overhead. Managing roles, permissions, and various authentication protocols requires continuous monitoring and adjustments to keep pace with organizational changes, such as personnel shifts or restructuring. This ongoing management is critical to maintaining alignment with security policies and ensuring access controls remain effective and relevant over time.

Improper implementation or inadequate updates of IAM strategies can introduce security vulnerabilities. For example, insecure storage of OAuth tokens or weak session management practices can facilitate unauthorized access, compromising the entire system. Regular updates and rigorous security practices are essential to mitigate these risks and protect user data against potential breaches.

Adopting new systems like SSO or changes in access management can meet resistance from users, particularly if the advantages and functionalities are not effectively communicated. Ensuring all users understand the benefits and how to utilize the new systems correctly is necessary for smooth integration. Communicating clearly and scheduling user training can help combat resistance and foster acceptance of new IAM measures.

Zero trust model

The zero trust model revolutionizes network security by adhering strictly to the principle of "Never Trust, Always Verify." This approach assumes that internal and external entities could potentially pose threats, and requires stringent verification for anyone attempting to access network resources. The principle of least privilege access complements it, ensuring that users are granted only the minimum levels of rights and privileges necessary for their tasks, significantly minimizing the potential damage in the event of a breach.

To help simplify this effort, zero trust advocates for micro-segmentation, a method that divides security perimeters into smaller, manageable zones. Each zone operates independently with its access protocols, ensuring a breach in one segment does not compromise the entire network. A segmented approach not only strengthens security but also enhances the manageability and isolation of network components, reinforcing the overall resilience of the infrastructure.

Core components. The zero trust model is built on a set of core components that deliver consistent security across an organization's network. They start with continuous monitoring and validation, which require real-time assessment of all network activities and security configurations. Comprehensive surveillance ensures the system remains secure against external and internal threats by continuously checking and adjusting security measures in response to network activity and threat intelligence.

Another core component of zero trust security is data encryption, both at rest and in transit. This practice secures sensitive information from unauthorized access and interception, protecting data integrity and confidentiality across all network communications and stored data.

Multifactor authentication is also necessary as it builds on the assumption that passwords can be easily compromised and that we need more assurance before we can trust an access attempt. By requiring multiple verification methods, MFA reduces the likelihood of unauthorized access, ensuring that only verified users can use network resources.

At the heart of the zero trust model is the policy enforcement engine, which acts as a central authority to scrutinize every access request against predefined security policies. The engine ensures that only requests that meet strict security criteria are granted access, maintaining tight control over network interactions.

Zero trust models are designed with the assumption that threats are not just external but are likely already on internal networks. Traditional hardware-based security perimeters, such as firewalls, were built to keep attackers out but are useless when they are already inside. Instead of continuing that approach, zero trust turns to software-defined perimeters. These dynamic perimeters adapt to real-time conditions, such as the user's location and device security status, providing flexible and context-aware security barriers.

As part of this awareness, zero trust relies on advanced analytics and intelligence to continuously analyze patterns in user behavior and access requests to identify anomalies and potential threats. The ongoing analysis informs dynamic adjustments to access controls and security strategies, enabling proactive threat mitigation and a more refined security stance.

While each of these core components is valuable for organizational security and reducing their attack surface, they need to be used together to achieve zero trust.

Implementing zero trust.   Getting to a zero trust architecture is rarely done through a major overhaul that happens all at once. It can be done in stages, implementing different layers that progressively improve an organization's security until the full architecture is achieved.

This effort often starts by focusing on access control mechanisms, as components like MFA are likely already part of the organizational architecture. Similarly, there are likely to already be access controls in place, but by auditing infrastructure and validating actual access needs, privileges can be scoped down to follow the principle of least privilege, ensuring that user access is strictly limited to what is necessary for their roles, minimizing potential exposure and the attack surface within the network.

Implementing zero trust architecture requires a robust framework of access control mechanisms to secure network resources effectively. MFA is crucial, enhancing security by permitting access to network resources through rigorous verification processes. Additionally, implementing least privilege access control ensures that user access is strictly limited to what is necessary for users' roles, minimizing potential exposure and the attack surface within the network.

Similarly, network security enhancements often build on capabilities that may partially be in place. Most larger organizations already have some network segmentation, dividing it into specific zones. Zero trust takes this a step further, dividing the network into secure, manageable segments governed by specific access rules that enhance security and control over data flows.

This segmentation is supported by continuous monitoring and adaptation technologies, which scrutinize network activity in real time and dynamically adjust permissions and security measures to respond to emerging threats and anomalies.

Finally, zero trust's integration and operational strategy involves aligning the new architecture with the organization's existing infrastructure. That ensures the zero trust framework cohesively interfaces with current IT systems and security protocols, streamlining implementation and enhancing security.

Successful integration requires careful planning and a strategic approach so that all elements of the zero trust architecture are effectively synchronized with established organizational processes and security frameworks.

Preventing data loss

Part of any complete security effort is preventing unauthorized transmission of data outside the organization. At one time, data loss prevention (DLP) was the de facto tool in this effort, as it monitors, detects, and blocks the leakage of critical data, and identifies sensitive information through content inspection and contextual analysis. DLP systems enforce security policies that prevent unauthorized actions and trigger alerts for potential breaches. This function supports compliance with privacy regulations and protects across networked devices.

However, DLP is only part of a comprehensive data protection strategy and relies on layers of security. A holistic strategy pulls in IAM and MFA to limit exposure so that only authorized users can access sensitive information. These methods leverage RBAC to narrow down permissions based on job functions, which is particularly beneficial in cloud environments where resources are widely shared.

Encryption provides an additional layer of protection, commonly applied to data at rest and in transit. This approach keeps data safe even if intercepted, which is especially important in cloud storage, email, and file sharing. For highly regulated industries, certain solutions enable encryption "in use," allowing data to remain secure during analysis. This lets researchers collaborate without needing to share massive sensitive data sets, keeping the data isolated and secure within its environment and limiting the attack surface.

With the expansion of the cloud and the dissolution of traditional security boundaries, data protection strategies had to evolve. Advanced techniques such as behavioral analytics and machine learning further strengthen DLP efforts by enabling real-time detection of unusual data usage no matter where it resides. These technologies analyze user behaviors, identifying deviations that could indicate potential threats. Unlike traditional, rules-based approaches, they adapt to evolving threat patterns, providing a responsive defense that is well-suited to cloud and on-premises environments.

A complete data loss prevention strategy relies on multiple layers to address threats at every stage and location. Cloud security posture management (CSPM) and cloud access security brokers (CASBs) help to prevent data loss and secure data by ensuring visibility and control across cloud platforms. CSPM continuously monitors for misconfigurations, while CASBs enforce data access policies, so sensitive information remains protected across hybrid cloud landscapes.

Security information and event management

SIEM is generally considered a strategic control because it supports long-term security objectives by providing comprehensive visibility, continuous monitoring, and compliance management across the organization. It primarily enhances security by providing real-time monitoring and comprehensive log management. The log management function aggregates and stores security logs across the network, allowing for systematic analysis and robust reporting. By monitoring security alerts in real time, SIEM systems enable quick detection of potential threats, ensuring rapid response to mitigate risks.

SIEM tools gather this data by integrating with other security systems. Using event correlation, they analyze and connect events from multiple sources to detect patterns that may indicate potential security incidents. Advanced analytical capabilities look for patterns in alerts to highlight more probable threats. They leverage forensic analysis tools to provide detailed context for security events, using data from previous investigations to expedite future efforts and resolutions to security incidents. This level of analysis is critical for identifying subtle anomalies that could indicate sophisticated cyberthreats.

However, to achieve this level of effectiveness, significant time and tuning are needed to remove the reoccurring noise of false-positive alerts.

SIEM supports essential compliance and alerting functions to maintain regulatory compliance and ensure organizational security. Many regulatory frameworks require continuous monitoring and logging of security events so teams can rapidly respond to incidents. Even for those not requiring it, the improved security posture helps prevent incidents that could lead to data loss, further enhancing compliance efforts.

Building on the robust capabilities of SIEM, its operational efficiency is driven by sophisticated data management and visualization techniques. SIEM systems can perform centralized processing by aggregating data from various sources, which is critical for comprehensive analysis. Visualizing this data through intuitive dashboards allows security teams to monitor network health in real time, quickly assess potential threats, and streamline the decision-making process.

Advanced threat protection

Similar to SIEMs, advanced threat protection (ATP) is a security solution designed to combat sophisticated and evolving cyberthreats across multiple vectors such as email, endpoints, applications, and networks. It delivers a proactive defense utilizing behavior analysis and real-time response capabilities to identify and mitigate unusual activities indicative of potential security breaches. This system operates in real time, offering immediate detection and response to potential threats, and integrates the latest threat intelligence to optimize detection accuracy and response times.

ATP implements protection mechanisms across several layers of an organization's IT infrastructure. Through a layered defense strategy, it ensures protection at the network, application, and device levels. For endpoint security, it detects and blocks malicious activities at devices used to access the network. It also provides email security to prevent phishing and malware threats, so that malicious emails are filtered out before they can cause harm.

ATP solutions analyze network traffic for to detect patterns or anomalies that may indicate cyberthreats. Through continuous monitoring, ATP can detect and analyze these activities in real time, flagging suspicious behavior for immediate action.

Training and awareness

Training and awareness programs serve as the first line of defense in an organization's cybersecurity strategy. These programs equip employees with the knowledge and tools to recognize potential security threats, such as phishing attempts, turning them into active participants in safeguarding the company. Empowering staff through training helps prevent breaches and reduces overall vulnerability by encouraging safe practices and adherence to security protocols.

When regularly trained, employees become more vigilant and can detect early signs of potential threats, enhancing the organization's overall threat detection capabilities. The proactive awareness ensures that threats are identified and reported early, allowing for a faster response to potential security incidents.

Regular training programs condition employees to act swiftly and correctly when a security incident occurs. By knowing how to respond appropriately, employees can help reduce the time between detecting a threat and responding.

Tactical Techniques

Tactical techniques are practical actions derived from strategic decisions, which include overarching security policies and long-term goals. Tactical actions such as implementing role-based access control systems help to drive the strategic objectives of a complete IAM framework. Similarly, firewalls, intrusion detection systems, and data encryption are all components of achieving defense-in-depth.

The effectiveness of these tactics offers valuable feedback that can lead to refinements in strategic planning, ensuring that security measures evolve to address new and emerging threats. Continuous monitoring and assessment play a key role in this iterative process, helping to align strategies and tactics against cyberthreats.

When looking at attack surface management, many of the practical risk reduction techniques will be tactical in nature. The following sections will cover some of the most commonly applicable tactical methods that can be utilized in an organization and how they help reduce the overall attack surface and mitigate risk.

Network segmentation

Network segmentation acts as a barrier that limits the spread of breaches within the network. It isolates critical systems and sensitive data into distinct segments, confining potential breaches to smaller, manageable areas and simplifying the containment and response process during security incidents. The targeted isolation helps control the scope of impact, making it easier for security teams to manage threats effectively.

Besides security enhancements, network segmentation also contributes to improved overall network performance. Confining network traffic to designated areas reduces congestion and helps essential services run smoothly without interference from non-critical operations. This setup is particularly beneficial in large organizations where heavy traffic could degrade network responsiveness and efficiency. Additionally, segmentation facilitates compliance with regulatory standards like PCI DSS, HIPAA, or GDPR by segregating sensitive data into secure zones, which is critical for protecting personally identifiable information and other sensitive data.

The strategic division of a network into segments enables more straightforward and effective management. It allows administrators to enforce specific security policies and manage measures tailored to the sensitivity and requirements of each segment. This capability simplifies administrative overhead and enhances risk management by allowing organizations to prioritize their security resources on segments that house the most critical assets, thus optimizing security investments and focusing protection efforts where they are most needed.

Effective network segmentation begins with careful planning and strategy. This starts with defining an organization's specific security and operational needs. Understanding these needs ensures that segmentation enhances security and supports and streamlines operational processes. Maintaining consistency in security policies, protocols, and practices across all segments is also essential. The uniformity helps manage and enforce security measures effectively, so that no segment is less secure than others.

The next step is robust policy management and security enforcement. Implementing strong firewall policies is critical to controlling traffic flow between segments, preventing unauthorized access, and mitigating risks of data breaches. The principle of minimal access, or least privilege, should be strictly applied to limit access rights across network segments to only what is necessary for specific tasks. Furthermore, implementing comprehensive security measures that span across segments helps monitor and control the flow of information, enhancing overall network integrity.

Finally, diligent monitoring and maintenance are key to sustaining the effectiveness of network segmentation. Utilizing automated security solutions aids in continuous monitoring and timely updating of segmentation rules, ensuring they remain effective against evolving threats. Regular updates and reviews of these rules are necessary to adapt to new threats and changes in the business environment. Regular testing and simulation of network segments also help identify vulnerabilities and strengthen defenses, improving the network's resilience against attacks.

Vulnerability management

As part of attack surface management, we examined our existing environment, identified our core assets, and prioritized them. With vulnerability management, we assess and take in vulnerability information from different sources, such as analysis tools and ethical hacking engagements, to determine the most effective method for mitigating them.

Often, mitigation is as simple as applying a patch. Still, in some cases no patches are available, so teams need to be more creative and implement compensating controls that may not entirely eliminate the vulnerability but reduce the risk until an appropriate patch is available.

Timely patching is a core component of a solid vulnerability management program, especially when there is a known exploit. In these cases, unless the patch requires an outage of services or comes with the risk of a disruption, a quick patch can rapidly reduce risk.

In these minimally invasive cases, an automated patch management system can streamline the process throughout the organization. Such a system can push patches to endpoints using a set schedule, such as Microsoft's well-known "Patch Tuesday," a practice where patches are released on a known cadence. Even for out-of-band fixes where an emergency patch is issued, these systems can push it out to applicable endpoints, reducing the manual effort required for legacy patching.

Patching is not the end-all of vulnerability management, but it is a good way to eliminate many of the easier attacks that cybercriminals turn to. Rapid patch management helps remove these attacks from their arsenal.

Automated patch management has added benefits beyond reducing the attack surface. It also helps ensure compliance with many regulatory standards, showing that the organization takes a proactive stance with how it manages its software security. By reducing the risk of a successful incident, especially one that compromises sensitive data, the organization minimizes the potential damage and associated costs of falling into noncompliance.

Patching is a fundamental part of vulnerability management. Yet, it's not the only method for safeguarding systems, especially where patches are not viable, such as in many industrial systems or IoT devices. In such cases, altering configurations can serve as effective compensating controls. This might involve disabling affected ports or services, which can isolate vulnerabilities and mitigate potential breaches. These compensatory actions are particularly crucial in environments where the affected systems may never receive patches due to operational criticality or compatibility issues. Sometimes, these adjustments become the permanent solution if they sufficiently contain the risk without impeding functionality.

In some scenarios, where neither patching nor compensating controls are viable solutions, continuous monitoring becomes the primary strategy. This is often the case when a patch is delayed or unlikely to be released, and any potential compensating measures could severely disrupt the functionality of critical assets. Under these circumstances, monitoring systems rigorously check for any signs of exploitation, which allows organizations to maintain operational integrity while being prepared to respond swiftly to security incidents. This approach makes sure that vulnerabilities are managed proactively despite the constraints on direct remediation methods.

Challenges. Vulnerability management efforts are frequently met with numerous challenges. Some involve resource and vendor challenges that can hinder effective vulnerability management. Limited personnel and budget constraints restrict the capacity for timely patching and updates, impacting the ability to swiftly address security vulnerabilities. Additionally, heavy reliance on vendors to deliver these patches can introduce delays, exacerbating the issue by exposing systems for longer periods.

Operational and environmental challenges further complicate the security landscape, adding to the complexities of vulnerability management. The diversity and complexity of IT environments make implementing a consistent vulnerability management strategy difficult, as different systems may require unique approaches. Even patch management in large organizations is fraught with challenges. Managing updates across numerous systems can lead to conflicts and even system instability, complicating efforts to maintain a secure and stable IT infrastructure.

Accurately detecting vulnerabilities is also challenging, as tooling is imperfect and may miss known issues that have not been updated into their data sets, leaving organizations believing they are safe when they are not. Alternatively, they may discover false positives, which detect vulnerabilities that are not an issue, due to their not being exploitable or simply misidentified. One creates a false sense of security, while the other generates more work for teams in validating findings only to discover they are on a wild goose chase.

Once actual issues are found, communicating the findings to different teams for resolution is still challenging. Security teams frequently pass on findings to technology owners with prioritization based on CVSS scores. While effective for security professionals who understand the jargon, this approach fails to paint a valid picture of the urgency for teams.

It's like telling someone who's never driven a car that their brake pads are down to 1 millimeter. Technically, that's a serious issue, but unless they understand how that affects stopping distance, wear, and risk of failure, the urgency doesn't land. Similarly, telling a nonsecurity team that a vulnerability has a CVSS score of 9.9 might suggest it's "high." Still, without context, like whether it allows remote access or impacts critical systems, they may not grasp why it should be prioritized immediately.

The same holds true for communicating vulnerabilities to different teams. To many nonsecurity teams, they can identify that a CVSS score of 9.9 is obviously worse than a 5, but they can't say why. Security teams should clarify how a given vulnerability is worse in terms they can understand—such as, the 9.9 could allow someone to remotely take over your servers, whereas the 5 may still allow a takeover, but it requires someone to physically touch the hardware. Without this context, teams may fail to prioritize efforts to eliminate a vulnerability, leading to disjointed management efforts and delayed responses. All of this increases organizational risk because the attack surface was not reduced in a timely manner.

Overcoming challenges. While many of these challenges may seem daunting, organizations can adopt strategic and technological solutions to help.

One way is through technological enhancements, such as integrating automated scanning and patch management tools. They streamline identifying and mitigating vulnerabilities, reducing the dependency on manual processes and the associated delays. Similarly, employing advanced detection technologies that utilize machine learning and artificial intelligence can significantly improve vulnerability detection accuracy, overcoming traditional methods' limitations.

From a more strategic direction, organizations may implement risk-based prioritization strategies to ensure that resources are allocated effectively, focusing efforts on mitigating the most critical vulnerabilities first. Organizations may also look to enhance internal capabilities through continuous training and the development of cross-functional teams. These efforts can improve communication and decision making across various departments, addressing the communication gaps that often hinder effective vulnerability management.

Forming external partnerships and engaging third-party security assessments can provide an external perspective on the organization's security posture, offering unbiased insights and recommendations. These partnerships can help validate internal security measures and ensure compliance with industry standards, further strengthening the organization's defense mechanisms against emerging threats.

Endpoint management

Effective endpoint management is crucial in maintaining a secure network environment, and controlling access points like ports is a key strategy. Closing unnecessary ports significantly enhances security by reducing potential entry points for attackers, effectively minimizing the network's vulnerabilities. This deters external threats and supports compliance with security best practices and regulatory requirements.

Prudent port management improves network performance and contributes to operational efficiency. By reducing the number of open ports, organizations can decrease the monitoring overhead, allowing security resources to focus on necessary ports. This approach not only bolsters security measures but also enhances the overall functionality of the network, ensuring that critical services run smoothly without unnecessary exposure to risk.

Removing nonessential processes from network endpoints also aids this effort by boosting operational efficiency. By eliminating unnecessary processes, your organization reduces the vulnerabilities that attackers could use, eliminating any known ones related to these processes and preventing the utilization of those that may be discovered down the road. This simplification comes with the added benefit of helping comply with regulatory requirements by minimizing the attack surfaces and mitigating potential security risks that could arise from unused or less-monitored processes.

Streamlining processes improves system performance and responsiveness by freeing up critical system resources. This improves endpoint efficiency, allowing quicker responses and smoother operation. Additionally, having fewer active processes means that endpoint management and monitoring become more manageable, reducing the complexity and overhead associated with security updates and system maintenance. The operational simplification facilitates the more effective and timely implementation of security measures, ensuring that the network remains robust against potential threats.

Configuration management enhances endpoint management efforts. Maintaining a comprehensive record of all system configurations aids in creating a trackable, auditable trail of changes, essential for verifying compliance and assessing security risks. This systematic tracking helps prevent accidental or improper modifications that could inadvertently expand the attack surface. By ensuring that only authorized changes are made, configuration management secures the system against external threats and guards against internal errors that could compromise network security.

Configuration management supports operational consistency and reliability by making sure all system settings are configured correctly and uniformly across the network. This uniformity reduces the risk of configuration drift, a common issue where individual systems become less secure over time due to untracked changes. It also simplifies rolling back changes if they introduce vulnerabilities, maintaining the integrity of the IT environment and reducing the likelihood of security breaches. This level of control is vital for organizations aiming to minimize their attack surface and enhance overall cybersecurity resilience.

Summary

The relationship between strategic and tactical techniques in cybersecurity is mutually reinforcing. Strategic methods set the overarching security blueprint, while tactical actions bring this vision to life by addressing immediate needs and operationalizing long-term objectives. As the organization executes the strategy, feedback from the tactical outcomes helps inform strategic adjustments, strengthening the organization's security posture in both proactive and reactive capacities.

However, merging these approaches can be challenging, particularly when bridging communication gaps and aligning resource allocations. Stakeholders may approach situations from different perspectives—strategic teams might advocate for overarching zero trust principles, whereas tactical teams may need to focus on short-term solutions to manage day-to-day operations and remediate high-risk vulnerabilities. This disparity can make it difficult for tactical teams to see the immediate value of resource-intensive strategic plans when they are already stretched thin while keeping the lights on.

Clear, two-way communication is essential to align these perspectives. Strategic planners must demonstrate how tactical implementations directly contribute to broader goals while also understanding the practical limitations tactical teams face. Structured implementation plans and open dialogue about constraints help foster collaboration, ensuring both teams know each other's overarching goals and can work together toward realistic and impactful security outcomes.

CHAPTER 10

Continuous Monitoring and Management

Continuous monitoring and adaptive security measures are essential for protecting organizational assets against evolving threats. This chapter explores the role of automated tools, artificial intelligence, and machine learning in enhancing anomaly detection, accelerating threat response, and ensuring compliance across diverse environments. As organizations expand into hybrid and multicloud infrastructures, traditional security methods are no longer sufficient to manage modern cyberthreats' scale, speed, and sophistication. Automated monitoring solutions enable security teams to identify real-time risks, leveraging AI for proactive threat detection and rapid remediation.

However, automation is not a complete solution. This chapter also addresses the limitations of automated processes and emphasizes the need for human oversight to validate high-impact responses and adapt security strategies to emerging threats. Balancing automation with manual control allows security teams to capitalize on AI's speed and efficiency while mitigating risks associated with false positives, system blind spots, and algorithmic bias.

Organizations can establish a resilient, adaptive security framework capable of responding to known and unforeseen threats through a layered approach that combines the strengths of automated detection and human analysis. A comprehensive continuous improvement strategy, automated monitoring, and cross-team collaboration provide a robust foundation for attack surface management.

The Dynamic Nature of Digital Ecosystems

Our digital ecosystems have evolved from relatively static infrastructure. Organizational IT is now driven by technological advancements, shifting business needs, and emerging cyberthreats. As organizations adopt cloud services, IoT devices, remote work solutions, and third-party integrations, their digital footprints expand, introducing new vulnerabilities and complexities. Each new system or connection creates potential entry points for attackers, who are quick to adapt to changes in digital environments. This interconnected landscape makes it essential for organizations to maintain a flexible, adaptive security posture that can respond to the increasing scale and scope of their digital operations.

However, businesses are not alone in leveraging technology to evolve. Cybercriminals have the same technologies at their disposal, allowing them to more quickly exploit gaps in defenses, be it an unpatched system, a misconfigured cloud asset, or a vulnerable third-party connection.

Organizations must go beyond traditional security methods to protect dynamic digital ecosystems. To keep pace with these changes, they must integrate advanced monitoring and automated threat detection, regularly reassess risks, and adapt to new technological and operational shifts to manage their attack surfaces.

Technological Shifts and New Integrations

As organizations increasingly migrate to cloud and multicloud environments, they encounter new layers of complexity in security monitoring and asset visibility. Hybrid and multicloud architectures offer flexibility and scalability but require that assets be managed across diverse infrastructures—some on-premises, others in various cloud platforms. This distribution makes it complicated to maintain a comprehensive view of all assets as data and applications continuously shift between environments.

Maintaining consistent security controls across different cloud providers also complicates the attack surface. Each provider—AWS, Azure, Google Cloud, or others—has unique configurations, compliance standards, and built-in security tools. The variation can create gaps in policy enforcement and increase the likelihood of misconfigurations, as security teams must adapt their controls to meet each platform's requirements. For example, an access control policy that applies seamlessly to on-premises resources might require customization to be effective across multiple cloud environments.

To address these challenges, organizations need cloud-native monitoring solutions that can seamlessly integrate with the native security features of each provider, such as AWS CloudTrail, Azure Sentinel, and Google Cloud's Security Command Center. Cloud-native monitoring tools are designed to align with the specific functionalities of each platform, enhancing visibility and enabling automated threat detection within each cloud environment. These tools allow security teams to centralize monitoring and unify threat intelligence, even as data moves between cloud providers.

Adding to the complexity is how organizations have evolved development in these environments. The adoption of microservice architectures enabled greater scalability and flexibility, but has also introduced a larger attack surface. In a microservices setup, applications break down into smaller, independent services that communicate via APIs. While this modular approach enhances efficiency, it also requires robust monitoring, as each service and API presents a potential entry point for attackers. This distributed nature makes maintaining a holistic view of security challenging, as threats may emerge from interactions between multiple services or vulnerabilities in individual components.

Containerization has become the preferred method for deploying microservices, but it brings unique security challenges, particularly in managing container security and orchestration. Containers, which package applications with their dependencies for consistent deployment, are often handled by platforms like Kubernetes that orchestrate container deployment and scaling. However, the security of containers is complex, requiring monitoring for runtime vulnerabilities, securing container images to ensure they remain unmodified and uncompromised, and maintaining secure configurations for orchestration platforms. For instance, Kubernetes needs careful oversight, as misconfigurations can lead to unauthorized access or exposure of sensitive resources.

Also challenging is the ephemeral nature of containers, which can spin up and shut down rapidly based on demand. This dynamic behavior creates difficulties for traditional security approaches that rely on static monitoring, as containers may not exist long enough to be thoroughly analyzed by legacy tools. Instead, organizations need container-aware monitoring solutions designed to operate within the fluid environment, capturing relevant security metrics and detecting anomalies in real time. These tools must also integrate with orchestration platforms to maintain visibility over rapidly shifting workloads, ensuring that transient containers are protected as effectively as permanent assets.

APIs connect applications and share data, but they create new security risks and integration challenges. They are gateways to application functionality and data, making them prime targets for attackers seeking direct access to sensitive information or system control. The proliferation of internal and external APIs opens up additional attack vectors, as each API endpoint represents a potential entry point for unauthorized access. With the rapid expansion of API usage, maintaining security becomes a priority, as even a single vulnerable or misconfigured API can expose an entire application to threats.

Continuous API security monitoring and testing is essential to secure APIs effectively. Organizations must address various elements, including authorization protocols, rate limiting, input validation, and data exposure policies. Authorization ensures that only permitted users and applications can access certain functions, while rate limiting prevents excessive requests that could overwhelm the system or signal a potential attack. Input validation helps safeguard APIs from injection attacks, such as

SQL injection, by ensuring that only valid, expected data enters the system. Additionally, thorough testing is necessary to confirm that APIs do not expose more data than necessary, which reduces the risk of accidental data leaks.

Further complicating API security is the complex integrations with third-party services that many organizations rely on for extended functionality and data sharing. Third-party APIs introduce a layer of security risk, as they may have vulnerabilities, data handling practices, and compliance requirements. A security breach in a third-party service could potentially compromise all applications and data connected through its APIs, creating significant risks to data privacy and regulatory compliance.

Adopting AI and ML in security monitoring has transformed companies' ability to detect and respond to threats quickly and accurately. AI and ML algorithms analyze vast amounts of data to identify patterns and anomalies that might indicate an attack, often catching signs that traditional rule-based systems could overlook. For example, AI-driven tools can detect subtle deviations in network traffic, user behavior, or application activity, enabling security teams to respond proactively rather than reactively.

The same technologies that bolster security are also being exploited by adversaries. AI-driven attack methods have led to more sophisticated and evasive threats. In phishing campaigns, for instance, AI can craft highly personalized messages, increasing the likelihood that targets will engage. Similarly, the technology can power brute-force attacks, making them faster and more efficient by predicting password structures based on common patterns. Attackers may also leverage AI to automate social engineering attacks, generating realistic interactions that evade traditional detection methods.

As organizations rely more heavily on AI for security, ensuring the integrity and security of AI models themselves becomes crucial. Attackers have increasingly turned to methods like adversarial attacks, data poisoning, and model tampering to manipulate AI algorithms and skew their outputs. For example, data poisoning can corrupt the data that AI models use for training, causing them to misidentify threats or overlook specific attack vectors. Adversarial attacks involve subtly manipulating inputs to confuse AI systems, leading to incorrect or missed threat detections.

Impact of Organizational Changes on the Ecosystem

Organizations evolve through expansions, acquisitions, restructuring, and technological adoption, and their digital ecosystem—and the challenges of securing it—evolve in turn. Each shift introduces new assets, systems, and processes, widening the attack surface and requiring adaptable, proactive security strategies.

Acquisitions, for instance, bring in a variety of new digital assets and third-party integrations, each with its own security standards and maturity levels. These additions often need alignment with existing protocols, creating coverage gaps and complicating threat detection. The disparate systems become vulnerable entry points without careful integration, demanding continuous monitoring and cross-functional collaboration to close security gaps and harmonize protective measures.

Business expansion, particularly through mergers, increases third-party and supply-chain risks. Each new vendor or supplier brings security practices that may not align with the organization's standards, introducing unmonitored vulnerabilities. Regular security assessments and consistent oversight of third-party networks are essential to mitigate these risks and maintain compliance across expanding supply chains.

Internally, organizational restructuring often reshuffles roles and responsibilities, leading to ambiguities in security ownership and potential vulnerabilities. Essential security functions may go unassigned without clear handover processes, leading to misconfigurations or overlooked assets. Structured documentation and updated access controls help maintain a secure environment during transitions, ensuring that every role is equipped to handle its specific security responsibilities.

Digital transformation, another driver of organizational change, enhances operational efficiency but simultaneously expands the digital footprint. Adopting cloud services, automation, and data analytics introduces additional entry points, each demanding unique security controls and monitoring. Integrating security by design into these new processes can minimize risks, so teams can manage emerging vulnerabilities as the technology landscape evolves.

Expanding into new markets often introduces stringent regulatory requirements, such as GDPR or HIPAA, which mandate additional monitoring and reporting standards. As regulatory demands increase, security practices must remain agile to provide the necessary audit data and adapt to changing compliance landscapes, allowing the organization to maintain transparency and accountability.

The shift to remote and hybrid work has further broadened the organization's network perimeter, requiring rigorous endpoint and device management. Employees accessing corporate resources from personal devices and unsecured networks introduce new vulnerabilities. Endpoint security tools and ongoing employee training are needed to minimize the risks associated with remote access and create a resilient security culture across distributed workforces.

All these changes place pressure on security budgets, often requiring organizations to make tough decisions about tool selection and resource allocation. A risk-based approach ensures that critical assets receive prioritized protection, even with limited funds. By adopting multifunctional security tools, organizations can maximize their impact, covering a range of threats while supporting a cohesive, resilient security strategy amid changing circumstances.

Setting Alert Thresholds

Proactive threat detection requires setting alert thresholds to enable security teams to focus on genuine risks without being overwhelmed by unnecessary alerts. By calibrating alert sensitivity based on historical data, user behavior, and asset criticality, organizations can fine-tune their monitoring systems to detect suspicious activities accurately.

For instance, creating baselines of normal behavior across network traffic, login patterns, and data access enables automated systems to identify deviations that may indicate potential threats. Properly calibrated thresholds help reduce the frequency of false positives, so security teams can dedicate their resources to incidents that warrant immediate attention while minimizing alert fatigue.

Alert thresholds must be dynamic to remain effective in a constantly evolving threat landscape. Automated systems equipped with machine learning can adjust thresholds in real time based on shifting activity patterns, user roles, or heightened risk periods. Thresholds might tighten during off hours, when abnormal activity is more likely to indicate a threat, while adjusting to allow for higher traffic during peak business hours. Feedback from incident response teams is invaluable for refining these thresholds over time, as it helps identify blind spots or overly sensitive settings.

Differentiating Between False Positives and Legitimate Threats

Distinguishing between false positives and legitimate threats is critical to maintaining a useful response system. False positives can have a significant operational impact if not managed carefully. When security teams are bombarded with false positives, they face operational overload, as time and resources are spent investigating alerts that ultimately pose no threat. An overwhelming influx of alerts can lead to alert fatigue, a condition where team members become desensitized to alarms and may overlook valuable signals. As a result, the system designed to protect the organization becomes inefficient, with security teams unable to focus on actual incidents due to the constant noise of false alarms.

The consequences of alert fatigue and excessive false positives extend beyond operational strain, directly affecting an organization's ability to respond to legitimate threats. When security teams are engaged in reviewing and dismissing false positives, they have less time and capacity to investigate actual security incidents. This delay in response time can be critical; the longer a genuine threat remains undetected or unaddressed, the more time an attacker has to infiltrate systems, exfiltrate data, or compromise valuable assets.

For organizations where timely response is key to mitigating damage, diverting resources to handle false positives can increase the risk of undetected breaches or prolonged security incidents. Setting appropriate alert thresholds helps security teams be alerted only to activity that genuinely warrants their attention, allowing them to focus on high-priority threats.

Beyond the operational and response impacts, false positives carry financial and resource costs that can add up, particularly for larger organizations with complex security infrastructures. Each unnecessary alert may require analysts' time, specialized tools, and computational resources to investigate, all of which incur costs. For enterprises with substantial security teams, accumulating staff hours spent on false positives translates to wasted budget, limiting funds that could otherwise be used for strategic investments or enhancements in threat detection capabilities.

Establishing baselines for normal activity across systems and networks is a critical step in reducing false positives and enhancing threat detection accuracy. By understanding what constitutes typical behavior, security teams can more effectively identify anomalies that may signal genuine threats.

Baselines serve as a reference point, capturing patterns of standard activity such as peak login times, common access locations, and average data transfer volumes. When an event deviates from these established norms, it triggers an alert, allowing the security team to investigate further. Without these baselines, every slight deviation could be misinterpreted as a threat, overwhelming teams with unnecessary alerts and making it harder to identify actual incidents amidst the noise.

Dynamic thresholds and adaptive learning help adapt to evolving ecosystems and maintain relevant baselines. Static thresholds—fixed levels that trigger alerts when crossed—often fail to accommodate natural fluctuations in user behavior, which can result in numerous false positives. For instance, seasonal changes in business activity or variations in access patterns as teams adopt new tools can cause legitimate deviations that static thresholds would flag as suspicious.

Adaptive thresholds that adjust in response to observed patterns allow the monitoring system to adapt to these changes, so it can recognize when variations are harmless. With machine learning and AI capabilities, these adaptive systems can analyze activity trends over time, refining thresholds to distinguish between routine fluctuations and behaviors that might indicate malicious activity.

Incorporating contextual awareness into baseline thresholds further improves them, since security systems can interpret behaviors with greater accuracy. Considering variables such as the time of day, the user's role, and typical access points, security teams can set more refined thresholds that account for legitimate variations. For example, an IT administrator may be expected to access sensitive systems outside regular business hours. Still, it is suspicious if a standard user attempts the same activity. A context-driven approach reduces the likelihood of false positives, as the system only flags unusual behaviors within the appropriate context.

Calibrating and Fine-Tuning Thresholds

As organizations evolve, continuous monitoring becomes essential for calibrating alert thresholds to balance sensitivity and accuracy. Through ongoing data collection, security teams can refine thresholds to filter benign activity while catching real threats, preventing outdated settings from leading to false positives or missed alerts (see Figure 10-1).

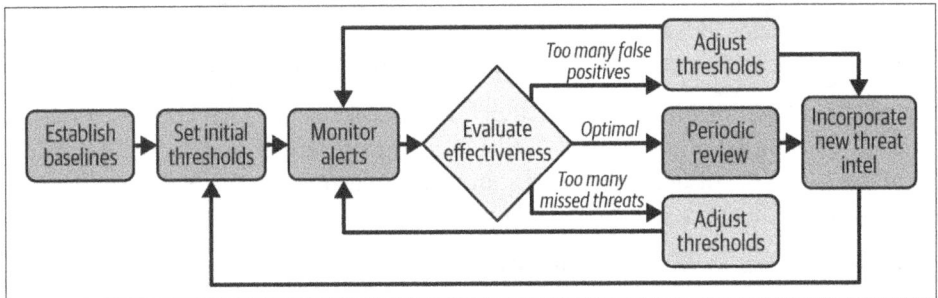

Figure 10-1. The process of establishing baselines, setting thresholds, evaluating effectiveness, and incorporating new threat intelligence to maintain optimal alert sensitivity.

Real-time traffic monitoring allows thresholds to adapt to seasonal or periodic spikes, ensuring legitimate traffic surges don't trigger unnecessary alerts. Feedback from incident response teams further fine-tunes thresholds by aligning them with real-world threat patterns and reducing false positives.

Customizing thresholds for specific network segments and user roles makes them more precise. For example, stricter thresholds can be assigned to high-risk areas like public-facing networks or high-access user roles, such as administrators, to better capture potential threats.

Threshold calibration also differs between cloud and on-premises environments. Cloud setups require more adaptable thresholds to account for dynamic traffic, while on-premises systems benefit from stable, consistent settings. Incremental adjustments help achieve the right balance between sensitivity and specificity, minimizing alert fatigue and ensuring genuine threats aren't overlooked.

Machine learning enhances threshold calibration by analyzing historical data to identify patterns and suggest adjustments. ML anomaly detection identifies subtle deviations from typical activity, revealing potential threats that traditional thresholds might miss. Self-tuning thresholds powered by ML further improve adaptability, automatically adjusting to changing behavior patterns to maintain optimal alert accuracy without continuous manual intervention.

Incorporating Contextual Awareness in Alerts

Imagine a bustling office where every employee has a unique role, from the IT administrator managing sensitive systems to the marketing specialist crafting campaigns. Now, picture a security system that doesn't account for these differences—flagging normal IT maintenance as suspicious or overlooking a marketer's unusual access to financial data. This is the challenge of setting context-aware alert thresholds.

Effective security begins with understanding who is accessing what and why. For instance, an IT administrator's midnight server updates might be routine, but the same activity by a marketing employee could indicate compromised credentials. Similarly, a flagged login from an unfamiliar location might seem benign—until it's cross-referenced with unusual data exfiltration, revealing a larger threat.

Our most critical assets, like databases housing financial records or patient information, demand stricter monitoring. Even minor deviations in usage patterns should sound alarms, while less critical systems can afford broader thresholds. These priorities come into sharper focus when organizations build historical behavioral baselines. What's "normal" for a user or system? Deviations from established patterns—like unexpected spikes in data access—can be a red flag for security teams.

Threats also evolve in stages, requiring dynamic responses. A surge of failed login attempts followed by odd file transfers might seem disconnected but could signal a coordinated breach when viewed through the lens of an attack life cycle. By layering alerts—where small anomalies combine into high-priority warnings—security teams can uncover malicious intent hidden within daily noise.

Even the time of day shapes threat perceptions. Late-night activity on a quiet weekend should raise eyebrows, especially in contrast to the predictable spikes of month-end reporting. Similarly, location matters: an access attempt from a high-risk region, like Eastern Europe or Southeast Asia, could signify an attack.

Tailoring alerts extends beyond people and places to the systems themselves. Cloud environments, with their ever-changing workloads, differ from the steadier rhythms of on-premises infrastructure. Recognizing these nuances ensures thresholds are neither too sensitive nor too lax.

Context isn't static. Using real-time threat intelligence, the tracking of malicious IPs or domains adds a dynamic edge, escalating alerts tied to known risks. Industries like health care and finance can refine their defenses further by monitoring sector-specific threats, such as ransomware or fraud.

Ultimately, a good security system tells a story: one of behaviors, contexts, and connections. By integrating these elements, organizations can turn fragmented alerts into a cohesive narrative, uncovering threats before they escalate into crises.

Integrating with Incident Response

For incident response (IR), decreasing impact comes from reducing response times. Integrating monitoring systems into the IR process, organizations can be sure that critical alerts trigger immediate responses by aligning alerting mechanisms with IR protocols, minimizing the time between detection and action. This integration enables automated systems to directly escalate high-risk incidents to response teams while providing valuable contextual information to guide their actions. Seamless communication between monitoring and IR workflows empowers teams to respond with greater speed and precision, significantly reducing the impact of incidents on the organization.

Effective integration with incident response also involves structured collaboration and periodic feedback loops between monitoring and IR teams to refine processes continually. Cross-functional debriefs and post-incident reviews allow teams to assess how well alert thresholds, escalation paths, and response actions support the incident resolution.

Coordinating Monitoring with Incident Response Teams

Good integration of monitoring and IR teams begins with setting incident-driven thresholds that prioritize meaningful alerts and streamline escalation. Input from IR teams allows for the fine-tuning of security thresholds, distinguishing minor anomalies from genuine incidents. For example, while a single failed login may be inconsequential, repeated failed logins from unusual locations could indicate a breach. IR teams offer valuable insights into behaviors that signal actual incidents, helping monitoring teams establish relevant thresholds.

A tiered alert classification system further improves coordination by organizing alerts by severity: informational, warning, or critical. This categorization aligns monitoring systems with IR workflows, allowing low-severity alerts to be passively monitored while medium- and high-severity alerts escalate with increasing urgency. Such an approach prevents IR teams from being overwhelmed by minor notifications, enabling a focus on incidents that warrant immediate intervention.

Incident-specific criteria and contextual triggers add precision, ensuring high-risk behaviors—like multiple failed logins from various locations or spikes in data exfiltration—automatically prompt IR involvement. These contextual triggers help prioritize alerts that need immediate attention.

Real-time alerting and notification systems ensure seamless coordination by providing direct communication channels for high-priority alerts. These systems are designed to push notifications to IR through secure platforms, so teams can respond to threats promptly. Additionally, clear incident escalation pathways categorize alerts by urgency, ensuring IR teams receive relevant alerts while minor anomalies remain monitored but deprioritized.

Regular check-ins and coordination meetings between monitoring and IR teams support the ongoing review of alerting trends, recent incidents, and response strategies. These sessions provide an opportunity to discuss adjustments to thresholds or escalation criteria based on real-world insights to reduce false positives and focus on critical issues.

Unified dashboards integrate monitoring and IR tools to allow IR teams to view real-time alerts, escalations, and responses in one interface. The consolidation streamlines threat assessment, reduces time spent toggling between tools, and enables quicker, more informed decisions.

Automated escalation workflows help coordination by forwarding high-priority alerts directly to IR platforms, such as security orchestration, automation, and response (SOAR) or SIEM systems. These workflows trigger predefined responses without manual intervention, accelerating the hand-off process and ensuring prompt IR action.

Bidirectional feedback loops between monitoring and IR systems create a closed process where each incident informs future threshold settings. If specific activities trigger frequent but nonactionable alerts, IR feedback can prompt monitoring adjustments to reduce noise. Conversely, new threats identified by IR can increase monitoring sensitivity.

Aligning monitoring and IR teams with shared key performance indicators—such as mean time to detect and mean time to respond—helps coordinate efforts to minimize detection and response times. Tracking false positive rates and escalation accuracy further refines processes, allowing adjustments that reduce unnecessary escalations and focus IR resources on genuine incidents.

Incident playbooks and standard operating procedures (SOPs) provide structured approaches for handling alerts. Playbooks outline steps for specific threats, while SOPs address routine responses to lower-severity alerts. This enables monitoring teams to manage common alerts systematically while IR focuses on significant incidents. Clear hand-off protocols within playbooks and SOPs facilitate a smooth transition of alerts, specifying when escalation is required, priority levels, and communication channels to ensure prompt IR action and minimize response gaps.

Simulating Breach Scenarios

Deriving actionable insights from breach simulations requires establishing clear objectives and success metrics, such as testing response times, evaluating alert accuracy, and assessing communication efficiency, focusing the simulation on critical areas. For example, if the objective is to measure response time, teams can track how quickly they detect, escalate, and mobilize resources. Monitoring alert accuracy can reveal whether current thresholds distinguish real threats from false positives effectively.

Breach simulations also help identify weak points in incident response. Organizations can observe how effectively their security framework responds to various scenarios in a controlled environment. Simulations may reveal vulnerabilities like delayed escalations, misconfigured alert thresholds, or visibility gaps that impede rapid response. For example, delays in escalation might indicate a need for clearer hand-off protocols or automated workflows.

Testing incident playbooks and SOPs is another key benefit of breach simulations. These exercises validate each step in playbooks, ensuring relevance and currency with the organization's technology stack and threat landscape. Simulations also allow the updating of outdated steps or addressing of gaps to maintain effective protocols.

Choosing realistic scenarios aligned with organizational risks and threat vectors maximizes the effectiveness of simulations. Common threats like phishing, lateral movement, or ransomware allow organizations to test detection and response protocols against incidents they are likely to encounter. For instance, a phishing simulation tests the speed of credential compromise detection, while a lateral movement scenario identifies any network monitoring blind spots.

Tailoring scenarios to the organization's specific context enhances relevance and ensures teams practice protecting high-value assets. A health care organization, for instance, might focus on ransomware attacks on patient data systems, while a financial institution may prioritize simulations targeting sensitive financial information.

Rotating between different scenarios and covering a variety of threat vectors further prepares teams for diverse incidents. By varying the focus between external attacks, like DDoS, and internal risks, such as insider threats, organizations expose IR teams to unique response strategies, reinforcing a culture of continuous learning.

Effective simulations require clear role definitions for both monitoring and IR teams. Assigning specific tasks—such as who triggers alerts, manages escalation, and leads investigations—helps each team member understand their responsibilities. For instance, when a simulated threat is detected, the monitoring team confirms and escalates the anomaly, while IR handles investigation and containment.

Real-time communication protocols help to coordinate simulations, mirroring the needs of actual breach situations. Testing secure communication channels, chat platforms, and incident management systems ensures information flows efficiently, identifying and addressing any communication breakdowns or delays that could impede response.

Simulations provide a valuable opportunity to practice escalation and decision-making processes, allowing both teams to verify alert escalation and IR's readiness to make quick, informed decisions. During simulations, monitoring teams practice identifying escalation indicators, while IR teams focus on rapid containment decisions.

Simulations also allow teams to observe alert thresholds in real time, offering insights into whether thresholds are properly calibrated. Monitoring teams track alert speed and severity accuracy, identifying delays or oversights. Simulated data helps adjust thresholds to balance sensitivity and specificity, optimizing future incident alerts.

Another critical skill is testing dynamic threshold adjustments within simulations. During an active breach, threat patterns can shift rapidly, requiring real-time threshold tuning to keep alerts meaningful. Practicing this in simulations lets monitoring teams adjust thresholds on the fly as incidents evolve.

Breach simulations are invaluable for practicing with security tools and platforms under real-world conditions. Familiarity with SIEM, SOAR, and threat intelligence feeds is crucial for effective detection, analysis, and response. For example, SIEM systems provide data visibility, while SOAR platforms automate workflows. Simulations reinforce team proficiency with these tools, building confidence in their use.

Testing automation settings in simulated responses ensures that automated actions—like quarantining endpoints or blocking malicious IPs—achieve intended outcomes without unintended side effects. This practice fine-tunes automation to ensure optimal containment while preserving essential functionality.

Simulations reinforce IR teams' forensic analysis skills, allowing them to practice tracing a simulated attack's origin, pathways, and impact. Using forensic tools to analyze log files, memory dumps, and endpoint data, teams gain insight into threat behavior and identify specific indicators of compromise for future reference.

Breach simulations provide measurable data on detection and response times, offering benchmarks for performance. By tracking from initial detection to containment, teams gain insights into process efficiency and identify areas for threshold adjustment or protocol refinement. For instance, threshold settings may need recalibration if an alert type consistently triggers slow responses.

Benchmarking simulation response times against industry standards, like MTTD and MTTR, allows teams to assess their performance relative to best practices. Significant deviations may indicate areas needing additional resources, training, or process improvements.

Tracking escalation speed and efficiency in simulations helps identify bottlenecks in alert handling and escalation pathways. Delays in reaching IR teams might suggest the need for streamlined workflows or enhanced automation. Simulations enable teams to pinpoint and resolve these issues before they impact real-world responses.

Rapid Response and Mitigation Strategies

An effective incident response plan is built on well-defined phases and close coordination between monitoring and IR teams. This structured process usually unfolds in four stages: detection, containment, eradication, and recovery, with each phase bringing a unique set of tasks and goals.

In the detection phase, monitoring teams work to identify and verify potential threats, flagging incidents that require escalation to IR teams. Once a threat is confirmed, the plan moves to containment, where IR teams focus on isolating affected systems and halting any lateral movement to keep the incident from spreading. The containment buys time and ensures other systems remain secure as IR progresses to eradication, thoroughly removing any traces of malicious activity. The final stage, recovery, involves restoring systems to normal operations and conducting a post-incident review to capture lessons learned, reinforcing the organization's defenses for future incidents.

Supporting this process, IR teams rely on playbooks—detailed guides for common incidents like phishing, DDoS, and ransomware. A ransomware playbook, for example, might outline steps to isolate infected systems, secure sensitive data, and initiate essential communication protocols. These playbooks streamline responses and provide a consistent approach, ensuring each team member knows exactly what to do, from the initial alert to the final analysis. Monitoring teams may manage alert verification and data gathering, while IR focuses on containment and forensic investigation, with each role predefined for clarity and speed.

Even with clear roles, effective real-time communication is essential for coordination. Centralized platforms, like secure chat applications, allow teams to share updates, document decisions, and maintain visibility in one place, ensuring alignment across all response phases. When incidents escalate, these platforms support immediate reporting to executive teams, legal departments, and external partners like managed security service providers (MSSPs), especially for high-severity incidents that could affect regulatory, financial, or reputational standing.

Many organizations implement automated responses to contain threats quickly. Automated systems can isolate compromised systems, disable suspicious accounts, or block known malicious IPs as soon as an incident is detected, limiting threat movement. SOAR tools take automation further, linking monitoring data with response workflows and handling repetitive tasks like logging, alert categorization, and containment. For instance, if a phishing attempt is detected, SOAR might disable affected email accounts and notify stakeholders, accelerating the response and minimizing human error.

Effective triage ensures the IR team can concentrate on the most pressing threats. Automated alert triage filters out low-risk alerts, so IR can focus on high-priority incidents. By categorizing alerts by severity, triage systems streamline IR's attention to critical threats needing immediate action.

Once containment begins, network segmentation enables rapid isolation of affected areas without disrupting the entire network. This approach, combined with endpoint quarantine and access control adjustments, prevents compromised devices from further network communication. Blocking malicious indicators, like IPs or file hashes associated with attacker infrastructure, adds a layer of containment, cutting off potential communication channels for adversaries.

With the threat contained, IR teams turn to root cause analysis through log analysis and data correlation, retracing the breach to its origin. Examining logs from network, endpoint, and application activity helps IR teams identify unusual patterns, revealing how the attacker gained access. Forensic analysis goes deeper, so IR can scrutinize compromised systems, uncover vulnerabilities, and determine the exact methods used. This phase often benefits from threat intelligence, which provides a broader context for understanding attacker tactics and prioritizing remediation steps based on the adversary's likely objectives.

Cross-functional collaboration strengthens each stage of the response. IT and security teams lead containment, while legal teams assess regulatory implications. Communication teams handle stakeholder messaging, especially when incidents involve sensitive data. Collaboration ensures that all aspects of the response are covered, reducing risk and supporting compliance.

When needed, external partners such as MSSPs and threat intelligence providers offer specialized support, like advanced forensics and 24/7 monitoring. These partnerships bring additional expertise and resources, which are particularly valuable in large-scale incidents. Threat intelligence vendors contribute insights on attacker behaviors and trends, improving the organization's ability to detect, contain, and mitigate threats. In coordinated attacks, these partners also facilitate information sharing, strengthening collective defenses.

Throughout the incident, timely updates to stakeholders and a well-prepared public communication plan help manage reputational impact and maintain trust. Executive teams need accurate updates for decision making, and in cases involving customers or the public, transparent communication reassures stakeholders and demonstrates accountability. Proactive communication mitigates reputational damage and reinforces the organization's commitment to effective incident resolution.

Periodic Reviews and Audits

Monitoring, incident response, and vulnerability management efforts must be assessed to remain effective. Periodic reviews and audits evaluate their effectiveness, enabling security teams to identify gaps in current defenses, confirm the accuracy and efficiency of detection mechanisms, and check that response protocols align with the latest threat landscape.

These reviews provide a structured opportunity to measure the organization's resilience against potential threats, track progress in risk reduction, and refine strategies to address emerging vulnerabilities. Regular audits validate the integrity of current processes and ensure that security practices stay in step with organizational growth and infrastructure changes.

Beyond internal improvements, periodic reviews and audits are crucial for demonstrating compliance with industry standards and regulatory requirements. As regulations evolve and enforcement becomes stricter, organizations must maintain thorough documentation and always be audit-ready. Consistent audits create a detailed record of security practices, allowing for transparent tracking of vulnerabilities, remediation efforts, and compliance adherence. This proactive approach strengthens the organization's credibility with stakeholders and regulators while reinforcing a culture of accountability and continuous improvement.

Scheduling Regular Vulnerability Scans

Regular vulnerability scans are essential for uncovering weaknesses in an organization's infrastructure. To ensure effectiveness, scanning tools should align with the environment—whether cloud, on-premises, or hybrid—since each setup requires different optimizations. Additionally, updating tools with the latest vulnerability definitions is crucial for detecting new threats. Reviewing scan accuracy and false positive rates periodically helps prevent security teams from being overwhelmed, letting them focus on actual vulnerabilities rather than low-risk alerts.

Prioritizing scans based on asset risk is key, especially for systems handling sensitive data. High-priority assets, such as customer or financial information databases, should be scanned frequently due to their impact on organizational security. Building a comprehensive asset inventory means teams can classify systems by their business impact, scheduling more frequent scans for critical systems and periodic checks for lower-risk assets. Differentiating between internal and external-facing assets further refines the process, as public-facing systems are more vulnerable and typically require more frequent scanning.

Integrating vulnerability scans into security audits allows teams to track risk trends and measure the organization's resilience over time. Aligning scans with annual or biannual audits provides a structured way to evaluate vulnerabilities, with scan results contributing to audit documentation and supporting compliance. Establishing SLAs for remediation prioritizes critical vulnerabilities, while coordinating scans with updates or release cycles helps identify any new vulnerabilities introduced by recent changes. Automated, continuous scanning in dynamic environments enhances real-time visibility, so that emerging threats are promptly detected and addressed.

Reevaluating Remediation Efforts and Efficacy

To keep vulnerability management aligned with security goals, organizations need effective ways to evaluate remediation efforts. By establishing key performance indicators, teams gain concrete benchmarks that drive a clearer understanding of their progress. Metrics like MTTR, vulnerability recurrence rate, and SLA compliance provide critical insights. MTTR measures how quickly vulnerabilities are addressed, reducing the time systems remain exposed to threats. The recurrence rate uncovers persistent issues, signaling deeper security challenges if vulnerabilities resurface. SLA compliance, meanwhile, ensures that high-priority vulnerabilities receive prompt attention, keeping teams focused on the most urgent threats.

Looking at historical data reveals trends in remediation performance, showing whether strategies are improving or stalling. A consistent reduction in MTTR or a decline in recurring vulnerabilities suggests effective processes. However, data showing repeated delays or high recurrence rates may indicate gaps that need attention, from revising protocols to addressing resource allocation.

Measuring residual risk post-remediation is equally essential, particularly for high-impact vulnerabilities where complete risk elimination may be challenging. Some vulnerabilities leave behind residual risk due to system complexity or limitations in existing controls. Evaluating this risk allows teams to determine if additional safeguards, like enhanced security controls or access restrictions, are necessary to fully protect critical assets.

Efficient vulnerability management also depends on identifying and eliminating workflow bottlenecks. Regular process audits highlight slowdowns in areas like patching, approvals, or cross-department coordination. If patch deployment is regularly delayed, it may point to a need for better communication or streamlined processes in patch management. Addressing these bottlenecks optimizes workflows, reduces vulnerability exposure, and enhances overall security.

Coordination and clear communication among development, IT, and security teams are vital for smooth remediation. Each team plays a unique role, from vulnerability identification to patch deployment, so maintaining clear channels and regular alignment meetings helps avoid misunderstandings or delays. Tools like shared tracking platforms provide visibility into each team's progress, so everyone remains aligned with the organization's security goals.

Resource allocation is another key factor, allowing organizations to focus on vulnerabilities that pose the highest risk. Regular evaluations help direct resources effectively, ensuring high-impact vulnerabilities receive the most attention while balancing workload across teams. SLAs also provide benchmarks, setting expected response times based on vulnerability severity. Comparing actual response times to SLA targets helps identify strengths and gaps in the process; if high-severity vulnerabilities are consistently remediated on time, it demonstrates effective prioritization. However, recurring delays for specific vulnerabilities suggest areas that need further investigation and optimization.

Adjusting SLAs based on recent incidents and asset prioritization ensures response timelines align with evolving security needs. Systems experiencing repeated attacks or becoming more frequently targeted may warrant shorter SLA targets, keeping attention on assets most vulnerable to threats. Escalation paths for SLA breaches help ensure adherence, specifying steps to take when critical vulnerabilities exceed their expected resolution times, including escalation to senior team members or executives when necessary.

Effective patch management is fundamental to remediation success, particularly for high-priority systems. Tracking deployment success rates helps teams assess patching practices' reliability and identify areas for improvement. Similarly, tracking vulnerability recurrence after patching reveals whether underlying causes are being addressed or if deeper issues remain, such as misconfigurations or structural flaws requiring additional intervention.

Balancing patch timing with business continuity minimizes disruptions while maintaining security. Some patches need immediate application to counter urgent threats, but implementing them outside peak hours or business-critical periods avoids unnecessary operational impact. Automating post-remediation verification scans further improves the process by quickly confirming that patches are successful, offering immediate feedback on eliminating high-risk vulnerabilities.

Continuous monitoring helps detect new vulnerabilities or the reappearance of previous ones in dynamic environments. Configuration changes can inadvertently reintroduce risks, and continuous monitoring ensures prompt detection, allowing for swift remediation adjustments.

A forward-thinking approach, predictive remediation powered by machine learning (*https://oreil.ly/_G6W-*), enhances vulnerability management by anticipating potential risks before they are exploited. By analyzing historical vulnerability data, machine learning identifies patterns and predicts future vulnerabilities, so teams can prioritize high-risk areas and plan resources effectively. This predictive capability supports a proactive stance, focusing attention on emerging threats and enhancing the organization's overall security posture.

Reassessing Asset Priorities

All assets contribute to the organization's success in a complex digital ecosystem. Some store sensitive customer data, others power critical operations, and many connect to external networks. Each asset carries risks, and effectively prioritizing them builds a stronger security posture, especially as AI introduces new vulnerabilities.

AI-driven systems holding sensitive data are among the most high-stakes assets. A breach involving customer or financial information can lead to significant costs and eroded trust. Endpoints like cloud resources, IoT devices, and APIs amplify exposure, serving as frequent targets for attackers seeking entry points into broader systems.

The role an asset plays often determines its security priority. For example, systems processing financial transactions or managing medical records are essential to operations and an organization's reputation. At the same time, legacy systems without modern defenses can become weak links, creating hidden vulnerabilities in otherwise secure networks.

Recurring vulnerabilities add another layer of risk. Assets with a history of issues signal weak points that require immediate attention. Meanwhile, new acquisitions often arrive with different security standards, needing careful integration to prevent gaps in protection.

As AI adoption grows, so does the complexity of managing its dependencies. AI models rely on vast data sets, often shared across interconnected systems. Third-party APIs and cloud providers add efficiency but also introduce potential vulnerabilities. These connections must be carefully monitored, as a single compromise can ripple through the entire ecosystem.

Emerging threats underscore the need for adaptability. Ransomware targeting cloud-based AI systems or attacks on IoT devices illustrate how quickly the landscape changes. By incorporating insights from incident response teams and threat intelligence, organizations can anticipate risks and adjust defenses to stay ahead.

Whether it's a cutting-edge AI system or a legacy platform nearing decommission, each asset contributes to the larger security narrative. Understanding their roles, vulnerabilities, and interdependencies ensures that security strategies remain agile and effective in the face of evolving threats.

Feedback Loops and Continuous Improvement

Structured feedback processes help organizations become more adaptive, learning from each incident, alert, and monitoring activity to refine and enhance their defenses. These loops allow for constantly assessing and adjusting alert thresholds, response playbooks, and detection criteria based on real-world insights. Security teams can reduce inefficiencies, address recurring vulnerabilities, and proactively adapt to emerging risks through this iterative approach. Feedback-driven refinements make the organization's security posture more robust and more responsive to nuanced changes in threat behavior.

Continuous improvement goes hand-in-hand with cross-functional collaboration, as teams from monitoring, incident response, compliance, and IT contribute diverse perspectives and expertise. Regular debriefs, incident reviews, and cross-team discussions create a comprehensive view of both successes and areas for growth, fostering an environment where insights are shared and integrated into daily operations.

Encouraging Cross-Team Collaboration

To foster a proactive and resilient security environment, it's essential to encourage joint ownership of security goals across departments. Assigning security responsibilities and setting collaborative goals that involve multiple teams—such as reducing vulnerabilities or improving incident response times—ensures that security becomes a shared priority rather than the sole responsibility of the IT or security team. When departments like development, operations, and compliance share accountability for security outcomes, they are more likely to incorporate security considerations into their daily activities.

Goal-setting based on shared metrics is a powerful tool for aligning teams under unified security objectives. By establishing clear, measurable goals—such as the percentage reduction in vulnerabilities or the average time taken to resolve incidents—departments can understand how their efforts contribute to overarching security goals. For example, development teams may focus on reducing vulnerabilities in code, while operations may prioritize system updates and patch management, contributing to improved security metrics.

These shared metrics provide:

- A common language and purpose
- Help for teams tracking progress and staying motivated toward achieving collective outcomes
- Clear, shared goals that help each team recognize its role in strengthening security
- A coordinated effort that aligns all departments with security objectives

Recognizing cross-team contributions helps reinforce a culture of collaboration and encourages continued engagement in security initiatives. Acknowledging the efforts of all teams in achieving security milestones—whether in vulnerability reduction, incident response, or successful audits—creates a positive feedback loop that promotes ongoing collaboration. Publicly celebrating these achievements boosts morale and reinforces the message that security is everyone's responsibility.

Establishing shared communication platforms fosters open team feedback channels and encourages real-time collaboration on security-related matters. Platforms like Slack channels, integrated ticketing systems, or other collaborative tools enable team members to quickly share security concerns, updates, and suggestions with relevant departments.

Secure and centralized communication channels create structured feedback loops that enhance continuous organizational improvement. When team members can easily access updates, insights, and suggestions in a safe environment, they can better adapt their practices and incorporate feedback into their workflows. For instance, a development team might use a secure channel to discuss recent security updates from the IT team, adding these insights to their code review process.

Encouraging informal collaboration opportunities further supports a culture of open communication and continuous learning. Virtual open-office hours, ad hoc trouble-shooting sessions, or cross-departmental coffee chats allow team members to connect and discuss security issues in a relaxed, less structured format. Employees can ask questions, share challenges, and brainstorm ideas that may not arise in formal meetings.

Dedicated collaboration sessions that bring together representatives from security, IT, development, compliance, and incident response also help maintain a unified approach to security management. These regular meetings provide a structured opportunity for each team to share updates on vulnerabilities, discuss recent incident patterns, and address emerging risks specific to their domains.

The benefit of real-time feedback sharing in these sessions is that teams can make immediate adjustments based on input from others. For instance, if the incident response team reports an uptick in phishing attacks, the development and IT teams can quickly implement or enhance measures to mitigate these threats. Immediate feedback allows for agile adjustments, ensuring security practices remain relevant and responsive to current challenges.

Moreover, building relationships across teams through regular cross-functional inter-action fosters trust and openness, increasing the quality of collaboration. When team members become familiar with each other's roles, priorities, and challenges, they are more likely to share constructive feedback and communicate openly about potential issues. A sense of mutual respect and understanding encourages departments to work together effectively, promoting a culture where security is a shared responsibility. Over time, these established relationships help teams coordinate more seamlessly, making cross-departmental efforts to improve security practices more impactful.

Cross-training sessions on security best practices are invaluable for raising secu-rity awareness across all departments, empowering nonsecurity teams to recognize and address vulnerabilities within their areas. These sessions let departments like development, IT, and operations gain foundational knowledge of security principles, giving them the tools to identify potential risks and incorporate security considerations into their daily workflows.

In addition to broad training, knowledge transfer of specialized skills equips teams with the technical capabilities needed to support security goals. For instance, teaching developers about secure coding or providing IT staff insights on incident response techniques prepares them to handle specific security responsibilities more effectively. This specialized training helps bridge skill gaps, enabling each team to contribute meaningfully to the organization's security efforts. When nonsecurity teams are proficient in these areas, they can collaborate with security professionals more seamlessly and take proactive measures within their domains.

Collaborative learning from external sources such as industry reports, threat intelligence, and security conferences further enriches cross-departmental knowledge and keeps teams updated on emerging threats and best practices. By collectively reviewing external insights, teams can discuss how to adapt these findings to their organization's unique environment, translating industry trends into practical security measures. For example, threat intelligence reports might reveal new attack techniques targeting cloud environments, prompting IT and development teams to bolster cloud security configurations.

Leveraging Lessons Learned from Past Incidents

A comprehensive analysis of incident causes is key to understanding the full scope of a security incident and effectively preventing future occurrences. Organizations gain insights into where defenses may have faltered by identifying the root causes, contributing factors, and specific vulnerabilities. This analysis goes beyond surface-level observations to uncover deeper issues such as process weaknesses, overlooked configurations, or user behaviors contributing to the breach. Understanding these detailed elements helps guide targeted preventive measures, allowing security teams to strengthen safeguards, address protocol gaps, and adapt defenses in response to evolving risks.

Cross-team participation in incident reviews ensures that all relevant perspectives are considered when analyzing an incident, providing a holistic view of what went wrong and how to improve. Including representatives from IT, security, operations, and any other affected departments creates a collaborative approach to dissecting the attack. Each department may have unique insights into the factors contributing to the issue or ways to address vulnerabilities within their respective domains. For example, IT might highlight technical problems in configuration, while operations could offer insights into workflow disruptions.

Structured debrief sessions are vital for creating a consistent, repeatable process for capturing lessons learned from incidents. Following a standardized format, these

---

sessions ensure that key details are systematically documented, from the sequence of events to the response actions taken and areas for improvement.

Structured debriefs make analyzing trends across multiple incidents easier over time, revealing patterns that may require ongoing attention. Additionally, a formalized approach helps teams reflect objectively on the incident, facilitating clear action steps and accountability for implementing improvements. Organizations can establish a continuous learning process through structured debriefs, refining their security posture with each incident and building a resilient, responsive approach to emerging threats.

Maintaining a centralized incident repository creates a comprehensive knowledge base that teams can refer to for future incident response and prevention. This repository should include detailed summaries of each incident, root causes, and actions to mitigate or resolve the issues. Over time, the repository becomes a critical tool for tracking the organization's progress in strengthening security measures while enabling quick access to historical insights that inform decisions on both proactive and reactive strategies.

Identifying actionable takeaways from each incident ensures that post-incident reviews lead to meaningful improvements. These takeaways should outline specific steps relevant teams can follow to prevent the recurrence of similar incidents or enhance response effectiveness. For example, if a phishing incident reveals weaknesses in employee awareness, one takeaway could be implementing additional training sessions. Actionable takeaways transform the findings from post-incident reviews into practical steps, bridging the gap between analysis and improvement.

Distilling lessons learned into playbooks and best practices formalizes improvements in procedures, so that knowledge gained from incidents translates directly into stronger protocols. By integrating these lessons into existing response playbooks and security best practices, organizations can create standardized approaches that address previously encountered weaknesses. For instance, insights from a ransomware attack might lead to updates in backup and recovery procedures or adjustments in access controls.

Gathering insights from incident responders—the analysts, IT staff, and other team members directly engaged in managing an incident—improves the response experience. Those on the front lines are uniquely positioned to identify what aspects of the response plan worked effectively and where challenges arose. Their firsthand knowledge provides critical insights into the practical execution of protocols, uncovering issues that may not be visible to higher-level strategists.

Documenting practical challenges and workarounds encountered during incidents adds another valuable layer to post-incident reviews. Frontline responders often develop on-the-fly solutions to overcome obstacles, whether these are tool limitations, unexpected system behaviors, or unforeseen access restrictions. Capturing these workarounds offers an opportunity to formally address gaps in the incident response plan and refine existing protocols to incorporate these solutions. For instance, if analysts had to rely on a particular tool configuration that wasn't initially supported, integrating this knowledge into future response plans can streamline the process.

Adjusting security policies based on incident trends keeps organizational defenses responsive and effective. When repeated incidents or patterns emerge, they often signal underlying issues in current policies that must be addressed. For instance, if multiple incidents reveal gaps in remote access security, this trend may indicate a need for stricter access controls or additional monitoring for remote connections.

Integrating lessons learned into security protocols reinforces the practical application of these insights across the organization. When incident reviews highlight specific vulnerabilities or procedural weaknesses, incorporating these insights into existing security protocols ensures that corrective actions are embedded into daily operations. For example, if an incident reveals that a lack of multifactor authentication contributed to unauthorized access, updating access control protocols to include stricter authentication measures addresses the root cause directly. Embedding these lessons into protocols, such as authentication requirements, incident escalation procedures, or even user training, helps create a more resilient security framework that actively incorporates real-world experiences.

Ensuring policy accessibility and providing training on updated procedures are critical steps for successful implementation. Updated policies should be documented clearly and easily accessible to all relevant teams, preventing miscommunication or knowledge gaps. Additionally, training sessions should be conducted to walk teams through new protocols, explaining the rationale behind changes and how they should be applied in practice.

Adapting Monitoring Strategies Based on Feedback

Adjusting alert sensitivity post-incident is crucial to ensuring that monitoring tools remain responsive to emerging threats. When IR teams analyze recent security events, they often identify specific characteristics or behaviors that may have been overlooked due to current alert sensitivity settings. By incorporating this real-time feedback, security teams can immediately adjust monitoring tools to capture similar threats more accurately in the future.

Integrating response feedback into alert threshold settings allows for a more efficient and targeted monitoring approach. Insights from IR teams about which alerts were helpful versus which led to false positives are invaluable for refining threshold levels. Having too many false positives can overwhelm security teams, distracting them from real threats, while too few alerts can leave critical issues undetected. Response teams' feedback helps strike the right balance by highlighting threshold adjustments that reduce noise and focus attention on genuine risks.

Incorporating feedback on missed indicators further strengthens monitoring strategies by addressing detection gaps that allow threats to go unnoticed. During an incident review, IR teams may identify specific indicators—such as unusual IP addresses or rare user behavior patterns—that did not trigger alerts but were crucial in understanding the attack.

Analyzing recurring incident patterns within historical data offers invaluable insights into monitoring gaps that may leave the organization vulnerable to repeated threats. By examining past incidents, security teams can identify specific vulnerabilities or threat behaviors not effectively captured by current monitoring settings. For instance, if certain phishing attempts have consistently bypassed detection, this trend suggests adjusting alert criteria to capture similar activities better.

Trend analysis of past alerts and incidents provides a strategic foundation for adapting monitoring approaches to align with evolving threats over time. As threat tactics and vulnerabilities change, historical data can reveal shifts in the alerts that require attention. For example, increased alerts related to cloud access or remote work may reflect broader industry trends and the organization's infrastructure changes.

Organizations can identify patterns that indicate overly sensitive or insufficient alert settings by tracking and comparing both metrics. Adjusting thresholds based on this data helps balance accuracy and coverage, reducing noise from false positives while capturing genuine threats.

Automating threshold adjustments based on real-time data creates a responsive and adaptable monitoring environment that continuously aligns with current conditions. Automated feedback loops allow monitoring systems to dynamically adjust alert thresholds without requiring constant manual oversight. For example, if a sudden increase in login attempts is detected during a heightened threat, an automated system can temporarily lower thresholds to increase sensitivity.

Self-tuning monitoring algorithms further automate adjustments by leveraging historical incident and performance data to refine detection criteria continuously. These algorithms analyze past alert performance, false positive rates, and incident patterns to determine optimal settings for threat detection.

As new data is collected, the algorithms adapt to current threat levels and usage patterns, creating a tailored and contextually aware monitoring system. Self-tuning technology reduces the burden on security teams by keeping detection criteria updated and relevant, freeing teams to focus on response and remediation rather than constant recalibration.

Automated alerts on potential monitoring gaps provide an additional layer of proactive security, flagging areas that may require further attention before they become vulnerable. These alerts give teams early warning, allowing them to address potential vulnerabilities in their monitoring configurations before attackers can exploit them. With continuous feedback on monitoring efficacy, security teams can maintain a responsive and agile defense posture, constantly refining their approach to stay ahead of evolving threats.

Automation and AI in Continuous Monitoring

Automation and AI have become essential components of continuous monitoring, helping organizations to manage security threats with unprecedented speed, accuracy, and efficiency. By leveraging AI-driven tools, security teams can detect anomalies, analyze vast amounts of data, and initiate automated responses—all in real time. This integration allows for continuous, around-the-clock monitoring across complex environments, from on-premises systems to multicloud infrastructures.

Automation enhances the scalability of monitoring efforts, reducing the need for manual intervention in routine tasks and allowing teams to focus on high-priority incidents that require human insight. With AI and automation, organizations can achieve faster threat detection and streamlined incident response, elevating their ability to stay ahead of emerging risks.

However, incorporating automation and AI into security monitoring requires careful balance and oversight to ensure these tools operate effectively without introducing new risks. Automated systems must be regularly calibrated, tested, and refined to adapt to changes in the threat landscape and avoid overreliance on algorithms that may miss context-sensitive threats.

By combining the speed and efficiency of AI with strategic human oversight, organizations can maximize the benefits of automation while mitigating limitations such as false positives and algorithmic biases. A balanced approach to automation in continuous monitoring enables a dynamic security posture that is both efficient and adaptable, ensuring that technology is an enhancement to, rather than a replacement for, human expertise in cybersecurity.

Benefits of Automated Monitoring Tools

Automated monitoring tools offer organizations a powerful advantage in real-time threat detection and response. Compared to manual processes, they significantly reduce the time it takes to identify and address potential security issues. These tools continuously scan networks, endpoints, and cloud environments, catching anomalies and vulnerabilities as they emerge and enabling security teams to respond before incidents escalate.

A major benefit of automation is its capacity to process massive data volumes from diverse sources, filtering and analyzing information across the network without getting overwhelmed. By efficiently managing this data, automated tools can detect suspicious patterns and prioritize alerts, freeing security teams to focus on complex, high-priority threats that require human expertise.

Automation also improves alert accuracy by leveraging data-driven precision and reducing false positives. By cross-referencing data from network logs, endpoint activity, and user access, automated tools generate insights that more accurately reflect genuine threats, especially when combined with behavioral analytics. By establishing baselines of normal activity, these tools quickly flag deviations, such as unusual login locations or unexpected data transfers, that could signal a threat.

Automated tools also adapt dynamically to changing patterns. With threshold adjustments based on real-time activity trends, they can respond to fluctuations in network behavior, such as higher activity during peak hours or more sensitive monitoring during off-hours, ensuring accurate detection across variable conditions.

One of the standout features of automated monitoring is its ability to provide unified oversight across hybrid and multicloud environments. As organizations adopt diverse infrastructures—including on-premises systems, private clouds, and public cloud services—automated tools bridge these environments, consolidating data into centralized dashboards for comprehensive visibility. This centralization enables scalability, allowing security monitoring to grow seamlessly with new assets and infrastructure as the organization expands.

The rise of remote work and connected devices has made continuous monitoring critical. Automated tools ensure that even distributed endpoints—IoT devices, mobile platforms, and remote workstations—are covered in real time, offering end-to-end visibility and detecting suspicious activity across all asset types, regardless of location.

With 24/7 monitoring, automated tools provide around-the-clock security coverage, eliminating potential detection gaps during off-hours or holidays. They maintain constant vigilance without fatigue, ensuring that any suspicious activity is immediately flagged and that response teams can act swiftly to contain threats.

Automation also enables proactive defenses by identifying emerging threat patterns early. Through advanced algorithms and AI, automated tools detect subtle indicators, like unusual access attempts or shifts in network traffic, that might otherwise go unnoticed. By integrating real-time threat intelligence, these tools stay current with the latest attack vectors and indicators of compromise, continuously updating detection parameters to match evolving threats.

Automation is also invaluable in compliance monitoring, continuously assessing configurations and practices against regulatory standards like GDPR, HIPAA, and PCI DSS. Automated tools instantly generate alerts for deviations from compliance standards and simplify audit readiness by providing detailed logs and reports that meet regulatory requirements. This consistency in monitoring reduces the risk of human error, ensuring that policies are uniformly applied across all assets.

Centralized dashboards offer a unified view of potential threats across on-premises, cloud, and hybrid setups, breaking down silos that can obscure visibility. These dashboards update in real time, giving immediate insights into conditions across the organization and allowing teams to monitor assets according to their specific needs.

Automated monitoring also reduces staffing requirements by handling routine tasks like data analysis, log processing, and basic threat detection, allowing organizations to achieve robust threat management with fewer resources. Automation lowers operational costs and frees security teams to focus on high-value tasks, from advanced threat analysis to strategic security improvements.

With real-time threat intelligence, automated tools continually adjust detection parameters to flag new threats, adapting dynamically to unexpected patterns in network traffic and user behavior without manual reconfiguration.

Automated monitoring tools streamline incident triage by prioritizing critical alerts, allowing response teams to address the most severe threats first. Additionally, automated incident playbooks initiate predefined responses for specific incident types. In the event of a ransomware attack, for example, an automated playbook can immediately isolate affected systems, block network access, and notify key personnel, ensuring a rapid, coordinated response.

Finally, automated tools facilitate cross-team collaboration by integrating workflow systems like Slack, Microsoft Teams, or ticketing platforms. This ensures that all necessary notifications and actions are seamlessly communicated across security and response teams.

Role of AI in Threat Detection and Analysis

AI-driven behavioral analysis for pattern recognition transforms anomaly detection by enabling systems to identify subtle deviations from typical user and network behaviors. Unlike traditional rule-based systems, which rely on predefined threat indicators, AI models can learn baseline behaviors across various parameters, such as login times, data access patterns, or network traffic flow. When activity deviates from these established norms, AI can flag it as suspicious, even if it does not match known threat signatures.

Self-learning algorithms enhance anomaly detection by adapting to dynamic IT environments, continuously refining their understanding of normal activity. As systems generate new data, AI models update their baselines and detection parameters, learning from recent interactions and adjusting for evolving usage patterns. For example, if a business expands remote work policies, AI models can adapt to recognize increased remote access as typical behavior rather than a potential threat.

In addition to improving detection accuracy, AI plays a critical role in reducing noise by filtering out normal activity. The technology can differentiate between routine and unusual actions by creating behavior-based baselines, minimizing false positives that would otherwise overwhelm security teams.

Real-time data processing through AI-driven analysis enables immediate detection and response to threats, allowing organizations to act the moment suspicious activity is identified. Unlike traditional monitoring, which can involve delays due to data collection and batch processing, AI models automatically analyze data continuously, instantly flagging unusual patterns.

AI also enhances threat scoring and prioritization, assigning risk levels to detected anomalies based on their potential impact. AI models can determine which anomalies pose the most significant risk by evaluating factors such as the nature of a deviation, its origin, and its historical context. This scoring system helps security teams focus on high-priority threats, addressing the most severe risks first. For instance, a series of failed login attempts on a critical server might be flagged with a higher risk score than an unusual but benign system event, guiding teams to allocate their resources where they're needed most.

Predictive analytics further strengthen AI-driven threat detection by anticipating future threats based on historical data and global threat intelligence. AI algorithms can identify trends and project likely threat vectors by analyzing past incidents and known attack patterns. For example, if certain attacks are becoming more frequent or targeted toward specific sectors, AI can flag these trends and alert security teams to prepare defenses accordingly.

AI-powered threat-hunting capabilities are particularly effective in identifying advanced persistent threats, which often elude traditional monitoring due to their stealth and prolonged attack strategies. APTs can remain hidden within an organization's network for extended periods, gathering data or gradually escalating their presence. AI's ability to analyze large volumes of data allows it to detect subtle, long-term patterns that are characteristic of APTs, such as slow data exfiltration or highly selective access to specific systems.

Correlating data from multiple sources enhances AI's effectiveness in building a comprehensive view of potential threats, allowing for more nuanced and accurate detection. AI can integrate data from network traffic, endpoint behavior, user access patterns, and external threat intelligence feeds to provide a fuller picture of network activity. For instance, an unusual increase in login attempts combined with suspicious IP addresses flagged by threat intelligence may indicate a coordinated attack.

AI's capability to uncover hidden attack indicators strengthens its role in detecting nuanced signs of compromise that might signal the early stages of an attack. Unlike conventional monitoring systems that focus on clear, defined threat signatures, AI can recognize low-frequency anomalies, such as slight deviations in network traffic or unexpected login patterns. These minor indicators may go unnoticed by traditional systems but could suggest a hacker probing for weaknesses or testing access to sensitive areas.

AI-driven systems are crucial in initiating automated responses to known threats, reducing response time, and limiting potential damage. AI-powered monitoring can immediately trigger preconfigured actions when a threat is detected, such as a malicious IP address attempting unauthorized access or a compromised endpoint exhibiting unusual activity.

AI-powered incident triage further enhances response efficiency by analyzing and categorizing threats, enabling faster escalation of high-priority incidents to response teams. AI can assess the severity and context of each alert, helping prioritize those that pose the most substantial risk to the organization. For example, if an anomaly is detected on a system handling sensitive data, AI can flag it as a high-priority incident, ensuring it receives immediate attention.

Integrating AI within SOAR frameworks allows for even greater efficiency in responding to security incidents. In a SOAR environment, AI works seamlessly with automated workflows to execute actions tailored to specific threats. For instance, when a phishing attempt is detected, the SOAR platform can activate AI-driven actions to quarantine affected email accounts, notify the security team, and start forensic analysis on the impacted systems.

Balancing Automation with Manual Oversight

Automation has transformed cybersecurity, offering speed and scalability in threat detection. Yet, it's not without vulnerabilities. Automated systems excel at recognizing known patterns, but sophisticated attackers often exploit their blind spots. By mimicking legitimate behaviors and escalating access slowly, multistage attacks can bypass automated defenses, requiring human analysis to uncover the bigger picture.

False positives and negatives are another challenge. Overly cautious systems may flood security teams with benign alerts while subtle threats slip by unnoticed. Advanced algorithms help, but their effectiveness hinges on the quality of the data they're trained on. Automation may misjudge priorities or fail to detect emerging threats if training data is biased or incomplete.

Layering automation with human oversight bridges these gaps. Automation scans vast data sets and flags anomalies, but human analysts provide the context needed to interpret complex scenarios and refine detection criteria. For example, while automated tools might quarantine a suspicious endpoint, a nuanced decision, like isolating a network segment, benefits from manual review to prevent unintended disruptions.

Automation isn't static—it requires continuous tuning. Feedback loops and periodic reviews ensure detection models adapt to threats like novel malware or social engineering tactics. These reviews also identify areas where automation might overreach, such as blocking critical services due to overly aggressive thresholds.

Fail-safe mechanisms add an extra layer of protection. High-risk actions, like isolating key systems, should include validation steps to prevent unintended consequences. Redundancies, such as backup monitoring systems, ensure critical issues are flagged even if primary automation fails.

Ultimately, automation's strength lies in collaboration with human expertise. By combining machines' speed with analysts' insight, organizations can navigate the complexities of modern threats while addressing vulnerabilities inherent to AI.

Summary

Security isn't just about setting up defenses and calling it a day. It's about staying one step ahead of an ever-changing game. This chapter explored the crucial role of continuous monitoring and adaptive strategies in managing modern threats. Automated tools and AI have become the workhorses of cybersecurity, scanning vast digital landscapes and spotting patterns faster than any human ever could. But as impressive as these technologies are, they're not infallible. Blind spots, biases, and those sneaky false positives remind us that machines still need human intuition to make sense of the chaos.

The secret sauce, as we've seen, is balance. Automation handles the heavy lifting, but collaboration with human expertise turns raw data into meaningful action. By layering machine efficiency with human insight, organizations can create defenses that are as agile as the threats they face. And let's not forget the power of learning—feedback loops, honest reviews of what worked (and what didn't), and a willingness to adapt and keep our security strategies fresh, which we will cover in Chapter 11.

The Future of Attack Surface Management

The cybersecurity industry has transformed from isolated, siloed security operations to a more collaborative ecosystem where attack surface management is at the heart of business and security intelligence. Back in 2015, sharing threat intelligence was like pulling teeth—organizations guarded their security data like state secrets. Now, we're seeing entire industry consortiums dedicated to intelligence exchange, recognizing that our collective security is stronger than our individual defenses.

Take the financial services sector, for example. Ron recently worked with a publicly traded FinTech company that created a shared threat intelligence platform where people anonymously contribute attack surface findings, vulnerability insights, and threat patterns. By pooling anonymized data, they could identify emerging threats faster and understand attack trends without needing decades of experience.

In this chapter, we will explore the future of ASM and how emerging technologies, such as artificial intelligence and machine learning, are set to transform our ability to predict, prevent, and respond to threats. Organizations that thrive will be those that view cybersecurity as a shared responsibility, breaking down the traditional walls of competition and secrecy. This means investing not just in technical infrastructure for threat sharing but in building trust, establishing clear governance frameworks, and creating incentive structures that encourage meaningful participation. The attack surface is becoming too complex and expansive for any single organization to manage alone, and collaborative data sharing represents our best collective defense against future cyberthreats.

Emerging Trends in Attack Surface Management

Honestly, it's always been a struggle to manage attack surfaces. Even before the cloud, large enterprises would onboard new technology and users by the minute. They frequently use multiple providers with hundreds of thousands of ephemeral assets spinning up and down daily. Each of these assets represents a potential entry point for attackers. The security game has fundamentally changed: we're no longer playing chess with fixed pieces, but rather trying to secure a board where the pieces multiply and vanish in real time.

Integrating artificial intelligence into our security operations started as a pipe dream and has evolved into a necessity. Every security team has woes and stories of drowning in alerts, missing critical threats, and chasing false positives. AI in attack surface monitoring promises a future where we can identify the most difficult attack patterns exploiting our API gateways. AI in security operations will assist with detecting anomalies across millions of requests that human analysts had missed entirely. But this power comes with its risks. We've seen firsthand how AI systems can be fooled by adversarial attacks and how quickly security challenges can appear after introducing massive data sets needed for effective AI.

The rise of edge computing has blown cloud network perimeters into smaller fragmented pieces. Edge computing, a model that moves computing and storage closer to the data source, is one of the best ways to introduce speed and scale worldwide as you are deploying entire applications and APIs in several regions. Each edge application is a potential gateway into your enterprise environment or customer data. The previous approach of content delivery networks was helpful when you were deploying static content, but our present and future consist of dynamic content that changes as rapidly as the needs of your users. We must completely rethink how we monitor and protect distributed attack surfaces, fundamentally reimagining a new world where edge computing is the new perimeter. Future-ready ASM practices must harmonize automated tools with human expertise to effectively oversee assets in a world where data is more decentralized and exposed than ever.

AI and Machine Learning in ASM

In the early days of AI in security operations, we were basically throwing every machine learning algorithm we could at log files and hoping they'd spot something interesting. Most of these early tools required a team of data scientists just to get them running, and even then, the results were hit or miss. What a difference a few years makes. Nowadays, a junior analyst can use an LLM to decode malware binaries in minutes—something that would have taken the most experienced team members hours. Adopting AI through these generative models isn't just making our jobs easier. It's completely rewriting the rules of what's possible in security operations.

But this accessibility comes with its own set of headaches. When we ask team members about best practices for data handling in AI applications, we get a lot of blank stares: "We just paste in what we need to get the job done." Such a casual approach to AI usage keeps security up at night. These models are black boxes and we're feeding them sensitive data with often little more than a privacy policy link and a checkbox. We've seen AI providers change their terms of service overnight, leaving organizations scrambling to understand if they've accidentally exposed proprietary or regulated information.

We're just beginning to grapple with the emergence of AI-specific attack vectors. As organizations adopt AI, either by deploying models internally or accessing third-party providers, a new class of attack vectors is emerging, one that's not yet fully understood. Attacks specific to AI systems, particularly those leveraging generative models, introduce new attack surfaces.

Let's consider the AI attack vectors:

Guardrail jailbreaks

Every AI system ships with safety controls and content filters designed to prevent misuse. Attackers bypass these guardrails through prompt-engineering tactics, forcing models to ignore their built-in restrictions. Once compromised, models can leak sensitive data, execute dangerous commands, or produce harmful content. The real problem? These jailbreaks are getting easier to execute and harder to prevent.

Prompt injection

Think of this as SQL injection for AI systems. Attackers craft inputs that manipulate the model's context window, tricking it into operating outside its intended boundaries. When successful, these attacks can make AI systems leak data, execute unauthorized commands, or produce dangerous outputs. The challenge is that prompt injection attacks are often indistinguishable from legitimate queries.

Information disclosure

AI models, especially large language models, can accidentally reveal fragments of their training data through their outputs. We see models reconstruct sensitive information, such as personally identifiable information, from their training sets when given the right prompts. The risk increases with model size and training data complexity.

Content manipulation

This involves tampering with AI systems to generate false or misleading outputs. Attackers can influence model behavior through adversarial examples or by poisoning training data. Some manipulations can be subtle enough to avoid detection while significantly impacting model outputs.

Denial of service

AI systems are uniquely vulnerable to resource exhaustion attacks. By forcing models to perform computationally expensive operations, attackers can degrade performance or crash systems entirely. These attacks are particularly effective against large language models, where each inference requires significant computational resources.

Training data leakage

Models can inadvertently memorize and leak sensitive training data. Through careful querying, attackers can extract this information piece by piece. The risk is highest in models trained on proprietary or personal data, where even small leaks can have serious consequences.

Training data poisoning

Attackers can compromise AI systems by injecting malicious data during training. Even small amounts of poisoned data can significantly impact model behavior.

Weights disclosure

Model weights contain the essence of what an AI system has learned. If exposed, these weights can be used to clone models or reverse-engineer training data. This attack vector could lead to intellectual property theft and expose model weaknesses.

Layers disclosure

Understanding a model's architecture gives attackers a blueprint for exploitation. Layer configurations reveal how models process information, making it easier to craft attacks. This knowledge can be used to develop malicious prompts or identify architectural vulnerabilities.

Next, let's consider the AI attack surface:

Data ingestion points

Every AI system is only as good as its input data. These ingestion points are where external data feeds, internal repositories, and real-time streams enter the model's architecture. The challenge for businesses is maintaining data quality and avoiding inaccurate or poisoned data streams.

User interface

Every text box, every upload button, every interaction point is a potential attack vector. UI attacks on AI platforms go beyond cross-site scripting and can lead to an attacker tricking the AI model into exposing sensitive data or executing unauthorized commands. To protect the UI, providers use traditional input sanitization along with content filtering to monitor the model's output.

Application programming interfaces
APIs are the backbone of any AI architecture and are prime targets for attackers. When it comes to LLMs, attackers are combining language with traditional API attack techniques to bypass security controls. Rate limiting, strict authentication, and pattern detection are a few tactics that AI providers are using to combat this new breed of API attacks on AI systems.

Training pipelines
Your training pipeline is ground zero for model security. One compromised training run can poison your entire model. These pipelines need military-grade security, strict access controls, versioned data sets, and automated validation checks at every step. When untrusted code or data enters your pipeline, your entire model is at risk.

Pretrained third-party models
Using pretrained models is like installing third-party code: you're inheriting unknown vulnerabilities. These models can contain hidden backdoors or biases that emerge only under nuanced conditions. Rigorous testing is a vital strategy to defend against inheriting compromised models.

Data storage
AI systems devour data, creating massive storage requirements that expand attack surfaces. AI systems leverage traditional databases and vector databases. Security and data teams are responsible for securing training data sets, model checkpoints, and operational logs.

Deployment environment and hardware
The physical infrastructure running your AI models is a critical attack surface. GPU clusters, specialized hardware, and distributed computing each bring unique vulnerabilities. Hardware-level attacks can compromise model integrity or extract sensitive information directly from memory.

Control interfaces
Administrative and control interfaces are your last line of defense and often the first point of attack. These interfaces control everything from model parameters to access controls. A compromised admin interface could lead to complete control of your AI system.

Quantum Computing

Quantum computing, an emerging technology leveraging quantum mechanics to solve complex problems beyond classical computing capabilities, is a topic that keeps cryptographers up at night. Right now, someone could record all your encrypted traffic—from banking transactions to Slack communications to Zoom calls. Why would they? Because while they can't decrypt it today, quantum computers will eventually be able to break our current encryption standards.

Let's consider a few implications of quantum computing:

Increased decryption risks

Transport layer security (TLS) is the backbone of our web traffic. It's built on the assumption that the mathematical calculations for encryption are too complex and expensive to reasonably solve. Quantum computing changes that equation entirely. For example, Shor's Factoring is a quantum algorithm that can potentially be used to find prime factors of a number. Decrypting a 2048-bit message on today's most powerful supercomputers would take thousands of years. It's expected that a quantum computer could decrypt that in less than a week.

Quantum-resistant encryption impact on key security protocols

The transition to quantum-resistant protocols would require updates to virtually every piece of infrastructure and application. This includes replacing all SSL/TLS implementations, updating digital certificate authorities, and revising key exchange pipelines. When the time comes, organizations will be required to maintain operational continuity while adding quantum-resistant protocols to their technology stack. The National Institute of Standards and Technology has created post-quantum cryptography standards (*https://oreil.ly/fgPcG*) to provide a framework for implementing quantum-resistant algorithms.

New regulatory and compliance requirements

As quantum computing technology becomes more viable, new regulations are expected to address quantum-related cybersecurity risks, particularly concerning encryption standards. While the technology becomes more realistic, compliance standards will likely mandate new quantum-resistant algorithms to protect sensitive data. Organizations will likely need to incorporate quantum compliance into ASM planning to avoid penalties and uphold data protection standards.

The best thing we can do now is brace for the possibility of quantum computing with a few practical steps:

1. Inventory your encryption dependencies and know where and how you're using cryptography.
2. Start testing post-quantum algorithms in noncritical systems.
3. Develop a crypto-agility plan for replacing legacy algorithms and protocols.
4. Review data retention policies against quantum timeline predictions.

By taking these proactive steps, organizations can better navigate the transition to quantum-resilient security and ensure they're prepared before quantum threats become a reality.

Edge Computing Challenges

Edge computing results in faster data processing and more pleasant user experiences by bringing computing resources closer to end users. Each edge resource becomes a potential entry point, and these resources are constantly spinning up and down across different geographic regions. Imagine trying to secure thousands of tiny offices that appear and disappear within minutes.

Here's what makes edge computing particularly tricky for security:

Resource constraints
> Current security tools don't fit on edge computing resources. Most edge providers enforce a strict 25 MB limit on deployments. It will be difficult for developers to tell your security team why their 200 MB monitoring agent won't be viable anymore due to size limitations.

Shift left or die
> Security has to move into the development pipeline. We need to embed lightweight security checks directly into CI/CD workflows. If an edge function isn't secure before deployment, it doesn't deploy. Period. This practice has already saved developers from accidentally embedding credentials directly into edge functions.

Ephemerality
> To grow with edge computing, we will need to stop trying to secure individual resources. Focus on patterns instead. An example of how this shift is already happening is teams focused on building detection rules around behavior rather than using signatures. When an edge function starts making unusual API calls, we terminate it and spin up a fresh one. No investigation needed.

Embracing and preparing for these realities will help ensure your organization can safely scale with the agility and speed required by edge computing.

Evolving Challenges in Cybersecurity

Our prediction is that the cybersecurity industry will continue to evolve at an unprecedented pace, with organizations facing challenges that extend beyond technical threats. One of the most pressing concerns is insider threats, which have become more nuanced and harder to detect as remote work becomes permanent for many organizations. Expanded access, combined with the rising phenomenon of "quiet quitting" and increased employee turnover, has made it harder to distinguish between legitimate work activities and potential data exfiltration attempts.

Meeting regulatory requirements has also become more challenging. It feels like each year, a new regulatory framework is introduced that demands organizations to become more secure and report security incidents faster. The challenge doesn't stop at regulatory compliance—there's also the challenge of making the right decisions that promote a healthy workplace that doesn't make employees feel like their company is spying on them.

Privacy concerns have evolved beyond simple data protection, and the public has a microscope-like view of how companies treat the rights of individuals and how algorithms make decisions to promote content. Organizations must now consider how they protect personal data, ensure transparency in automated decision-making processes, and maintain individual privacy rights while leveraging data for business intelligence. This has created tension between security requirements and privacy rights. For example, detailed security logging might capture personal data that individuals have the right to have erased under privacy regulations. The challenge extends to third-party relationships as well, since organizations must ensure their vendors and partners maintain the same level of privacy protection while still allowing for effective security monitoring and incident response.

Staying Ahead in ASM Practices and Technologies

Having spent over a decade watching attack surface management evolve, we can tell you that continuing to work in security requires us to change how we think about security. We remember when ASM meant running a vulnerability scanner once a quarter and calling it a day. Now, we're watching companies invest millions into continuous monitoring solutions that can detect and respond to threats in real time, and even that's starting to feel inadequate for tomorrow's challenges.

What excites us most about the future of ASM is the potential for collaboration and shared intelligence. We're seeing a shift away from the old mentality of keeping security information close to the chest. Forward-thinking organizations are participating in threat and information sharing with companies in a similar vertical and contribute to open-source security projects that their organization uses. Collaboration is so effective because no single organization can keep up with all the emerging threats and attack vectors. During Ron's time at Intel Corporation, they participated in Information Sharing and Analysis Center groups, which were formed so that companies could confidentially share specific threats they'd been impacted by with their peers. The future of ASM will belong to those who can afford to invest in collaborative intelligence to stay one step ahead of future threats.

Continuous Learning and Skill Development

The skills that made us effective in attack surface management five years ago are barely scratching the surface of what's needed today. Many security practitioners have spent their evenings learning Python to automate enriching alerts and studying how to write effective prompts in ChatGPT to create agents for detecting social engineering attempts.

Here are a few strategies that individuals and entire security teams can take to stay ahead:

Attack simulation and tabletop exercises
A common saying in ASM is "you can't defend what you don't understand." Regularly running attack simulations focused on the most relevant attack vectors is one of the best ways to anticipate adversaries' next move. With this strategy, you can identify when your security controls and detections have gaps.

Cross-functional rotations
Now that security is no longer an isolated program, rotating security engineers through development sprints can be a gateway for reducing critical vulnerabilities for the most important assets. According to the Cloud Security Alliance (*https://oreil.ly/ARDFw*), in 2023, a third of cloud breaches were due to misconfigurations.

Community engagement
New threats emerge too fast for any one person to keep up. Teams that present at security conferences and contribute to open source projects can get more actionable insights from a wide range of security professionals on ways that they can improve. Some of our best security lessons have come from hallway conversations at conferences.

Stay Hungry, Never Give Up

Nobody can master all of the fundamentals or esoteric details overnight. We've been in security for almost two decades and still feel like we're drinking from a fire hose some days. The key isn't knowing everything, it's knowing how to learn and adapt.

The future belongs to security professionals who can adapt quickly, break down complex challenges into manageable chunks, and automate the actions that become repetitive. It also belongs to those who realize that security is no longer a specialist's game, it's a team sport where continuous learning is the only constant.

Remember: The attack surface you'll be securing tomorrow hasn't been invented yet. The best skill you can develop is learning how to learn.

Index

A

acceptance, of potential impact of risk, 60
access control, 191, 197
   AI pipelines and, 56
   misuse of, 8
   network security and, 166
access rights, misuse of, 8
account life cycle management, 167
accountability, 34
acquisitions
   prioritization of assets and, 156
   risks associated with, 30, 225
active directory, 49
adaptation, 19
adaptive malware, 13
adaptive thresholds, 227
administrative interfaces, 257
advanced persistent threats (APTs), 11
advanced threat protection (ATP), 213
AI (artificial intelligence), 254-257
   in continuous monitoring, 246, 248-250
   dependencies of, complexity of managing, 239
   exploitation of for adaptive malware and automated attacks, 13
   models and neural network architectures, 55
   pipelines and infrastructure, 56
   risks and opportunities of, 224
   in threat detection and analysis, 248-250
   user interfaces (UIs), 56
alerts, 197
   automated, 31
   incorporating contextual awareness in, 229

   setting thresholds for, 226-229
alignment, strategic, 141
Amazon ECS (Elastic Container Service), 44
analytics, 131
anomaly detection, 31
APIs (application programming interfaces), 11
   AI APIs, 56
   API attacks on AI systems, 257
   assessing, 170
   continued monitoring of, 223
   identifying, 126
   SaaS integration with security managed by customer, 47
   scanning, 191
   security risks and integration challenges., 223
   third-party, 224
applications
   third-party, 53
   unauthorized, 98, 99
APTs (advanced persistent threats), 11
artificial intelligence (see AI)
ASA (see attack surface analysis)
ASM (see Attack Surface Management)
Assess phase, NIST Risk Management Framework, 4
asset criticality analysis, 24
asset enrichment
   asset type details, 102
   configuration data, 103
   data classification and, 103
   environmental data, 105
   integrating into business strategy, 108-113
   interdependencies, 106

About the Authors

Ron Eddings is the cofounder and executive producer at Hacker Valley Media. Ron holds expertise across the cybersecurity domain with over 15 years of experience. His passion for making cybersecurity accessible and entertaining has established him as an influential voice in the industry. With hands-on mastery across IT and security, his career has spanned consulting at top firms like Booz Allen Hamilton and security architecture roles at Intel Corporation and Palo Alto Networks.

Ron's writing and perspectives have been featured in notable publications, including *Dark Reading*, *The CyberWire*, and *Black Hat*. He continues to push the boundaries of edutainment through initiatives like Hacker Valley Studio, bringing cybersecurity into mainstream entertainment.

MJ Kaufmann is the founder and principal consultant at Write Alchemist. She holds a master's degree in information security (MSIS). Her passion and vision have solidified her as a trusted authority in cybersecurity content. With over two decades of practical IT expertise, her experience ranges from trailblazing enterprise-level projects to ghostwriting for global tech giants and shaping the next generation of IT professionals. Her hands-on technology mastery includes architecting applications, pioneering system designs, and deploying enterprise-grade solutions.

As a college professor, MJ taught programming and cybersecurity courses. She championed the importance of cybersecurity education, resulting in the creation of both associate's and bachelor's degree programs in cybersecurity.

As a content and product marketing consultant specializing in technology and cybersecurity, her ghostwritten work has been published in respected magazines such as *Forbes* and *Dark Reading*. Her articles are published in industry publications like *Helpnet Security*, *Network Computing*, and *Security Magazine*.

Colophon

The animal on the cover of *Attack Surface Management* is a soldier crab (*Mictyris longicarpus*), which is native to beaches from the Bay of Bengal to Australia.

Adult soldier crabs are 1 inch across. They are mostly white, with powder blue backs and purple spots on the joints of their legs. They mostly eat detritus found in sand.

A soldier crab spends most of its time buried in sand. A few hours before low tide, some or all crabs will emerge from the sand. Temperature, wind, and rainfall affect which crabs emerge, with males and females responding differently to different conditions. Within minutes of their emergence, the crabs walk together toward the ocean in a straight line. *Mictyris* species walk forward, unlike most other crabs, which walk sideways. Their common name stems from this behavior of marching together in "armies." The crabs feed for 1–2 hours and then walk to a new spot and burrow themselves back into the sand.

There is no conservation status for the soldier crab, but it is not considered endangered. Many of the animals on O'Reilly covers are endangered; all of them are important to the world.

Color illustration by Karen Montgomery, based on an antique line engraving from *Pictorial Museum of Animated Nature*. The series design is by Edie Freedman, Ellie Volckhausen, and Karen Montgomery. The cover fonts are Gilroy Semibold and Guardian Sans. The text font is Adobe Minion Pro; the heading font is Adobe Myriad Condensed; and the code font is Dalton Maag's Ubuntu Mono.

O'REILLY®

Learn from experts.
Become one yourself.

60,000+ titles | Live events with experts | Role-based courses
Interactive learning | Certification preparation

**Try the O'Reilly learning platform
free for 10 days.**